What they're saying...

"My Silver Tongued Devil friend Tim Ghianni and his comrade Rob Dollar take readers on a laugh-and-tear-filled private tour of what it meant to be a newspaperman before corporate cancer killed the profession."
—**Kris Kristofferson,** Country Music Hall of Fame member, much-honored songwriter for classics like "For The Good Times," "Me and Bobby McGee," "Help Me Make It Through the Night," and "Sunday Morning Coming Down"; actor in "Pat Garrett and Billy The Kid," "A Star is Born," "Cisco Pike," "Lone Star," "A Soldier's Daughter Never Cries," and many more.

"All newspapermen are journalists, but not all journalists are newspapermen. Not many of them are, these days. Tim Ghianni and Rob Dollar are two of the last, and this is a report from the long-ceded front lines, complete with Lamar Alexander's T-shirt wearing daughter, Chico the dead monkey, Potsie's future sister-in-law, a little murder, and a lot of mayhem. All that's lacking is pulled punches."
—**Peter Cooper**, musician, journalist, and winner of the Charlie Lamb Award for Excellence in Country Music Journalism.

"You can always count on The News Brothers *to stir up things nicely."*
—**Bob Frost**, prominent Clarksville, Tennessee, businessman and political insider.

"Lord, please keep an extra eye on The News Brothers, *for they are subject to run amok if not looked after. Amen."*
—**Rich Liebe**, Kentucky Colonel, former mayor of Hopkinsville, Kentucky., retired police officer, decorated veteran, private eye.

IN THE EARLY 1980S, the citizens of Clarksville, Tennessee, were traumatized by the unrelated disappearances and random murders of two All-American teenagers, whose bodies were found within 24 hours of each other in the most shocking and mind-numbing of circumstances imaginable.

Having a job to do, but emotionally affected by the double tragedy, reporters and editors at the city's daily newspaper wrestled with their sanity while they pursued for their readers a trail of never-ending stories about the darkest underside of the human spirit.

In seeking solace, there was little choice but to replace tears with an undeniably fine madness, laced with mirth and mourning.

With that remedy, *The News Brothers* were born…

Two of the last great newspapermen, Tim Ghianni and Rob Dollar, take readers back to the days when newspapers actually mattered in America…When journalism was all about making a difference, not making huge profits at the expense of the reader…When reporters and editors searched for the truth, wherever it took them and at whatever cost.

Ghianni and Dollar—the Mickey Mantle and Billy Martin of the newspaper world, with nearly 60 years of experience between them at daily newspapers in Tennessee, Kentucky and North Carolina—earned reputations in their careers as award-winning "outlaw" journalists who always stood up to wrong-doers and wrongdoing.

In the early days of their friendship, while working together at *The Leaf-Chronicle* in Clarksville, Ghianni and Dollar detected a recklessness in the air and saw Korporate Amerika for what it was and what it would become…To no avail, they warned their colleagues that the day was fast approaching when their beloved profession would hang by a thread on life-support.

This book is a story about their love for newspapers…What went wrong…And why. It's also about those two long ago murders that continue to haunt them to this day.

Their story is dark. It's funny. It's honest. It's brutal. But, most of all, it's the truth—and in the end, that's all that really matters to two old newspapermen who never backed down.

WHEN NEWSPAPERS
MATTERED

The News Brothers & their Shades of Glory

By Tim Ghianni
& Rob Dollar

PUBLISHED BY WESTVIEW, INC.
P.O. Box 605
Kingston Springs, Tennessee 37082
www.publishedbywestview.com

© 2012 Tim Ghianni and Rob Dollar
All rights reserved, including the right to reproduction in whole or in part in any form.

ISBN 978-1-937763-23-7 Perfect Bound
ISBN 978-1-937763-33-6 Dust Jacket

First edition, March 2012

Good faith efforts have been made to trace copyrights on materials included in this publication. If any copyrighted material has been included without permission and due acknowledgment, proper credit will be inserted in future printings after notice has been received.

Printed in the United States of America on acid free paper.

TABLE OF CONTENTS

Foreword ix
The darkest underside of the human spirit 1
The birthday bash 31
Let's wear shades 43
In a place called Camelot 53
The road to Clarksville 65
High proof news coverage 85
The Royal screw job 91
My pal The Deer Hunter 97
C'mon all you big strong men 101
'Death Waits in the Dark' 113
Fore and 30 years ago with a few sports legends 121
Back on the subject of pigeons 133
Been there, done that, got the T-shirt 137
Monkey see, monkey do 157
The Right Stuff 163
Miracle on Commerce Street 167
Have a damn nice Christmas 175
'The birds shit on me' 181
Always the fools 187
Fired up and fired 195
The years in the wilderness 227
Life's defining moments 245
A letter to the Parole Board 251
It was the chemistry, stupid 255

The World According to Tim "Flapjacks" Ghianni 261
This is the End 303
The business of being heartless 317
11-11-11 327
The dearly departed 343
An Afterword from Tim Ghianni 375

Dedication

The authors had to exercise much restraint in resisting the urge to dedicate this book to the greed of Korporate Amerika, including the enablers who started out with journalistic intent only to follow The Almighty Dollar and destroy what was the best and most important of professions. We seriously mulled over the idea of expressing our "thanks" to such evil-doers by wishing them a red-hot poker up a part of the body where the sun doesn't shine. But, after careful consideration, we realized they surely will feel a lot more heat in Hell, so the poker would only be redundant and probably even mild in comparison.

So instead, this book is dedicated to our beloved "brother"— Scott "Badger" Shelton, a loyal friend and inspiration for everything good and decent in this world.

It's also for some of our most respected colleagues — the true and tested journalists who gave their hearts and souls to newspapering before departing this earth for The Big Newspaper in the Sky: Harold Lynch, Tony Durr, Richard Worden, W.J. Souza, Joe Caldwell, Bob Battle, Fred Russell, Jerry Thompson, Eddie Jones, C.B. Fletcher, Bill Roberts, Joe Dorris, Robert C. Carter, David L. Riley, E.L. "Lynn" Gold, Pete Wright, John Bibb, Jimmy Carnahan, Edgar Allen, Kent Heitholt, Kevin Paulk, Ken Litchfield, Cecil Herndon and, of course, Chico The Monkey.

FOREWORD

Once upon a time in America, newspapers thrived. Journalism was a most honorable profession made up of honorable men and honorable women. Most of them had gone to college, where they learned of pica poles, F-stops and holding their liquor.

Their contemporaries ventured out into the world in pursuit of riches, and that's fine, if making money is what you want to be remembered for when you're gone. But these men and women entered journalism because it was a time when the mission of newspapers was more about making a difference than making huge profits. At least that's the belief that drove them.

Reporters and editors did not clock out at 5 p.m. They slaved away to put out newspapers filled with information necessary to help an informed public make decisions, learn about what had happened, prepare for what was to come. Perhaps, occasionally, even give them something to smile about in a too-often bleak, corrupt and violent world.

The public good—not the size of paychecks and year-end bonuses that were inflated by "keeping positions dark" to save money while hurting coverage—was what mattered in the end.

Remember this is a profession that was, and should still be ... or at least could be... called upon for greatness. But who would answer that call when phones ring endlessly in desolate newsrooms?

The Founding Fathers were not talking about bean-counters when they wrote: *"Congress shall make no law respecting an establishment of religion, or prohibiting the free exercise thereof; or abridging the freedom of speech, or of the press; or the right of the people peaceably to assemble, and to petition the government for a redress of grievances."*

Perhaps someday the public will rise, tote torches to the glistening "Information Centers," rail against what has happened and why the simple daily newspaper no longer exists.

But it will be too late. Pressrooms will be hollow caverns filled with skeletal reminders of the days of hollering: "Stop the Presses!"

And, as for the Founding Fathers, bless them, but what good is freedom of the press when there are no presses left, no newspapers printed?

Not long ago, there were hundreds of thousands of newspapermen and women, journalists and editors and even publishers who not only could handle the truth, they reveled in being able to tell it to the public.

Somehow in the dying days of the Twentieth Century, this began to change.

Today's newspapers look good. They also look the same. It's not one corporation, but many. It's said, though not proven, that they all gather quarterly in corporate sweat lodges someplace outside of Barstow, tequila and fear streaming from their pores, trading code words and secret handshakes, talking about branding and demographics and sharing copy so the story gets told to everyone by the same voice. It may not be news, but it's "Pretty Paper," four-color splash, pie charts and links to online extras or what once were called morgue files. Often an advertisement dominates, right in the middle of what could laughingly now be called "news hole."

Speaking of asses, there are holes involved in what's happened all right. But that's another story.

Instead of toiling to provide great newspapers in newsrooms, the often good men and women—who remain shackled to these discouraging daily shoppers because they are in need of paychecks—are forced to operate with blue tooths and work in Information Centers.

The damn nice guys—and we are talking both genders here—who tried hard, who strived with life's blood, have either been laid off, bought out, "retired" or have died. A few, of course, remain, hidden in Information Centers, keeping their heads beneath the cubicle dividers, their backs to the wall and their butts firmly anchored and protected in their chairs.

Not everyone went quietly into the night while Korporate Amerika slowly, but surely, destroyed tens of thousands of lives in The Fourth Estate.

Some fought back, like Tim Ghianni and Rob Dollar, the heart and soul of *The News Brothers*. They were hard-charging but compassionate newsmen who gave it their all, and never backed down, during distinguished newspaper careers.

Ghianni and Dollar never thought twice about sacrificing the security and riches that would have been theirs for a lifetime of just going along and getting along. They battled the bean-counters, flesh-eating weasels and scurvy kiss-ups every day for what they believed to be right and fair. They never turned a blind eye to wrongdoing in the public sector nor in the boardrooms where news coverage was plotted out with polished-lead dollar signs and Monopoly money.

There have been and are others who fought and lost, but this is not their book.

But have Ghianni and Dollar lost?

Well, they don't have fancy cars and sharkskin suits. But they know about sharks.

The truth is, to the bitter end, *The News Brothers* kept their souls and senses of humor.

And they can look at themselves in the mirror every day, and sleep well at night.

Leaf-Chronicle staffers gather at G's Pancake House in Clarksville, Tennessee, after putting out the Sunday morning newspaper sometime in the summer of 1982. From left are: John Staed, Jerry Manley, Billy Fields, Tim Ghianni, Rick Moore, Rob Dollar (standing), Dennis Richardson, Larry McCormack, and Denny Adkins.

Chapter 1
(Tim)

THE DARKEST UNDERSIDE
OF THE HUMAN SPIRIT

When a dog carried what appeared to be an empty gallon milk jug out of the woods in Houston County, Tennessee, on March 1, 1982, it really was helping to launch *The News Brothers* from what had been a tongue-in-cheek brotherhood full-speed ahead on the quest for truth and what's right in the world. What we found along that path guides and haunts us to this day.

My name is Tim Ghianni. My friend and *News Brothers* co-founder, Rob Dollar, and I didn't know at the time how profound an effect that discovery three decades ago would have on our lives.

All we knew was that a woman, Christine Bell, 61, spotted near the road a strange-looking object that appeared to be an innocent empty milk jug to passers-by. She decided to check it out. And, because she did, countless lives were changed forever.

Holding the hand of her 4-year-old granddaughter, Michelle, she walked from her mobile home out in the country along Tennessee Highway 49, about seven miles from Erin, Tennessee, and discovered the object was a head. Well a skull, really.

At least, most of what was left of it.

"It had been laying there for two or three days, and I thought maybe it was a piece of paper that had blown over from the road," Mrs. Bell said.

When we got the word from investigators at the nearby sheriff's department, Rob and I looked at each other.

We knew it had to be the remains of Kathy Jane Nishiyama, the Clarksville, Tennessee, teenager whose mysterious disappearance about 3½ months earlier had traumatized our city. Her purse had been found only five days earlier, about 200 yards from the nearby Yellow Creek Bridge on Tennessee Highway 49.

The skull found that day did turn out to be that of Kathy Jane Nishiyama, 16, and it was dreadful proof of a beautiful and wonderful life cut short. The discovery was made the day before what would have been her 17th birthday.

In a way it was too bad the skull was found and the two or three bones from the skeleton—apparently scattered by the dogs through the woods—did end up to be Kathy Jane's.

Because up until the moment we learned the empty gallon milk jug was a skull, we still had hope that the vibrant girl with the pretty smile and the trusting spirit, the daughter of a proud Japanese-American Army veteran and a genuinely good guy, was still alive.

Well, it actually was up to Dr. William M. Bass, the forensic anthropologist at the Body Farm at the University of Tennessee in Knoxville, to prove it was the skull and a few hound-chewed bones of our beautiful Kathy Jane. But those of us who had lost sleep over her disappearance— even though deep inside we realistically figured she'd been abducted, raped and murdered months before—still held out hope.

For me, that little shred of hope was the last line of defense against the black dogs of depression that had begun consuming my soul.

Always, when a pretty girl or handsome boy disappears, the first thing everyone assumes is that they've taken off on a fling.

Girls—and boys—just wanna have fun, you know.

Problem is that when the law and the media think that way, it gives those killers a chance to get away, the trail to grow cold, allows torture to take place. Ever hear a cop talk about the first 48 hours after a murder? They know, because they've learned.

Even today, more than 30 years since her disappearance, I think about Kathy Jane often and with pain and sweat. Thrashing in the night.

And while it ended in deep trauma that still haunts my soul, I can't help but hope she had fun earlier on the evening of her disappearance —Monday, Nov. 16, 1981— that she was able to laugh, kiss, have ice cream, whatever made her happy. Be a carefree teenage girl enjoying her life.... One final time.

Because the hours that followed, leading up to her death, will always paint pictures of terror in my still troubled and dark brain.

Kathy Jane, a Northwest High School junior, left a note for her parents after school on the day of her disappearance, informing them she was going to visit her boyfriend, David Lin, 17, and would be home by 10 p.m. She left Lin's house in the Shiloh community between 8 and 8:30 that mid-November night, in her 1978 Ford Mustang, heading home. She never made it. Her car was found around 11 p.m. in the parking lot of a church, only blocks from her home on Charlemagne Street in North Clarksville. The car was locked, covered with dew and the engine was cold.

The teenager lived close to Fort Campbell, the massive Army post straddling the Tennessee-Kentucky line near Clarksville, because her pop was a military retiree. Our town was filled with retired vets and their families. Still is, although I can't force myself to go back up that way much anymore. Too many reminders of that winter that still devastates me, at times that should be happy, peaceful.

As far as we can figure, because no one really knows for sure, Kathy Jane was driving home on Fort Campbell Boulevard, near the Lafayette Street intersection, when she saw flashing lights in her rear-view mirror.

Maybe she was going too fast. We all do. Heck, on that highway, chances are good, if you didn't speed, you'd probably get run down by a soldier in a Trans Am with red-and-yellow flaming decals.

Anyway, on that autumn night, Kathy Jane pulled off Fort Campbell Boulevard into the parking lot of one of those big, fundamentalist churches where they still speak in tongues. She probably had her beautiful smile primed when she rolled down the window for the man she believed was an approaching "officer."

Nah, he won't give me a ticket, she likely thought, taking one last look into her mirror, checking for smudges and the like.

She didn't know it wasn't a cop who walked toward her car, of course.

This was the 1980s, when people still trusted the lights. Still trusted at all. Believed the good guys won. That The Lone Ranger still rode to the rescue and no one had bombs in their underwear.

Later that night, Kathy Jane's boyfriend, David Lin, found her car in the church parking lot. Concerned—after telephoning the Nishiyama residence three separate times after she had left his house, only to find out she still had not made it home safely—Lin went out looking for her. She was never heard from again.

But, it wasn't long after her disappearance that I got a call from a pretty reliable source about a bloody necklace rumored to have been found in a police car that "was returned" the morning after Kathy Jane disappeared without a trace.

The law enforcement agency involved—the sheriff's department in a nearby county—had allowed a trusty serving time on a burglary conviction at the Dickson County Jail to use the car to run an errand the day of her disappearance, and the convicted felon instead had apparently taken the vehicle on a "joy ride" to Clarksville and Montgomery County.

I called that department after hearing the tale of the bloody necklace. Officials denied the story. Now, I never saw the bloody necklace, but I believed the person who gave me the information. I also thought the department could be covering up a murderous mistake.

To this day, I think it's possible someone—an officer or perhaps a trusty, even THE trusty—shampooed the blood out of the vehicle's interior rug and perhaps got rid of the floor mats and the necklace. You know…it's not easy, or convenient, to admit a prized trusty, who had been out joy-riding in a government vehicle, might have committed a heinous crime while in your custody. So go ahead and yell at the newspaperman. How many times do you deny things before it becomes the truth?

That stone-walling probably delayed any sense of closure for the Nishiyama family, dragging out the uncertainty about what happened to Kathy Jane for another 3½ months. Investigators might have solved the case that November, simply by a forceful interrogation of the trusty.

Instead it was months of hoping, with all of Clarksville, she was safe, but perhaps having wild sex, maybe even being a sex slave in South Florida, tragic sure, but not usually deadly. That latter one is what they always throw out there when missing girls are particularly attractive. Crazy thoughts, for sure... I don't know.

Been a long time ago... OK. Some of the details are kind of hazy. Others, though, are crystal clear. Those details frequently shake me from slumber. I awaken with bruises on my hands from the clenched-fist tension and terror.

I do remember that around the time Kathy Jane disappeared, *The Leaf-Chronicle* newsroom helped Jerry Manley and I celebrate our 30th birthdays. Well, actually, Jerry and I helped the newsroom celebrate our birthdays. We had one heck of a party.

Our close-knit group even managed to get together one afternoon for a game of touch football, where Rob amazed us while playing quarterback.

Rob (He celebrated his 25th birthday on the very day of Kathy Jane's disappearance) could throw a football. He thought he was pretty good at making passes at the ladies, too. His problem, and he admits it, ruefully, is that too often there weren't enough eligible wide-open receivers... in either game.

Me, I used the game to try to hurt people, work out my own pain and anger. Same way I did in high school, when I ran full-on into a running back and delighted in the collision and ruptured spleen. In the "Newspaper Bowl," I delivered much more than an arm tackle to a reporter I didn't particularly like. No use naming him here. He probably remembers. At least I didn't kill him.

And, I remember like it was yesterday that Kathy Jane's skull was found in a rural ridgeline of woods the day after another teenager's body, that of Rodney Wayne Long, a football star for the small local university, was found along a creek just north of Clarksville, near Interstate 24 and not very far from the state line and Guthrie, Kentucky

He had been missing for 17 days.

Rodney was a good kid from Rainbow City, Ala. A talented young receiver—No. 86—with a lot of promise and even more character.

He was last seen alive by friends on the campus of Austin Peay State University on Thursday, Feb. 11, 1982.

The 19-year-old freshman had just spent the evening refereeing youth basketball games in the massive gym of the local mega-Baptist church.

After he got back to his dorm around 11 p.m., he ran into some of his buddies playing cards. He joked around a little and then said he was going to go down the road for some burgers and bring them back to the dorm.

He never returned from his late-night trip to the burger joint.

Instead, well…I don't know how far to get ahead of myself… but Rodney was a Good Samaritan…A fine, young man. And it cost him his life.

His mom, Barbara Mack, called me at *The Leaf-Chronicle* newspaper offices the very next day after his disappearance. She didn't know me, but she knew her boy. She was angry and she wanted someone, anyone, to listen.

The local cops told her Rodney went out to sow his wild oats.

"Probably holed up with some girl in a hotel over near Camden," more than one cop joked. It was no secret that plenty of other teens in Clarksville and elsewhere had disappeared in the past, only to turn up with sheepish grins on their faces days or even weeks later.

I only wish that had been the case with Rodney, that he would have been there or wherever, doing what young men and young women enjoy, exploring the pleasures of life, laugher, kisses, happily dancing in the dark.

Rodney's body was found on a peaceful Sunday—Feb. 28, 1982—in the weeds of a creek bed. He'd been shot to death, execution-style. When his bloated body was recovered, bloodstains marked the referee shirt he'd had on for the church basketball games. Who knows what happened to his whistle….

Lawmen summed up the slaying as a tragic case where the victim—Rodney—had simply been "in the wrong place at the wrong time."

To this day, I think a lot—too much—about them... Rodney and Kathy Jane.

Sometimes it's when I'm sleeping. And suddenly I'm awake. Hot and cold. Sweating and chills.

Sometimes it's when I look at my own kids and triple-check the security alarm on the house.

Gotta admit that even when my kids are not at their most pleasant, I don't breathe easily until they are inside our locked, bolted doors.

My daughter is away at college. ... and my heart grimaces when she tells me she walks across the campus, alone, at night, to go to the library or the rec center. "It's safe," she says. "Nothing will happen."

Same thing the kid who went for the burgers thought. Or the girl who stopped for the "cop" in a church parking lot.

Back then, the discovery of the football player's body in the ditch and a day later the "gallon jug" that was what was left of the beautiful 16-year-old girl, dragged from the woods, were really grim realities.

Part of our business, I guess.

This was the business we'd chosen for our life's work.

We were young, and we were newspapermen...Soon to become *News Brothers*.

Looking back on it, I think it was during the search for those two young kids—among Clarksville's best and brightest—that something began to change in me.

Rob, too...

Oh sure, we still got a laugh out of a good shootout or drunken gunplay out at one of the GI bars on Fort Campbell Boulevard. How many bodies of 101st Airborne Division (Air Assault) warriors were they pulling from crunched vehicles off U.S. 41A or Tiny Town Road, out near the post? By the way, you ever have a human brain squish when you stepped on it? Get back to that later....

Had to laugh or go crazy. It's called "Gallows Humor," no stranger to doctors, EMTs, firemen, coroners, cops and reporters, those who have chosen lives punctuated by death.

Nah, you don't court death. But it's there. You deal with it. Except when two beautiful teenagers are murdered and their parents cry on your shoulder. And you want to join them.

In our profession, though, a good murder trial brought out the jokes, as we coped with grisly details, often dramatized by Rob, who was our cops and courts reporter. Me, well my turf included the victims' families, tales of heartbreak, columns about survivors and the bereaved that often were packaged with his straightforward tales. Parents in pain, even GI widows sought me out as a guy who could tell their stories, allow them to mourn, describe their losses. Tales of widows and moms. Sudden orphans and grandpas burying their kinfolks.

And, of course, the crimes, the regular prostitution stings and pervert roundups at the public parks had to be covered. It was news, and we worked for a newspaper.

But something changed with these two kids. It was hard to make a joke.

Sure, we still tried to cope. We laughed away our tears when we could. "He got a burger to go, and then he was gone," was one line I would insert into the stories about the last sighting of Rodney at the drive-thru window of Wendy's Restaurant on Riverside Drive.

With the unfolding of the two tragic deaths, I noticed my smoking had picked up. I'd always had a taste for tobacco. And this was back when newsrooms were hidden beneath a cloud of blue smoke.

But a pack of Camel Lights became two. And then three.

And if the machine in the break room was out of lights, well, Marlboro Reds would do just fine. Let's have another one. Just like the other one.

In the meantime, my coffee drinking became out of control. I didn't stop until my heart was racing and sweat poured from my forehead. I actually sought that combination of feelings.

A simple coffee break between editions, when we walked down the street to a café, turned into two or three breaks during the morning rush to deadline and the press run. At one point, we counted my intake of coffee at an average of 40 cups a day.

Needless to say, the nights weren't much easier. While normal people slept, liquor was my late-night pal. I drank alone. All by myself. Until I could sleep. " I started out on Burgundy, but soon hit the harder stuff," Dylan once sang, as if he was describing my life.

Many evenings I exercised by walking to the local liquor store—Pal's Package—where I sought conversation and recommendation. Jimmy Maddox talked about how his brother had been murdered after a botched robbery long ago and recommended the whiskeys I should try when I got home.

But then, there were nights when I needed someone to join me……

Anyone. Eventually, it became Rob. And Jerry Manley.

Sometimes other guys on the staff, photographers and the like, when they got too close to the flame that was this double-edged news story…

Liquor to come down at night. Coffee to come up during the day. Cigarettes and death the constants of daydreams and nightmares.

Sometimes I'd stop and worry about me.

About us.

All of us.

But I'd shake it off and order up another round of the appropriate, for the moment, intoxicant or lubricant of choice.

The News Brothers—you can still see some of our adventures on YouTube, Facebook and other places on The Internet—had been around a little while, our camaraderie beginning several months before the official naming of this Band of Brothers.

It was while we were making merry that things began to change forever.

This is a school portrait of Northwest High School student Kathy Jane Nishiyama, who was abducted and murdered in mid-November 1981.

Rodney Wayne Long, who played wide receiver on the Austin Peay State University football team, went missing in February 1982 after going out for a late-night hamburger. He was later found dead, shot in the head execution-style.

Charles Edward "Eddie" Hartman, originally sentenced to the death penalty in the brutal murder of Kathy Jane Nishiyama, died in the Tennessee State Prison May 24, 2007. He was 49 years old.

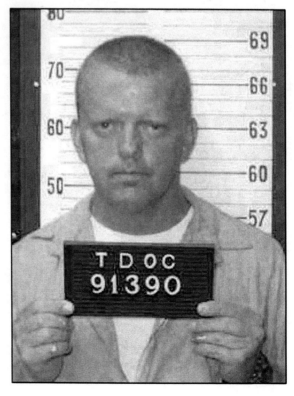

Stephen Drake and David Frey were apprehended on the East Coast within weeks of Rodney Wayne Long's slaying. Their trial in January 1983 was moved to nearby Springfield, Tennessee

We became deadly serious in our live-for-tonight, merrymaking once the two bodies were found, one right after the other in a numbing and shocking fashion.

It was our responsibility to tell the city that it was not safe to be young, pretty and a teenager any more. Heck, it wasn't safe to be out at a burger joint or church parking lot at night. A TV reporter looked at me at Kathy Jane's graveside service and said: "People must be terrified here in Clarksville."

At first I ignored her. TV only came up from Nashville for the gruesome stuff, the big stories. They didn't cover the dead soldiers out on Fort Campbell Boulevard or the plight of military widows.

Still the reporter was striking—many of them are—so I volunteered "I don't know about the rest of the town, but I'm scared shitless and sleepless." Didn't make the 6 p.m. news with that clip.

In addition to various management roles, my favorite task had always been writing columns about how wonderful most people are, no matter their walks of life. Yep, Clarksville was kind of like a happy TV show, where the good guys won, the bad guys went to jail and the cops and the press were friendly antagonists. Lots of hugs and High-Fives in the air.

All of a sudden, though, I discovered this city—and I'd lived in Clarksville for going on eight years when the kids were slaughtered—was nothing resembling Andy Griffith's Mayberry. Lock your doors, mothers and fathers. Darkness looms. And it's not just at the edge of town any more. They are coming for all of us. Me too.

"Death Waits in the Dark" is the way "The Night Stalkers" at Fort Campbell put it. And it's true. But in this case it wasn't covert missions with fast copters and well-trained guys doing it full-metal-jacket-style.

Rodney's death was at the hands of the boys next door. Literally in my case, as it turned out Long's killers had stayed with an aunt in the neighborhood butting up against the parking lot of my apartment complex.

When the deaths began to darken my already brittle psyche, I continued to write slice-of-life columns. But suddenly I began to notice slugs crawling up the sides of dank walls, dead birds in front of favorite restaurants.

Vultures tearing at dog carcasses on Madison Street....

These dark details were included in my columns. I suppose the slugs had been there before. But they emerged to my consciousness as I experienced the darkest underside of the human spirit. These excursions began to take me into the rougher parts of town, where I had been told I was tempting fate. "White people don't go down there at night," I was cautioned. I would fire up a smoke and laugh, climbing into the Duster to find moonlight and crap games. Gunfire and laughter. Slugs on walls.

I'm as safe here as in my apartment parking lot or at a burger joint, I'd tell myself, as I wandered among the dice players and numbers runners, barbecue smoke lifting my spirits a bit as I heard soft blues licks coming from guitars on porches and backyards.

Readers, who had grown accustomed to the happier images of dancing butterflies and clear blue skies that appeared in my works, seemed to be disturbed by the slugs. They began to send me prayers. I would read them and cry.

Then I'd light up a cigarette and say "The Hell with it." I still have some of those prayers, though. May need them when the call comes from up yonder or whatever. Or wherever.

Of course, at the newspaper, we at first had to accept it wasn't a safe place before we could tell the rest of our town.

We had to come to terms with the fact this was a frighteningly real time in our lives and those of our townspeople, the ones we served.

And the other ones we ultimately buried....

It was not just me, as associate editor and columnist, and Rob, the police reporter, who had to try to shake it off. This was different than covering a drunken-driving death or a red-neck shooting. This was innocence being slaughtered.

Our own innocence as much as anyone else's....

Jerry Manley, the copy desk chief, and a wonderful friend, had to force himself to read and edit the stories, write headlines, while perhaps thinking about his young son at home.

Sometimes if I had a day off, I'd pick up his son at the day care and haul him out to the Poor Man's Country Club on Madison Street, where Jerry would come out for beer and pickled eggs. Little John sat on the counter and seemed not to be bothered by the cigarette smoke. The barkeep would slide us a Pabst and Little John would watch the frosty mug slip down the bar.... and giggle. Sometimes that giggle was all I had to keep me going. That and the fact he'd lick my suds-covered index finger.

But other journalists were pulled into the death swirl.

A young guy named Jim Lindgren, also a copy editor, had to edit some of these stories. Pretty much fresh out of Indiana University, he has since told me that the errant behavior of me, Rob and Jerry while putting out prize-winning newspapers filled with crime coverage, at first scared the shit out of him.

He thought we were old.

He thought I was nuts.

He's still a great friend, because he leaped into the fray once he realized our way was the only way to handle what was happening in this little city along the Cumberland River. He still thinks I'm old and nuts by the way.

Course he's some sort of Star Trek super-geek, but a good fellow. Married to a young woman (not so young I guess now) who I first trained in developing film and getting coffee and pulled pork barbecue at Red's when I was a sports writer and she was my Saturday intern back during her high school days. We even went out with other reporters from my earlier days at the newspaper for the occasional drunken dance at the VFW, where apparently everyone was of age.

Like I've already mentioned, there were plenty of others who were shaken and stirred by what 30 years later seems like The Mother of all Murders, Mayhem and Nightmares.

There was our city editor, W. Wendell Wilson, whom we jokingly referred to as a "newspaperman" when it really wasn't a compliment. Those who are fans of the popular 1970s television series, "M*A*S*H," would have no trouble whatsoever picking out Wendell Wilson in a crowd. He was our "Major Frank Burns," or "Ferret Face"—someone who many people found difficult to like and respect.

Wendell didn't care about much as long as deadlines were made and the City Council and County Commission coverage didn't suffer as we tried to put out balanced newspapers. When he was a reporter, he was known to begin every story with the same breath-taking words "The meeting of (name your government body here)." Once, he actually got three leads like that on the front page. Maybe the feat is somewhere in the Guinness Book of World Records.

I remember early in Wendell's career when the rest of my pre-*News Brothers* comrades—many if not most of them dead now—sat with me at Red's, a barbecue and stuffed-baked potato joint on Riverside Drive, near the Cumberland River, during a snow day. We'd gotten to the office that day at 4 a.m. instead of 5:30 and had the paper done early for delivery purposes.

The "newspaperman" declined our offer to join us for a late breakfast. He said he had to go get some tires for his old Camaro. I remember we all were looking out the window onto Riverside Drive when the Camaro's front wheels rolled into sight... followed by the "newspaperman" in the rest of the crippled vehicle, its nose at first traveling above the pavement, defying gravity, like in one of those cartoons. Then it settled into the asphalt with a screech and sparks.

"Lug nuts weren't tightened," Wendell yelled at us, as we raced out to roadside and applauded his feat, after first assuring ourselves he was OK.

Anyway, Wendell eventually got himself promoted to a position where he taught other people how to write...It happens sometimes...Like a quarterbacks coach who's never stood under center. Or a general who never has actually seen combat. Ever hear of The Peter Principle?

In his new job, Wendell preached his "the meeting of" lead-writing philosophy, which sure didn't make him a hit with the young reporters or anyone else for that matter.

So, I guess it's true that not all bad things about journalism began when the corporations bought the newspapers and gutted them.

The last I heard of Wendell, he was living somewhere in Arizona, where he's actively involved in anti-death penalty protests. He's no longer practicing journalism, Thank God.... Course if he writes for the anti-death penalty cause and an execution, he could write about "the meeting of the condemned man with the needle."

When the Nishiyama and Long murders were in the headlines, our county government reporter at the time, Harold Lynch, didn't quite understand what was happening around him. He was busy pleasing the "newspaperman," now the city editor, while we danced with death. Harold, a one-time rodeo star who always wore a black cowboy hat, couldn't understand the reason we were perhaps running on fumes and tiptoeing the fine line between laughter and tears.

But he was dealing with his own demons.

Once when his car was broken down, he called me to come and pick him up. On the way home, he asked if I'd stop at the market so "I can get myself a beer for tonight." He came out of the store with a case of beer. He'd already downed a couple Sterlings by the time I got him to his rooming house on Golf Club Lane.

The News Brothers had an editor, Tony Durr. He cared ... at least as long as he didn't have to work hard. He cared enough to turn us loose on the story and stand behind our work. He wanted to sell papers and look good, of course. But he also was a father of two children, one of whom lived with him (and his next wife-to-be) after a divorce.

During those dark days, the routine became familiar. Rob and I would show up for work, track down clues, follow up on anonymous tips, talk to suspects and friends, talk with family and friends....

Ladle out stories of love and tragedy while Jerry Manley asked us questions, making sure the copy was clean and made sense.

And then we went for coffee.

Because of my intake, Durr referred to me in print as "The Caffeine Kid." "Nobody, but nobody, drinks more coffee than Tim Ghianni, The Caffeine Kid," he wrote once in one of his newspaper columns.

Some people misread that as "Cocaine Kid." Not true, but it didn't bother me, the way I fidgeted and roamed, smoking and cussing, going sleepless and surly, I could understand that misconception. I figure it only added to the outlaw mystique that began to build around me and my friends.

Durr, for example, one day looked around my Saturday newsroom, filled with cigarette smoke and fellows who liked to drink, liked to laugh, liked to work. "You know, Tim, you remind me of Hawkeye Pierce in M*A*S*H. You amaze me.

"You come to work in that Hawaiian shirt and you help keep everyone sane because you are appropriately insane. It really helps you put out the newspaper."

He cautioned me that what would be my undoing is that while I helped others deal with their stress by perking them up, "you wear your feelings on your sleeve. It's gonna get to you sometime." It wasn't the first or last time he offered that caution.

Then he went out to play golf while I fired up another Camel and choked down some lukewarm coffee.

Rob (my "Trapper John"), back then an occasional smoker to deal with the pressure and stress of deadlines, couldn't handle the Camels, but he took up Kools, and we smoked plenty while we drank our coffee at The Royal York Hotel's cafe, a meat-and-three diner attached to what could only be called a flophouse.

Jerry had an odd vice. His wife at the time—his first, but who's counting?—smoked Virginia Slims. Here was this thick, bearded, short, mountain (or maybe foothill) of a tough-guy from Redneck Country smoking women's cigarettes. Yep, we've come a long way, baby.

Like I said, The Royal York Hotel, once Clarksville's grandest hotel, became something of a clubhouse. It was around the block and only a three- to four-minute walk from our desks in the newsroom.

More than one cowboy star and perhaps even a horse or two stayed at this hotel back in the golden matinee days of the 1940s.

The one-time General of the Army, Omar Bradley, was a guest in the 1950s.

This old hotel still had the elevator with the gate you closed as you rose and you drove it by pulling on the lever and looking at the floor numbers painted on the doors to the shaft.

Course there was no elevator operator. And the rooms, concrete cubicles, were filled by mostly old men, fellows who had tried to make their marks in the world, like we all do.

This hotel was as far as they got, a long layover en route to death.

Or perhaps it was where they landed on the way down. An existence where they swapped dog-eared Zane Grey novels and watched game shows on the TV in the lobby by day, cop shows at night and Johnny Carson would end their day.

A room for maybe $5 a night, including electricity and water …. No TV. No phone, no pool, no pets. Private bath and a thin mattress mounted on a cement riser.

"Fireproof," bragged the neon sign out front … when it was working.

The hotel would figure more into our lives as the weeks and months progressed. But while we knocked down cup after cup of coffee and filled up ashtrays, we started fantasizing about our own "15 Minutes of Fame," talking about deadly crimes while at the same time looking for ways to make fun of ourselves. We needed to find a coping mechanism.   Hey fellas, I know what we'll do: We'll make a movie!

Yes, crying about whatever happened to Kathy Jane and Rodney somehow led us to begin plotting a movie that would cast us in the starring roles....

Our friends from the newsroom laughed at us. I don't think they questioned that we would do our movie. Some probably worried that young Rob had fallen in with the wrong friend or friends. He'd beg to differ, of course.

Here is a close-up photograph of Tim Ghianni, taken by him with his trusty camera sometime in the early 1980s.

Leaf-Chronicle Reporter Rob Dollar shakes hands with Al Gore in 1982 shortly before the young Tennessee congressman announced his plans to run for the U.S. Senate.

But I think those other newsroom folks just figured we were nuts and a mess....what with coming to work every day wearing sunglasses and our high school letter jackets.

The Hawaiian shirts and football jerseys....

The deadness in the circles beneath our eyes....

The constant amber nicotine stains on our fingers....

While *The News Brothers* already had been born, and were alive and kicking, this—the depressing and gut-wrenching days after the discovery of the bodies of Kathy Jane Nishiyama and Rodney Long—was our official "Coming-Out Party."

We couldn't just sit there and cry. We had to tell stories and talk to the bereaved. I had funerals to cover. Rob had more dead bodies to go out and see get scraped off the highways.

Perhaps it was some sort of Post-Traumatic Stress Disorder that was triggered in Rob and me. That's our only explanation all these years later. How frequently I wake up, sweating, trapped in the middle of those days. My wife has to shake me as I scream the foulest obscenity and murder threats into the night.

Rob and I both had been swamped in covering these sensational murders, along with our many newsroom cohorts, for weeks. Months even.

And now, the inevitable had occurred, the bodies—or "skeletal remains," the acceptable newspaper euphemism for the state of what was left of Kathy Jane when the dogs and weather were done with her—had been found on successive days.

I had befriended the parents of the two teenagers, as associate editor and general interest columnist, and had been writing columns and news stories about the dual mysteries. If a news item was about to break that may expose the parents to more hurt—if that was possible—I would pick up the phone and forewarn them.

Rob, too, had prided himself on being polite and courteous. Unlike me, he had to report the news in straightforward fashion, where I could cry in print, help the town fear and come to terms with what had happened and grieve for the young people.

But we couldn't cry ourselves. If we'd been able to....it's quite possible *The News Brothers* never would have been set free to make a mark on the city. For what replaced those tears was an undeniably fine madness, laced with mirth and mourning.

This was our city, Rob and I reckoned.

And these criminals had stolen its innocence. Ours too....

Oh, we were hardened by our trade. But, this was the Perfect Storm.

In the preceding months, it seems like scores of people died on the highways of Clarksville and Montgomery County, so many that the county set a traffic death record. Many of the fatalities were soldiers from nearby Fort Campbell, home of the 101st Airborne Division (Air Assault).

Seldom did a Friday or Saturday night go by that some soldier didn't drunkenly run into a post or bridge abutment. Sometimes they even lived. Many times these men and women, trained in the art of killing, bled out on Tiny Town Road or U.S. 41A, the deadliest of the city's roads.

Rob had been to many of the fatal wreck scenes as a reporter. I helped get the stories in the newspaper. I'd seen plenty of bodies, often going out to cover the cops after my last reporter had gone home, and really didn't need to see more.

There were so many wreck pictures, depicting policemen with flashlights examining a burned, torn vehicle, perhaps with a body covered by a blanket nearby, that the Mr. Big of *The Leaf-Chronicle*, Publisher Luther Thigpen, had actually mandated that no more wreck pictures appear in the newspaper. We liked to call Mr. Thigpen "The Big Guy."

Now, The Big Guy's "new rule" was issued two decades before Gannett took over *The Leaf-Chronicle* and sanitized the news, making it bland, and mostly filled with stuff appealing to white, upper-class women looking for coupons, teeth whiteners and satin nighties.

The Big Guy didn't explode when he came into the newsroom to announce such weighty decisions.

He would stand there and jingle the change in his pockets as newsroom managers made their daily decisions about where to place the news stories and pictures.

Mr. Thigpen was a pretty good guy, we reckoned, but surely the Chamber of Commerce must owe him a plaque or two. He was Mr. Good News long before it became a corporate mantra for Gannett and other Information Center chains.

Nothing against good news....It's just that most "news" is bad news, by nature. Or it's no news at all, as you'll notice if you look at your local corporate-owned paper.

Rob and I were numbed to violence, or perhaps by it.

I mentioned the squish of cerebral matter earlier. Well, a cop told me once at an accident scene that the slippery matter I had just stepped in was part of a brain. I think he probably was lying. I shared a sour laugh of the damned as I scraped my shoes off on the edge of the asphalt. Probably was just garbage....Or a possum.

I never wore those shoes again, regardless. Started wearing red Converse All-Stars instead. I still wear them sometimes. Except nowadays they hurt my feet. Not enough support for an old, burnt-out relic of the news business and life in general.

A car full of young women I knew, who were somehow connected to the Austin Peay State University Athletic Department, burned to death one night when their car caught fire after a crash out on the Boulevard. They pretty well melted.

When cops and reporters arrived at that grisly scene...Well, the only thing they found that did not burn...that was left uncharred, without a scratch on it, was the Holy Bible.

I had asked one of them out a few months before the accident. Never had a date, but we talked a lot of basketball.

Rob had been to fires and market robberies, written of rotted corpses and seen bullets in the head, exploded eyeballs. It was all part of the day's work. It was the same for other staffers.

One of our photographers brought in a murder photo one night that was a close-up of a man's testicles. A bullet had entered the inside of the thigh. Nervous laughs rang out in the newsroom, even while our stomachs turned.

It was just another day in The Life and Death of Clarksville.

We tried to shrug it off. Sometimes I'd sing "A Day in the Life"... "I read the news today o boy,'" goes the great Beatles song, celebrating the cheery side of death.

Still, there was something that happened to us during the searches for Kathy Jane and Rodney, something that ached in our respective souls.

"Why?" Rob and I asked each other when we looked at the picture of the body bag carrying the football player's remains.

He had given two out-of-town strangers, David Frey and Stephen Drake, a ride after they asked for his help during a chance meeting at the burger joint... A helping hand...."Good shot!" Drake yelled out after Frey shot Rodney in the back when he tried to run as the two men robbed him of his car. Frey then walked up to the wounded Rodney and fired a second and fatal bullet into his head, execution-style.

A tough football player is no match for a bullet. No match for evil. They stole his car and made their getaway to the New Jersey-Pennsylvania area on the East Coast, leaving the young man to spill his life's blood along a creek in an isolated field.

"Why?" Rob and I asked each other, whenever we visited that site. That area's been developed now. Doubt the folks in the big, modern mansions know what happened there, what I lost there and why.

Recreational drives would lead us to this spot of darkness at the edge of town.

Perhaps to grieve. Hell, sometimes it was the laugh of the damned that echoed over the creek as we amused ourselves, dulled the pain, with sick jokes and cheap beer. But we ached.

Somehow these two tales of murder, of beauty and promise of youth snuffed like slugs by evil, helped fuel what was to come.

Both the good and the bad. The madness and the joy that still, I believe, guide our lives all these years later.

The adrenaline rush of the big story, the newsman's cynicism, Gallows Humor offered up in heaping doses to cope with the deadlines and the headlines, carried us through.

So did the whiskey and the cigarettes. And, of course, the coffee....

The stories we told when a bartender would let us in after closing and let us drink until it was time for dawn's stumble home for a fitful night's sleep before getting back on the trail of murder and teenage tragedy early the next morning.

But what happened would leave us still, a third of a century later, talking, weeping, and even laughing. People say we're crazy.

Old pain still aches when I think about those two kids.

There was not then nor now any levity directed at the dead youths or their families. Heck, we didn't even smile years later with the deaths of two of the killers. Charles Eddie Hartman, the jail trusty who was convicted in the Nishiyama case, died of natural causes in prison instead of death by electrocution. Stephen Drake, convicted and sentenced to a lengthy prison term along with David Frey in connection with the Long slaying, eventually was shot and killed by another inmate in a Tennessee prison.

But our laughter remains as we reflect on how we dealt with those stories.

"Laugh for a Good Cause," screamed the marquee on the night our names "Tim Ghianni and Rob Dollar, *The News Brothers* (in) Flapjacks: The Motion Picture" glistened in neon above the once-abandoned movie theater, a beacon in the night of Nov. 12, 1982 ... nearly nine months after the teenagers' bodies were found.

The movie that enabled us to help find peace within our own souls, scarred by too much violence and loss, was showing at The Roxy on Franklin Street in downtown Clarksville. People were paying to see it.

There was a military band playing in front of the theater. The Clarksville High School cheerleaders performed for the crowd. We arrived on a fire truck instead of limousines. Photographs from that night show friends and relatives, most of them now dead, sharing in our joy.

Somewhere, along the way of this long, strange trip, probably when we were making our movie, we gave ourselves "*News Brothers*" names.

Tim Ghianni and Okey "Skipper" Stepp watch the world on parade while sitting on a bench outside the Royal York Hotel in downtown Clarksville, Tennessee in 1982.

Leaf-Chronicle staffers Sandy Smith (left) and Pam Fleming sit with Okey "Skipper" Stepp on his bench, while two News Brothers (Rob Dollar and Tim Ghianni) make a spectacle of themselves in the Royal York Hotel lobby.

I became "Flapjacks." The name came from one of our favorite late-night treats, going out for pancakes and coffee with Okey "Skipper" Stepp, an old merchant marine we had befriended in the early summer of 1982.

Rob, who had to deal with the deadly and tragic side of life daily as our police reporter, was "Death."

Jerry Manley, a funny and good man who took to wearing a yellow aviator's cap to work, was dubbed "Chuckles." Rounding out the original quartet of *News Brothers* was Jim Lindgren, who was "Flash." Others enlisted in the "fun" as well, when the spirit moved them. John Staed was "Street," Ricky G. Moore was "Dumbo," Billy Fields was "StrawBilly," and last, but not least, Harold Lynch, who stole the show in our movie with his portrayal of an aging gunfighter, was "The Stranger." I think the rest of the guys just made up names for themselves that they thought sounded cool or funny. In later years, after our movie was showing to raves as a cult classic on cable television, the newest additions to *The News Brothers* arrived on the scene: "Badger" (Scott Shelton) and "Teach" (David Ross).

"You know, Flap, we should just drive off into the Cumberland River tonight and die," said Rob, "Death" *News Brother*, as he passed another $2 bottle of champagne to me while our friends hooted and hollered at that memorable movie premiere so long ago.

"Yep. It'll never get any better than this," I said.

"This probably was our 15 Minutes of Fame," Rob added, with a big grin, just before he jumped into a black Trans Am—driven by a hot redhead, *The News Brothers'* first official groupie—that sped away from the theater, headed for what most certainly was a rendezvous with destiny if the liquor didn't get in the way.

Now, *The News Brothers* are—and always have been—for full disclosure. But, *News Brothers* don't kiss and tell.

Some things should remain private so as not to distract from the real message.

Rob Dollar, Jerry Manley, and Tim Ghianni stand outside The Roxy in downtown Clarksville, Tennessee, only days before the Nov. 12, 1982, world premiere of *The News Brothers* movie.

As Rob disappeared into the darkness, I rounded up the other late-partiers, locked up the theater, and men and women, some who had at least late-night crushes on an old *News Brother* and his yellow-aviator-cap-wearing pal, went for something to eat. Flapjacks as dawn approached. Hold the bacon.

The night turned into day and a quick shower was the remedy, the spark, that got me back into the newsroom, sleeplessly composing my budget. Laughing at myself. And crying in my heart.

And so, while we've chosen to live, to try to help others, to not back down to evil and corruption, that one night was pivotal in the lives of *The News Brothers*.

It was the culmination of our struggle to come to terms with death in terrible times by laughing in its face, along the way risking our careers by disregarding authority or at least not bending down, or over, to suit management's selfish whims.

For some of it, we paid the price. Perhaps still are.

"Why?" you might ask.

Because we were, and still are, the men who played chess with tragedy, checkmating it with levity. Or trying, at least.

We, who helped compose the headlines that screamed the horrors that shocked a city, chose to fight back against the carnage of the soul by playing chicken with "The Grim Reaper" publicly, hiding the raw scars inside our guts.

We remain, to this day, *The News Brothers*.

This is our story as we remember it. There is a certain haze that settles in over time, so the retelling might have a date or detail wrong, here and there.

But the story you are about to read is true. The names have not been changed because nobody is really innocent. Tell me if I'm wrong about that.

Chapter 2
(Tim)

THE BIRTHDAY BASH

In newspaper parlance… or at least in old-time newspaper lingo… the number "30"—often scrawled with a wax pencil—meant the end of a story.

Don't think that's even a part of the terminology these days, when call centers in Bangalore are pretty much responsible for a lot of news decisions.

Actually, there are a few good newspaper people left. It's just that they don't have much contact with me. Never have since the day I was "bought out" a few years ago.

But that's not the story I want to tell today. Instead I want to focus on how back in 1981 "30" was the beginning of something that we really didn't expect.

In a lot of ways, the "30 mark" was responsible for at least fueling a sort of camaraderie that would help birth the notorious *News Brothers*.

But I'm talking about "30" as in "30 years old." Remember when Jerry Rubin and Bob Dylan popularized the phrase "Don't trust anyone over 30"? They were right, of course.

Nov. 13, 1981—four days after Jerry (soon-to-be "Chuckles") Manley's 30th birthday and five days before my own—started out inauspiciously enough, even for a Friday the 13th… It was going to end with a helluva birthday bash.

A couple weeks before Jerry and I—who had been drinking and listening to music together for a number of years—looked around the newsroom at *The Leaf-Chronicle*.

I arrived in this room a couple of years before him, as he actually began his career in Gallatin, Tennessee, where he worked with a guitar-strumming fellow we called "The Rhinestone Fatman." I'm not sure if the Fatman made it to the 30th bash, but I think he probably was there...at least in spirit if not in economy-sized glory...

Anyway, Jerry arrived at the *L-C* not long after the first wave of my colleagues there were beginning to leave. Richard Worden was ready to jump ship (but not dead yet ... you'll read about him later). Richard McFalls was soon to depart as well, to become "Telegraph Editor" at the *Memphis Commercial-Appeal.* My friend Steve Jones, with whom I shared a passion for Rastafarian music and rituals as well as Colorado beer, had also moved on to Memphis and actually by this time may have been living in Hong Kong and working for the *Wall Street Journal.*

Even Ron Taylor, who back then was a pretty good guy, soon left for some small manure-producing town in Southern Illinois.

Jerry and I were now the old relics on the staff. Or at least the old relics among the "young" staff. One other old-timer, W. Wendell Wilson, I guess, was still there, but no one really cared, one way or another.

There had been some changes, though, by November of 1981. Notably that *The Leaf-Chronicle* had a relatively new editor in Tony Durr, a guy I came to love even if Jerry didn't like him. "He's a liar," Jerry would tell me.

"I know. A lot of people are. But I like the guy." Tony, by the way, had taken to noticing that not only was I the editor of prize-winning sports pages and a damn good and much-honored daily sports columnist, but I also had begun writing stories for the features and news sections. I did a melancholy Weekend cover story about my failed search for America—with a guy named "Wizard—the length of Route 66 and then some in the summer of '73. I also wrote about Waylon and Willie and the Boys. But I think it was my appreciation of Bob Marley—after cancer consumed his marijuana-addled brain—that caused Tony to take notice.

Soon, I was his special projects editor and actually became his running buddy of sorts, as we tried out our two-man "investigative" team.

One night, he'd gotten a late-night call about alleged patient abuse at a nursing home and he called me. It probably was midnight, and he asked me to pick him up. We were going to raid the nursing home.

And we did. The two of us, bluffing our way past the guard and then entering, where we were greeted by a Nurse Mildred Ratched-like woman who was wondering what two newspapermen were doing in her facility in the middle of the night.

We were coldly but politely asked to leave after "interviewing" one sleepless patient who was drooling in front of a television set. Heeeeeere's Johnny....

We didn't expose the home in print at all, although the big cheeses did call on Tony and me to come back for a meeting and a tour of their facility, allowing us to talk with the patients unescorted.

Never did find out if there really were any problems. But the patient who called Tony said later that the conditions had improved drastically since the midnight raid by the little guy with a beard and the big, young guy with the long curls.

We'd similarly gone out to expose the litter problem in Clarksville, and I was working a little with Tony on a story about prostitution in North Clarksville.

It was during this time, by the way, that the city's best-known madam became a close friend of mine. This was strictly a business friendship. She liked the stories and columns I began writing about people in need and she'd call me, at odd hours, to have me meet her. She'd give me $100 bills to give to various people I'd written about.

"Don't tell them where it came from," she'd say. "Just give it to them from you. They wouldn't want it from me, knowing how I make my money." I always did as asked, and noted that the $100s were always crisp and as bank-fresh as some of her clientele.

The madam with the big heart also was an expert in local history and art, a nice woman, extremely attractive, almost elegant and well-educated. She'd simply found her niche in life and learned how to use it.

Through me, she even managed to contribute to some sort of history project which involved Montgomery County Historian Ursula Smith Beach. Miss Ursula was, by the way, a wonderful woman, a member of Old Clarksville who welcomed all newcomers as long as they loved her city and county.

Now, she actually knew who my generous friend was and what she did for a living, but it didn't matter to her. Of course, I suppose it is an historical occupation—the oldest known to mankind.

Getting off-topic here, but talking about Tony often brings up the thought of whores. Joking, folks. I loved the guy. One of my life's favorite people.

Anyway, Jerry and I not only had a new boss in Tony, we also had a few younger fellows in the newsroom, particularly a young cops and courts reporter I'd taken to joking around with a little in the five or six months he had been with the newspaper. He was a good kid (remember I was almost 30, after all), and he had the passion for newspapering that I still retained at that point.

There were a few other scattered relatively new fellows and women.

But Jerry and I didn't know them well and had taken to just drinking with each other, a habit that would carry on for decades until I pretty much dried up (or is that out?).

We also felt a little melancholy because our old friends were gone. I was known then as now for doing a good Joe Cocker impression at parties and also could be Elvis with a batch of Jordanaires (Jerry, Worden, McFalls, Taylor and even Wendell) singing behind me wearing hardhats. I can't remember why they wore hardhats.

Anyway, Jerry and I were turning 30 and no one was around to help us celebrate or even really care. The idea hit us both that we would throw our own 30th birthday party, roughly halfway between our two birthdays, and invite the whole newsroom. Hell the whole town could come, we didn't care.

We particularly didn't care because on the Friday the 13th we chose for our evening party we'd both left work a little early. We'd already recorded 8-track soundtracks of our favorite party songs, many about birthdays and others about death, to play in the clubhouse of the apartment complex where Jerry lived and first hung up his old aviator's hat.

But before we could set up the sound system, part of it my stuff, part his, we had to pick up our refreshments.

We'd ordered a full 15-plus gallon keg of Budweiser (remember, light beers were then as now for only the weak and elite). We picked it up at 11 a.m. over at the beer store next to Pal's Package and we carted it out to the clubhouse.

Always worried about our guests' happiness, we decided that we should tap the keg and "drink off the foam."

Which began an afternoon-long marathon in which we set up the sound system and vacuumed the clubhouse while making sure the beer still retained its full body.

It was sort of like the end-of-school-year coaches parties I used to organize with my first hire—assistant sports editor Larry Schmidt. Larry—who, with his Clarksville childhood chum Jeff Bibb (now a successful marketing exec) nicknamed me "The Italian Stallion"—and I, joined by No. 3 sports writer Ricky G. "Dumbo" Moore, were especially dedicated to making sure the evening's beverages were well-tested during the party set-up phase.

Larry, who now is a big-shot bank dude in Clarksville, left for a newspaper in Paducah, Kentucky, well before the big 30 celebration. The fact that, when Tony promoted me to columnist and newsroom leader status, he handed the sports editor position first to an out-of-town crony (who failed miserably) and then to a government reporter rather than to him angered Larry into leaving his hometown. Tony made a number of personnel miscues, but this was his worst.

Back to the party for the 30th birthday boys: By the time the guests arrived at 5 or 6, Jerry and I had made sure the keg was in good shape and we were jolly hosts. Heck we'd even had time to take naps on the clubhouse couches in preparation for what we were sure was going to be a long and happy night.

The guests only needed to bring chips or some such item worthy of eating. There wasn't as much variety in crackers and the like back then. And Jerry and I already had some bags tossed here and there for munching. Course we'd eaten some of them, too.

Even Tony, who had told us he couldn't attend because it wouldn't be proper for an editor to see what we might or might not be doing, showed up at about 8.

Former *L-C* staffer Greg Kuhl, perhaps fresh from witnessing an execution in Mississippi—for his reporting job, not for fun—even showed up. (He's now "retired" and running marathons for fun through the mountains of Calgary, where last I heard he was living with his dog, Blue.)

The party itself was a dance-a-thon, most memorable for the line-dancing sing-along to Edwin Starr's "War" and The Beatles' "Happy Birthday" and the Stones' "Gimme Shelter" mixed in with a little roots, rock and reggae.

That dancing and frivolity provided a perfectly relaxed atmosphere in which the two old codgers of the night got to mingle with the younger members of the staff. Most of them left by 11 or midnight.

Jerry and I noted that one of the young single guys stayed in there, step for step, beer for beer, shout for shout and song for song, well into the night.

That was the new police reporter, Rob Dollar, who immediately was branded as "one of us." That in our mind was either a mighty high honor or a curse. You could still view it that way three decades later.

I should mention here that I had bought the keg and Jerry was going to pay his half later. If you are reading this, old friend, well, you know our 60th birthdays have come and gone and I'm still awaiting reimbursement.

This party, by the way, and the staff football game mentioned earlier, marked the last real, carefree weekend for what were to become *The News Brothers*.

You see, the day after the party—I'll get back to its conclusion in a minute—was spent at the newspaper. Bleary-eyed and cotton-mouthed, to be sure, washing down vending machine Honey Buns and M&Ms with black coffee while chain-smoking and laughing.

That night, as they say, was a time for hair of the dog at a place called Camelot. It really couldn't get much better or happier, really. Ignorance is bliss.

The Sunday was the day of the football game in which Rob's passes and my own natural-born aggression (we both are of Italian descent, by the way), shined on the gridiron.

Damn, here I was 30 years old and I had life by the throat. What a wonderful world, indeed, as Satchmo said.

Monday, Nov. 16, Kathy Jane disappeared. We didn't know it right away, but that perfect world for young journalists was going askew. It soon was a full-blown freefall, as described earlier. A year in Hell, with a few jokes for the devil along the way.

A fellow I am proud to call a good friend, the genius songwriter Kris Kristofferson, once wrote a song, "To Beat The Devil," that kinda describes the year that was ahead for us.

Here's a verse: *"You see, the devil haunts a hungry man,*
If you don't wanna join him, you got to beat him.
I ain't sayin' I beat the devil, but I drank his beer for nothing.
Then I stole his song."

We didn't beat the devil either. Kathy didn't come back. Rodney went missing and both turned up dead. We consoled parents and cajoled cops. We saw a never-ending string of death on the highways.

A great friend—despite his shortcomings, physical and professional—Tony left the paper under less than wonderful circumstances. I lost a soulmate and a colleague—Tony and I were in the middle of writing a book when he left. Rob lost a boss who understood him.

Thirty colleagues left the newspaper, most disgruntled, many fired.

Then there was the case of Chico The Monkey....

Anyway, I don't need to roll it all out here. But during the next 12 months ... until, Nov. 12, 1982, the night we had our grand

and glorious world premiere ... we faced the devil and he smiled at us.

We were hungry for answers, for solace. But we didn't get them.

No, even now I can't say we beat the devil. But we drank his beer—oh boy did we drink his beer. And then, as this story goes along, you'll see we stole his song.

I have a habit of getting too far ahead of myself, so before we go any farther, let's go back to the big "30," the party that preceded the fall.

There really isn't much reason to detail the party. You may have been at one like it, perhaps a presidential inauguration or something less significant.

It was wildly enthusiastic, lasted until near dawn and kept us pretty well occupied cleaning up until it was almost time to go to work the next day, which was Saturday. We had to be there by 2 p.m.

But one image sticks with me forever. Sometime around 3 a.m., Tony wanted to leave. The rest of us were going to ride it out in the clubhouse. We were in no shape to drive.

Oh, this reminds me of something about "Tony The Journalist" that I don't believe Rob even knows. I don't think Rob was in Clarksville at the time the serial rapist was striking the trailer parks out near Fort Campbell.

These rapes were coming once a month, when the moon was full.

I don't think the rapist ever was caught, though his cruelty was reported, in good taste, of course, to protect the victims of this worst-type of crime. I only bring this up now because, in a second, I'm going to make fun of Tony.

Did you ever wonder how serial killers and rapists got their nicknames? Remember "The Green River Killer," "The Son of Sam," "The Boston Strangler" ... names that still make goose-pimples rise when we read about their butchery and savagery.

Well, one night, as the Sunday paper was being put together, Tony decided to lead again with the latest crime of the serial rapist, including details about how everyone was scared and neighbors were looking suspiciously at each other. You know, you've read the story a million times.

"We need a nickname for this rapist," said Tony, as he started thinking about the similarities between the rapes. All of them—at least those that were reported—occurred, as I noted earlier, when the moon was full.

Being a sports editor on deadline with scores and stories to work, I looked up and offered: "Let's call him 'The Full Moon Rapist.'"

From that point on, every time the moon is full, I think of that beastly criminal. And I smile in amusement that a sports editor gave the moniker to a savage who had a town traumatized. Of course, you have to remember sports reporters gave names to guys like "Slammin' Sammy" Snead, "Hammerin' Henry" Aaron, Ed "Too Tall" Jones and Joe "The Brown Bomber" Louis, to name a few.

So, who knows who dreamed up the name for "The Boston Strangler"? It might have been an intern or an obituary writer in his first week on the job or a bored sports editor, looking up for a moment while proofing "The Agate Page." (Now generally just called "The Scoreboard Page," since no one really knows what agate is any more.)

Anyway, back to Tony and his inebriated exit—though he claimed otherwise—from the big "30" party for Jerry and me.

We reminded our boss we were staying there at the clubhouse. Course most of us really had no better place to be at that time of the day and really didn't want to die on the highways. We'd already begun to be inundated with those kinds of stories … and it was going to get worse very soon.

Tony said he was fine. He was a pipsqueak, 5-5 or so, but he said he could handle his liquor. So he went out into what had turned into a cold, rainy night. I kept watching out the window as he got in his car, a black Ford sedan.

He kept on revving his engine, but the car would go nowhere.

So I went out to help. Rob may have as well.

Anyway, Tony was sitting behind the wheel of his car, repeatedly pulling on the lever to control his windshield wipers. "I can't get this thing in gear," he said. "Transmission messed up."

He kept working that lever and the windshield wipers kept on going on and off. Finally I pointed out that he needed to use the lever on the other side of the wheel, the gear shifter, and he'd be OK.

I told him to put it on the "little R" and back up carefully. Instead, he jammed it into drive and jumped the concrete curb, bottoming out his car and shooting sparks into the night.

"The R, Tony, the R," I said. "But maybe you should stay here with us."

"Nah, I'm OK," he said. "Sober."

He finally got the car into reverse and drove away backward for perhaps 100 feet before pulling down on the lever, without braking, and driving into the cold and rainy night. (We didn't know it at the time, but he made it as far as Don's Donuts, maybe a half-mile away, before pulling in and parking, calling his current wife-to-be to come pick him up. He didn't admit that to me until a long-distance phone call from Kodiak, Alaska, years later.)

Anyway, as we stood there smoking in the rain, Jerry shook his head and his belly.

"He says he's sober, see I told you he was a liar," said Jerry, as we watched the car disappear into the mist. There even was worry in Jerry's voice, although I think he also was drooling at that point.

"You know, Tim, I think old Tony might be a little drunk," said Rob, as he fired up a Kool.

"Nah, kid," I said. "This is the way he acts all the time."

It was the beginning of a perfect friendship.

Clockwise, from left, Billy Fields, Tim Ghianni, Tony Durr and Rob Dollar get ready for a road trip, probably to nowhere in particular.

News Brothers (from left) Tony Durr, Billy Fields, Tim Ghianni and Rob Dollar share some fun and a few beers in Ghianni's Clarksville basement.

This was the first official photograph of *The News Brothers*, taken in the late spring of 1982, outside *The Leaf-Chronicle* building in downtown Clarksville, Tennessee.
From left are: Jerry Manley, Rick Moore, Tony Durr, Tim Ghianni, Rob Dollar, Billy Fields, and John Staed.

Chapter 3
(Tim)

LET'S WEAR SHADES

Up until the early spring of 1982, *The Leaf-Chronicle* didn't publish on Saturdays. We were an afternoon newspaper, Monday through Friday, and then published a Sunday morning paper.

Saturday papers everywhere always have been poorly read.... even by today's standards when poorly executed papers are poorly read.... But we're talking decades ago here, when newspapers flourished. ... Except on Saturdays.

Why tamper with history and success?

After all, we were Tennessee's oldest newspaper, founded in 1808, and we'd done OK. We beat the big Metropolitan papers (such as they were) down in Nashville on most of the important news. Remember this was decades before the Internet, Fox and *USA Today* helped kill journalism. So people relied on their hometown newspapers.

About the only thing we didn't deliver under this publishing strategy were Friday night sports scores on Saturday morning. Instead, we spread out our staff and stringers over about a five-county (and two-state) radius, covering football or basketball or baseball and we spent our Saturdays massaging the stories and photos into perhaps 16-page broadsheet sections that not only covered all of the college and pro action but were at least half-devoted to the local stuff.

No one touched the locals in the "big" papers, save for a box score perhaps, so we were the definitive and well-written choice even if a day late.

Ah, but then came the early taste of Korporate Amerikan infringement into the affairs of what had been, in essence, a family paper.

Sure the family—Mr. and Mrs. James Charlet (I loved them both, by the way)—had sold the paper to Greenville, S.C.-based Multimedia Inc. years before. But as long as they were in the building, the family flavor prevailed.

As is the case with most people, Mrs. Charlet eventually died, her open coffin displayed in the living room for all mourners to see and pay tribute.

Mr. Charlet retired, to spend his remaining years tending the massive rose garden at the Catholic Church, and the Korporation gradually pushed its way in.

As an aside here, I need to salute Mrs. Charlet, who hired me in 1974 and who always took time to brag about me and to be kind to me in her acerbic fashion.

I also was fond of the old man. He was a newspaperman in his soul, having run papers in Nashville before striking it rich in Clarksville.

And, of course, a part of his wealth came from his ... shall we say, frugality? ... when dealing with the newspaper staff.

I went to work for a princely sum of $125 per week in 1974. "Don't turn in overtime," I was told by the sports editor, Gene Washer, who would eventually become publisher, long after my time in Clarksville was done. He actually gave his life to the newspaper, spending a total of 45 years there, including his first 17 as a sports editor who at first didn't know a strike from a touchdown and then the last 17 as publisher. He retired in 2008.

He was better-known perhaps, at least in his sports writing days, not for how well he wrote, but for how he dressed, in multi-colored sport coats, leisure suits, boots and hats. Kind of a down home and extremely white cornbread version of "Superfly," Washer always had shades on his head. He didn't often use them over his eyes, just used them to keep his permed "Afro" in place. Come to think of it, if he hadn't gone into management, he'd have made a finely dressed *News Brother*.

Speaking of attire, the day I accepted the job, I had waited for my interview in the reception area with a tall black fellow with an ankle-length white rabbit-fur coat. I have no idea why I remember it was rabbit fur.

James "Fly" Williams, a troubled legend of the basketball court in New York City and who had come to play at Austin Peay State University in Clarksville for two years, had that day inked a gazillion-dollar contract (I don't know the figure, but it was a bunch of money) with the old American Basketball Association's raucous Spirits of St. Louis franchise.

So, while I was going to work for what turned out to be less than $3 an hour, my first acquaintance in Clarksville was well on his way to becoming a rich man. Of course, he later was chased from the league because of his antics and eventually he spent time in jail after being involved in what he termed a "misunderstanding" with a shotgun-toting off-duty court officer in New York City. The shotgun roared, leaving the guy who some say ranked among the best basketball players of all time near death and eventually recovering at Attica, where he served a part of his stint and signed autographs for hero-worshiping fellow inmates.

I always liked Fly, though. Still do. When he was on the skids back in New York—in the years before he became a guest at Attica—I'd occasionally call him. He was a man of the streets and the playgrounds, after his fall from grace in professional basketball.

Every once in awhile when I was sports editor of the newspaper and even later when I was writing a regular general-interest column for the news pages, someone would ask about Fly. So I'd go through the same routine. I'd call his mother in Brownsville in the city. Fly didn't live with her.

Instead, she told me, he was living in a series of condemned buildings, I think with this little, round guy he brought to The Peay with him. His mother didn't know where he'd be, but she'd put the word out on the streets.

I'd call the next day or two and she'd tell me how to get him. It may be a pay phone or a friend's apartment phone at a designated hour, usually very late at night. Of course this was long before cell phones. In New York City, the guy who could have been one of the great pro basketball players of all time was invisible, a phantom of Brooklyn.

One time when I called him he said: "Hey, Tim, brother, whatever happened to that little-bitty white guy with the 'Fro and who always wore the f---ked-up clothes?" I told him Gene Washer was in management, which seemed to surprise Fly, who responded by laughing and using the "F" word loudly. Old Fly, rabbit-fur-cloaked basketball legend, liked to use the word a lot. In spending time with him over the years, I found it necessary to employ it as well, to punctuate my conversation so he'd know I was fully engaged and deadly serious about giving my readers the wit and wisdom of the guy who found heaven on inner-city playgrounds.

Anyway, back to Mr. Charlet. Even in those days, $125 a week didn't go far. And it was cut into even more when someone stole the battery from my 1965 Ford Falcon one night outside my $125 a month "efficiency" flop. The best thing about that apartment, in a converted house, was that the train tracks ran, literally, through the yard. I told my friends that "The Last Train to Clarksville" actually passed by my place several times a day.

But the battery incident was tough on me. So, Saturday morning, after the police dusted for prints and even took me to a shop to buy a new battery and helped install it, I sat in the office and wondered how I was going to make it to the next payday.

Mr. Charlet heard my comments—I'm not a soft-spoken guy—and summoned me into his office, where he reached into his pocket and gave me a $20 bill. "Not a loan. You earned it. You've gotta eat," he said.

OK. It wasn't a fortune. But it was kind.

Kindness is not a word heard often in today's world of Korporate Amerikan Journalism.

Anyway, I digressed. Let's get back to the story about Clarksville's first-ever Saturday morning newspaper. It was Saturday, April 3, 1982, and we were standing outside the building sometime after midnight, just by the docks where the trucks picked up their bales of newspapers. It had been a long night.

For the first time, a crew, other than sports writers, had been required to work Friday night. And that meant that most of us had also been in at 5:30 the morning before to put out the regular Friday afternoon edition of the newspaper.

Of course, eventually the shifts would be split, but this was a show of force.

Korporate wanted a Saturday product and all of us, including a Korporate pimp or two, were there to deliver. Sometime after the last baseball score came in and the last body had been pulled from a deadly traffic wreck on Fort Campbell Boulevard, we all went home or maybe to a bar.

But our boss, our editor Tony Durr—who became a dear friend, but who came to us as a Korporate appointment/infiltrator—had mandated the news staff return after only a few hours of sleep and be down by the docks early the next morning for a celebration of the new Saturday product.

And, so it was…Instead of five afternoons and a Sunday morning paper, the bean-counters decided that a Saturday morning edition would be the ticket to wealth and happiness. Nope, don't increase the staff. Yeah, some of them may have to come in to work at 5 a.m. Friday to get the afternoon paper out and then return at 7 p.m. for the next morning's paper but they are young. They don't know any better. If they don't like it, they can leave. "Reporters are a dime a dozen," is the way one editor whore/pimp/genius/wizard phrased the new corporate philosophy.

After all of our moaning, though, which as usual did no good, the morning of the Saturday newspaper launch arrived. And we all followed orders and reported to the newspaper to pose for a picture with our new "SATURDAZE" T-shirts. The photograph was quickly slapped into the next day's newspaper, showing everyone what a dedicated crew of young people had done.

But I'm getting ahead of myself.

Slitted eyes stared into the morning sun to get the photograph. We all were supposed to smile. Some of us wore sunglasses, to hide the red eyes of the night before, or at least offer protection from the sun.

News staff, big shots, advertising execs, publisher, Korporate pretenders, everybody showed up. None of them were stepping on a brain or watching a fire rescue five hours earlier.

None of them had to be in the office later that afternoon to put out the Sunday newspaper.

But, the bigwigs wanted us at The *L-C* for their dog-and-pony show, looking pretty for the camera. So, we were there. On that early Saturday morning, we all walked in, stinking of gin and cigarettes, we all assembled, some of us without a wink's sleep, because it was a big deal. And because it had somehow become a job mandate.

Like I said many of us not only had already worked two shifts in 24 hours, we were also going to have to come back in by 2 p.m.—I always came in at noon—to begin putting out the real money paper, the Sunday edition.

Now, I had advanced to something like "Special Projects Editor" under Durr's guidance, later ascending to associate editor. My job was the same in both cases: I was the fellow who made sure the paper got put out while Tony talked dreams, sat in his living room and made up columns about "real-life" encounters with desperadoes and complained about his migraines.

Or went out to play golf with a lard-ass nice guy reporter who was incompetent enough to go on to have a great career in government. Some claim he'll be mayor of Nashville one day very soon.

I had advanced by hard work. Butt-kissing was never in my arsenal, unfortunately for my long-term career and the good of my eventual family, it turns out. So the idea of us all being required to be there on that day in the spring of 1982 bothered me.

I also felt badly for the others who, like me, were going to be back in for maybe a 12-hour shift in a few hours.

Korporate Amerika has been our bane. But it also helped lay the foundation, at least the cosmetic foundation, for *The News Brothers*.

No, they didn't tell us to laugh at death and as Kris Kristofferson says "smoke too much, drink too much, do every blessed thing too much..."

The bosses told us that on top of all of our other work, we were going to have to put out one more edition of the newspaper each week...More work for the same low pay and same lack of appreciation and respect. And, pssst: Don't turn in overtime.

This new chapter in the history of *The Leaf-Chronicle*—a Saturday morning newspaper—began only 4½ months after the disappearance of Kathy Jane Nishiyama, and just over a month from the exact day her skeletal remains were found in Houston County. The Rodney Long saga, too, was fresh in everyone's mind since he had disappeared and was found dead within a three-week time span, two months earlier in February.

Although *The News Brothers* had had their "Coming-Out Party," they still were without an official name when *The Leaf-Chronicle* launched its Saturday morning newspaper.

A sunny day and stroke of brilliance or two, really, it always took a pair, would change all of that.

I already was wearing sunglasses the morning of the "SATURDAZE" event, because of lack of sleep and perhaps a smidge of alcohol now and again. OK...Maybe hourly. Anyway, I gathered those few around and I said: "When we come in to the office today (this afternoon), everybody must wear shades."

I was deadly serious. It was as big an executive order as I ever made. I threw a cigarette into the gutter as a bit of smoky punctuation.

A light bulb—or perhaps even a cherry bomb—flashed and exploded inside the head of police reporter Rob Dollar. Wild-eyed, he added: "Hey, we'll call ourselves *The News Brothers*."

Now, official in every way possible, it was time for *The News Brothers* to make their mark on the world of journalism and try to save it from falling deeper into the clutches of greedy, Korporate Amerika.

At noon, I was back in the office preparing the news budget for the following day's paper. For some sleep-deprived reason, I began writing the news budget as a series of stream of consciousness tales. For example, the simple listing of court agate—the week's court highlights—became on my budget the life-and-death courtroom adventures of attorney Court Agate, counselor at law.

Even something as simple as the weather forecasts took on characters and stories. During the next several months, before the dream/nightmare ended, these budgets consumed an increasingly greater amount of time. Often I'd come in as early as 10 a.m. to begin writing them, so that they would be there for the 2 p.m. news meeting.

Even if you were a friend of mine, if you died on the road the night before, you may have been the subject of depraved humor in the news budget while cigarettes burned and beery-breathed laughter roared. My budget was a cheery ice-breaker from "the boss" (yes, they entrusted this paper to me on Saturdays), and it loosened us up for producing regularly excellent Sunday newspapers.

Anyway, that day, as I did my first installment, I was a little pissed. And I also knew my guys were a bit down and tired. So I began composing. I wore my shades the whole time I was typing. I wondered how *The News Brothers* would respond to the idea Rob and I had planted in their heads.

At 1:45 p.m., Rob came in from his first visit to "The Cop Shop"—the Police Department/Sheriff's Department down the street—and he was wearing shades.

Then came Jerry Manley, the copy desk chief. He was wearing shades.

Jim Lindgren, the fresh-faced kid who worked on the copy desk, awkwardly wore shades.

The senior sports reporter, a chubby and soft fellow named Ricky G. Moore, who loved greasy hamburgers, was wearing shades and shoving a burger into his bulging cheeks.

Even Billy Fields, the previously mentioned lard-ass who reported the news by throwing facts onto a computer screen and letting editors unscramble them, was wearing shades, though he had no clue why. Still doesn't ... almost 30 years later.

I can't remember where Moore's boss, Sports Editor John Staed, was that day, but I'm damn sure he was at least considering wearing shades. He may have called in sick and sought treatment and recovery while getting a nice tan and playing golf.

Harold Lynch also was missing that Saturday. It was his weekend off. Harold, of course, needed thick eyeglasses just to see, so he wore shades when he could, but only to make us happy.

I nodded at the boys and fired up a smoke. I think we all did. Maybe even Billy. *The News Brothers* had shown up in full force. Korporate Amerika would never, from this day forward, go unchallenged.

It was a heady time, indeed. Rob and I couldn't help but think of the famous quote from Gold Hat, the outlaw leader in Humphrey Bogart's 1948 movie, "The Treasure of the Sierra Madre."

"Badges? We ain't got no badges! We don't need no badges! I don't have to show you any stinking badges!"

No. *The News Brothers* didn't need no stinking badges—or the smiling approval of Korporate Amerika, for that matter—to rise to the occasion and get the job done, and done right.

They had shades…Many thought shades of glory.

After putting out the paper and having a few beers, (from left) Jerry Manley, Tim Ghianni and Rob Dollar pose outside The Camelot on a balmy late Saturday night or early Sunday morning in the spring of 1982.

Chapter 4
(Tim)

IN A PLACE CALLED CAMELOT

That first night after we wore shades to work, it was natural to wear them to our favorite after-work locale.

It was a decent bar, sometimes with live music—Lee Greenwood was a regular before he finally broke big and then capitalized the rest of his career on being "proud to be an American" at every tragedy and sporting event. Shit. At least he knows he's free.

Yep, the Twin Towers have fallen down. Let's bring Lee Greenwood in to sing at Yankee Stadium. Oh hold it, can't we get Toby Keith to sing that "kick a boot up your ass" song to soothe the troubled Mideast? Hold it. Getting way ahead of myself here. Just Lee Greenwood got me going. By the way, give peace a chance, folks. My politics haven't changed much since 1967.

Anyway, The Camelot, just off Madison Street, was a few blocks from the newspaper. It really was an old-fashioned nightclub, with a stage and waiters.... A pool room off to the side...It also was the hangout of choice for newspaper reporters, even before the birth of *The News Brothers,* and for "Clarksville's Finest."

There was, of course, always a certain tension between cops and reporters as we did our jobs. But come midnight or 1 or 2 a.m., with plenty of drinks...all was not only forgiven, it was pretty well forgotten.

No longer were we enemies. We were partners playing our roles in a play about life and death, violence and decay.

The Camelot was where we went to ply cops with liquor to get them to spill about a story we were working on. By the end of the night, they were spilling both information and whiskey.

I told you *The News Brothers* could be sneaky, if that's what it took to get the story for the people of Clarksville.

It also was where the cops went to ply us with drinks to make sure we got an accurate spin on the heroism in their department or perhaps how unfairly they were being treated by the mayor. Fortunately, the cops often forgot when it was our turn to buy a round, so they kept ponying up. Bless them, every one.

Some 2 a.m. liquor-fueled exchanges turned into real stories told by "reliable sources inside the police department" by Monday.

Later, when we were chasing the murderers and trying to chase away the scars in our souls, it just became a place to get drunk. Rob liked the bar because he got to practice his football, there....

You know, making those 2 a.m. "Hail Mary" passes. Now and then a seemingly beautiful woman would stop by our table to flirt with one of us.

Then, she'd leave, and we'd watch the departure. "Damn. I hate to see her go, but I sure as hell love to watch her leave," Rob liked to quip, before signaling for another drink.

One of the single and available women from work spent a lot of time at The Camelot with her best friend, a leggy blonde. The two would prance around the nightclub, giggling and flirting with all the guys, including us. Then, they'd stop in their tracks, point at each other and say in unison: "Remember...KLC."

The routine drove Rob crazy, and finally one night, he jumped up and said he was going to investigate the meaning of "KLC" and find out what these two ladies found so entertaining about it. "You know, maybe I'd like some KLC," he declared. Of course he really wanted some TLC.

Rob kept sending drinks over to our lovely co-worker until she was tipsy, and then he sweet-talked her into going outside to sit in his sports car. About 30 minutes later, they returned to the bar.

It was obvious Rob had been given a hard time. "Well," I said to my frustrated wing man. "Did you find out what KLC is?"

Rob nodded his head and replied sheepishly, "KEEP LEGS CLOSED... Boy, I really need a drink."

I pressed for more details. But, *News Brothers* don't kiss and tell.

The local disc jockey, a pretty good guy, was always at The Camelot, often passed out over his Scotch, at least by the time we got there. Sometimes he would look up and order us a round, say something unintelligible even to us and put his head back down. I was a semi-regular drop-in guest on his show over the years. He shoulda been a contender for the big time.

The bar also had something of a Wild West feel to it. You see, this was not a polite little college bar, with game machines and bowls of peanuts.

Nor was it a GI bar, with men in fatigues hoisting rounds to whatever battalion or whatever stripper they seemed to feel like saluting or shooting.

Nor was it a biker bar. You know what happens there. Sometimes I even like it.

No, this was a night spot where all layers of drunken society met and where, when the last call was ordered and the liquor sales must stop, the owner would signal for a few of his regular customers to stay. He'd lock the doors and the drinks were on the house.

Anyway, it was here where we met Tennessee Williams. He was, well, how do I put this? He was "a character." For some reason, *The News Brothers* always attracted characters, just like honey attracts bees.

Tennessee was a proud member of Clarksville society, so he told us, living in one of the mansions down on Madison Street.

I never knew if that was true, but he had that soft, almost Virginia-flavored drawl of a man of wealth and grace.

One day he just sat down with Rob, Jerry Manley and me as we were sitting back watching chairs fly and listening to fists hitting jaws across the room.

Anyway, this was common entertainment for the kind of crowd at The Camelot. The bouncers would let the fighting go on just long enough to make sure everyone had some fun and then they'd break it up. At least that's how it seemed to us in our drunken haze.

I'd seen a lot of bad things in my life, traffic fatalities, murder victims and mean-spirited bosses, but I'd never before seen a guy get picked up and thrown across a barroom, landing on and breaking a table. I liked the sights and sounds.

In other words, this was an exceptionally good night at The Camelot when Tennessee Williams sat down.

"I know you've been talking to me in your columns," he said, quoting passages from various columns I'd written for the paper. "And I know you've been communicating with my girlfriend there. Wow, man."

Of course, I wasn't communicating with anyone, other than readers. One time I had quoted a bit of graffiti from a railroad overpass, and he swore that the message was for him. And perhaps, he mused, I had actually painted it. And then written about it. Maybe, he thought, I surely wanted his girlfriend. I have always loved women, sometimes to the point of danger and excess and perhaps worship. But I never would be interested in one of old Tennessee's loves.

At first I didn't know what to make of old Tennessee. Neither did Rob. Jerry, I think, figured he was nuts. It was his answer for anyone unusual. Perhaps he even thought that of Rob and me later on. May to this day. Probably right, Jer.

It wasn't until old Tennessee told us of his great bank massacre that I realized he maybe was a virtual genius.

You see, when we met him, he'd just returned from some treatment (I'm not sure if it was in a jail or perhaps a more suitable facility), after he was arrested for waving an ax in a bank and hollering "Reaganomics."

Yep.

One day, this little rich boy who wore a hat and a tie and shorts as he rode a skateboard around town—I'm not sure if he ever got a driver's license—decided that the country was in a shambles because of the trickle-down theory of economics of the relatively new president.

So Tennessee decided that it was time to make a statement. He went to his closet and got a ski mask to cover his face.

And he got an ax. To hear him tell it, it was an ax like those used by the knights of old, but it probably was just your typical Paul Bunyan ax.

And dressed like that, he went into the downtown main branch of the bank where he did his business.

Waving the ax around he shouted "Reaganomics!" and then he turned and fled. In a city like Clarksville, well, everyone knows everyone. And Tennessee was recognized despite his mask and ax.

After all, he and his family banked there. His eccentricities were well known, if not fully appreciated by polite society.

He didn't threaten anyone nor break anything. He just turned and ran down Franklin Street to a nice little restaurant and bar called Austin's.

He went up to the upper-level dining room and set down his mask and his ax, ordered a sandwich and a beer, and waited for the police to come and apprehend him. I think he was eating one of Austin's apple-crunch ice cream deserts by the time the friendly coppers arrived.

Of course, stories told at 2 a.m. at bars by guys who are not only drunk but seemingly unbalanced often don't match any sort of reality.

Trouble was, we were reporters and we were intrigued. We later did some checking and found out that the story was almost true.

Tennessee and his soft drawl and his darting eyes were a part of many of our Saturday nights. Sometimes he would just listen. Sometimes he'd tell his ax story again. Other times he'd tell me how he knew my most recent column was about him. That most recent column, by the way, had been about a World War I veteran named Adam Cantlon, who lived near the railroad overpass where the graffiti had long since been covered over. He was one of two WWI doughboys I had the pleasure of befriending in Clarksville, the other being a great pal named Smith Keel who often would talk about his adventures with a soldier named Harry Truman. Even after I moved on to Nashville, I'd make quick jaunts to a nursing home at Clarksville's southern edge to visit my beloved old friend who I tried to call "Mr. Keel," but who insisted I call him "Smith."

That's all a WWI aside brought on by memories of Tennessee Williams and the Camelot. Journalists…Hell, people in general, today probably think doughboys are that chubby little mound of Pillsbury dough with the irritating laugh.

It was at The Camelot that an officer came to me one night with a request that I meet him the next night, or rather at 2 in the morning, in an abandoned parking lot behind a mall and near the Red River.

I was stupid enough to do it, even though there had been a blizzard and the snow made it tough for me to drive the old Duster into the unplowed lot. I can't remember the tip he had for me now. It was either about racism in the police department and city government or perhaps it was about the mayor having made a fool of himself by appearing completely drunk on Wild Turkey or vodka and lemonade at a public event.

Both were stories the cop eventually tipped me to, but I can't remember which one was the 2 a.m. meet-me-in–the-parking-lot, and blink-your-headlights-twice, French Connection- type of meeting.

Here in the same bar, Rob negotiated stories from the various sheriff's deputies and police officers. The Vice Squad officers were regulars, even having their own booth. I never could figure out whether they were working undercover or just trying to well, get under covers....

And Jerry, ever a great copy and news editor, would listen to it all, sorting through the stories that had been told for holes that needed filling and he'd ask questions to fill those holes.

Anyway, again, I got ahead of myself here. When we arrived at The Camelot with our shades on that early April night, people didn't really even blink. It was just those crazy newspaper guys. Or perhaps they were too blind drunk to notice. It was the beginning of the night on the town for us, but the end of theirs, of course.

For the next year or so, shades were in fashion after midnight at a place called Camelot. Like The Rat Pack in Vegas, although perhaps a bit seedier-looking, we entertained hundreds of Clarksvillians with harrowing tales of our profession. Because we were reporters, they assumed we knew what was going on, and we had the dirt on everyone.

Often it was in The Camelot that I mentally had to relive one of my toughest moments as a journalist. I'd see the Vice Squad guys there, and we all knew what had happened a year or so earlier when everyone was just doing their jobs.

They had a stakeout at a city park.

At their invitation, we'd sent one of our reporters out there to chronicle what was happening ... after parents had complained that this nice park had turned into a place of disgrace and sadness.

The Vice Squad photographed men, many from the respected community, who had turned the park into a meeting place for sex. It wasn't that they were "doing it" that was so bad, as I had no problem with sexual preference. It was that the activities were occurring out in public, at a family park, and the participants were leaving their bowel movements along the paths...There were even more sordid details involved in this case that I really don't care to get into here. But, you get the picture.

Eventually, the investigation was wrapped up and arrests were made, some based on surveillance photos from the scene and others due to caught-in-the-act circumstances involving suspects. Also, the reporter we had at the park had chronicled the names, the acts involved and frequency of visits.

With the arrests, the Vice Squad wanted a big story in the newspaper. After all, they'd allowed a reporter in on the stakeout. The names of those arrested, of course, were public record. But Tony Durr, Managing Editor Max Moss, and I—along with input from "The Big Guy"—debated for more than a day whether to run the list of names.

Another consideration was that there were so many names being floated around in the rumor mill, for surely the tale of the roundup at the park was fodder at every meat-and-three and pancake house in town, that putting the facts out there might be the only real choice. We kept looking at the list and debating.

In the end, we decided it was our obligation as a newspaper to identify every suspect arrested in the undercover operation. But, the decision wasn't easy. I knew some of the men. I knew some of their families. The case drew a national spotlight, and I was interviewed by several publications, including *Editor & Publisher* magazine, on our decision-making process.

I still think it was the right decision, that what these men were doing was not only risky to them, but was ruining a peaceful park that was needed by many in a more urban part of the Clarksville community. Families could enjoy the trails without stumbling on piles of human feces and send their little boys to the public restroom without worrying what scene they might encounter inside.

Whenever I saw the Vice Squad guys at The Camelot, I always thought about those men, our agonizing decision and apparently some deadly aftermath. Rob will pick up the rest of the story later, as he inherited some of the fallout that put me for a time on the speaking trail defending the newspaper's decision. But suffice it to say, not all of the news judgments we make are black and white. Still, we must live with them.

For the most part, when *The News Brothers* held court at The Camelot, seldom was there a serious note or an empty seat. We were there to have fun and to entertain our fans.

And we always had something to offer. But sometimes it might take us a few minutes to come up with it.

If nothing new was going on to report, we didn't want to disappoint the crowd.

So, when people stopped by our table to talk to us, we would start making things up....One lie, after another...It became kind of a game to us. Most of the conversation was outrageous, but when someone is stone-cold drunk, it's hard for them to connect all of the dots.

One night, some total stranger named "Joe" was having the time of his life, listening to Rob and I recount one adventure after another...The lies had gone on for about 30 minutes, when I began mentioning my strong friendship with Willie Nelson and the fact I had a big adventure planned with him. I actually had met

Willie by then and know him better now, but, well, at times like that, red-eyed, pre-dawns, he was always on my mind. That's when Rob fed Joe something he couldn't digest... "Flap, we better get going. We've got to get up early tomorrow morning to fly out to Australia. When Willie Nelson invites you to go kangaroo hunting, you better be on time."

With that line, Joe stood up, of course, in disbelief, and let out a big, "Shi-i-i-i-it!!" and stormed off.

Back for a minute on the subject of Tennessee Williams. Since he likely won't figure much more in this story, I did encounter him one more time several years later. He called me at my next newspaper employer from the Nashville jail, because he could get to the pay phone and he knew I was working at the *Nashville Banner*.

Old Tennessee Williams wasn't the only jailbird who used his early morning telephone rights to call the *Banner* newsroom, by the way. James Earl Ray—then serving time in Brushy Mountain prison for the 1968 assassination of Dr. Martin Luther King Jr.— had somehow formed a "friendship" with my chief state reporter, Charlie Appleton. Problem was I came to work at 4:30 a.m. or earlier and Charlie didn't get in until 6. Sometimes the phone would ring at the state desk and I would pick it up. It could be drunks settling a bar bet about how many points Julius Erving scored or a legitimate police tip. But sometimes it was James Earl Ray, wanting to talk with Charlie. "Just tell him I called, will you Tim?" the strangely soft spoken piece of scum would say.

Of course, I was well-accustomed to such vile creatures by then, having dealt with child killers, father rapers and the like because of all the crime encountered in Clarksville. And, before I forget it, some of Ray's ideological pals, the Ku Klux Klan, once protested outside *The Leaf-Chronicle* building. I can't recall ever feeling my stomach roll like it did when I went outside the building on that hot summer's day to talk with these cowards, their faces covered by sheets. My stomach may have equaled that roller-coaster of nausea, I suppose, whenever I had the "good fortune" of beginning my day by having a chirpy morning chat with the man who killed Dr. King's body, but who couldn't kill the dream.

Anyway, back to Tennessee Williams. He'd been thrown out of Clarksville, he said in his phone call. And he still saw messages to him in the columns I was now writing for the *Banner*.

We talked briefly and that was it. He wasn't asking for bail money or anything. After he got out of jail, he began to hang around the building, telling the guards what a great friend of his I was. But they didn't let him inside to visit me. One guard, Johnny Sibert—who is in the Steel Guitar Hall of Fame for his touring work with my friend Carl Smith and also worked sessions with Lefty Frizzell, Little Jimmy Dickens and The Everly Brothers—used to let Tennessee sleep just inside the door on really cold nights.

Last time I'm sure that I saw Tennessee, I was looking out the front window of the *Banner* newsroom. Walking across a parking lot a few yards away, leading to the front of the building, he was painted head to foot in red paint and had it highlighted with war paint. He had feathers in his hair. He was waving a spear that had feathers on it. And he was angrily shouting as he walked toward the front door.

The guards, who knew him by then, stopped him and told him they'd get him help. Within seconds, a Metro Police cruiser arrived and carted a handcuffed Indian Chief Tennessee Williams off. He was still screaming, unintelligibly. I think he was shouting "Reaganomics." But I wasn't sure.

I was not allowed by the cops and the guards to go out there because of fear of danger. I guess they thought he was stalking me. Maybe he was, I don't know. I wasn't really afraid, but it was strange. I didn't sleep well that night. But that wasn't unusual.

Actually, I am pretty sure I saw Tennessee Williams one more time. It was a few years later and I was in a hurry to get to the hospital south of Nashville where my mother was desperately ill with the disease that eventually took her.

As I came down the ramp from the interstate I had too much gravity behind me and I didn't stop in time, butting the car in front of me.

It was a time when people were terrified. There had been a number of robberies set up on highways that began with someone butting into the rear of the victim's car. The car I slightly rammed took off before I could write down the license number. No real damage anyway.

As I rolled back into traffic, to the point of no return, I saw a fellow holding an "I'm Hungry" sign at the roadside. He was pointing at my car and clapping.

I couldn't stop, because I needed to get to see Mom. But I'm pretty sure I heard "Reaganomics" echoing into the night.

Rob Dollar joins lawmen from the Clarksville Police Department and Montgomery County Sheriff's Department on the firing range in April 1982.

Chapter 5
(Rob)

THE ROAD TO CLARKSVILLE

It was May 1981, and I found myself at the proverbial Fork in the Road. Graduating the year before from Eastern Kentucky University in Richmond, Kentucky, I was slaving away as a reporter for *The Morehead News*, a twice-a-week newspaper, in the eastern part of the commonwealth, when two good opportunities came knocking at my door.

My name is Rob Dollar. I answered the door to greet those knocking opportunities more than 30 years ago. Now, it's my turn to pick up the story about the birth of *The News Brothers*. Sit back and take your shoes off…Relax…Boy, do I have some stories to tell you…

In the waning days of typewriters, Morehead already was my second job as a professional journalist. My first had been the summer after graduation, when I went to work in Cynthiana, Kentucky, for the weekly *Cynthiana Democrat* for a pitiful sum of $150 per week. But, these were the years right after Bob Woodward and Carl Bernstein broke "Watergate" and brought down the Nixon presidency. I wanted to be just like the two *Washington Post* reporters and right all the wrongs in the world. So, money didn't matter. It was about the pursuit of the truth, wherever it took you.

Funny thing, more than 20 years later, in mid-November 2002, I actually met Bob Woodward at the start-up meeting for Military Reporters & Editors (MRE) in Washington, D.C. He was still chasing down the truth, but on this particular occasion, he sure got it wrong. The Pulitzer Prize-winning reporter, in a luncheon speech, predicted that George W. Bush *would not* go to war with Iraq the following year. Well, those of us who can handle the truth, know what actually happened, don't we?

From my earliest days as a reporter, I wanted to be on the right side and always get the story right.

Once, while in college, as the editor of *The Eastern Progress* my senior year, I got called on the carpet and was ordered to report to the University President's Office. I had written a controversial editorial, questioning the efficiency of the Richmond Police Department and also maintaining that a murder at a market might have been prevented had officers not been spending so much time looking high and low for drunken students to put in jail. The city manager, who years later became a powerful senator in the Kentucky Legislature, wanted my scalp — and bad. (Nowadays, that wouldn't worry me much, but back then I had a darned nice scalp.)

"Rob, you were a little hard on them, don't you think?" EKU President J.C. Powell asked, reminding me the people of Richmond were our neighbors and we had to get along with them. "No, I don't think so," I responded. "I said something that needed to be said…And I said it, only because the Richmond daily newspaper wouldn't say it."

With that response, Dr. Powell smiled and said, "OK, Rob. Go get 'em!"

It was one of my first lessons in what would become my mantra as a journalist: *Don't Back Down. Ever.*

At *The Morehead News* for just five months, I received a pleasant surprise with an invitation to interview for a reporter's job at *The Leaf-Chronicle*, a daily newspaper in Clarksville, Tennessee. Now, working for a daily newspaper was one of my most immediate goals at this point in my life. So, I was happy about the invitation — and location of the paper. I was very familiar with the Clarksville area since it was only a hop-and-a-skip from Fort Campbell and Hopkinsville, Kentucky, where I had spent most of my life prior to leaving my family ties for college and career.

A day after hearing from the Clarksville newspaper folks, I also received a letter from Uncle Sam. THE Uncle Sam. Well, one of his relatives, a recruiting officer for the CIA (Central Intelligence Agency). The government, it seemed, wanted to know if I wanted to become a spy. While the potential for lots of undercover work intrigued me, since I'm told I'm good under the covers (at least I like to think that's what they say), I decided not to make a snap decision and to check out the Clarksville job first since I already had a scheduled interview. I would see what this fellow, Max Moss, the newspaper's managing editor, had to say before I made up my mind on whether to meet up with R. Stephen Gunn of the CIA.... Have you ever noticed that spies and assassins, for some reason, always get identified by an initial, middle name and then last name? Strange.

And so it was that I made a five-hour road trip to Clarksville, where I met with Max at his home on a Saturday in early May 1981.

He was a nice man, small in stature, in his 40s, who wore glasses and had gray hair that made him look much older than his true age. My visit included a quick trip to *The Leaf-Chronicle* offices, where the staff was busy putting out the Sunday edition. The interview went well, and Max decided right then and there I was his man for the job.

I think what impressed him was my response when he asked whether I could spell...I told him I was OK at spelling, but it didn't really matter because I owned a dictionary and knew how to use it.

With my answer, I became the only person ever to be hired, at that point, by *The Leaf-Chronicle*, without first taking and passing a spelling and grammar test.

I'd already conquered new territory and hadn't even accepted the job or gone to work yet. While Max was doing something I'm sure was important, he asked someone out in the newsroom — it turned out to be Tim, then the sports editor — to come and visit with me. So, a guy who eventually would become my best friend for life was one of the first people I met at *The Leaf-Chronicle*. I hit it off with "Flap" the moment I met him. He had an easy-going manner and long hair, just like me. He also liked The Beatles, Bob Dylan and Johnny Cash, so I knew, again like me, he had to be an outlaw. And, he didn't try to talk me out of taking the job. That was a good thing, I think....

I knew my heart was in newspapering, and when *The Leaf-Chronicle* made me an offer I couldn't refuse—$10 more a week than I was getting in Morehead — I accepted that very day right there in the editor's office. Tony Durr was the editor. He was the kind of guy who comes across as a prick the first time you meet him. Anyway, Tony told me matter-of-factly he wasn't going to get into a bidding war for my services, even if I was "special" and the only guy they never made take the spelling and grammar test. I thought his comment was pretty funny. What kind of bidding war? This little newspaper trying to outbid the CIA? Like I said, the guy seemed like something of a prick. I wasn't in it for the money...Little prick.

With a handshake, it was official: I was coming home to practice journalism near my family instead of going to work for the CIA. I was happy with my decision, which R. Stephen Gunn later learned about in a letter I wrote to him. Heck, R. Stanley Dollar sounds more like the name of a damn nice guy than a murderous spy, and I know for a fact I could never kill anyone or anything other than a six-pack of beer, anyway. But, all these years later, I have to admit I wonder whether I might have become that CIA agent who helped SEAL Team Six and "The Night Stalkers" track down and kill Osama bin Laden — if only I had taken the other path in my Fork in the Road in 1981.

I arrived for work at *The Leaf-Chronicle* on a Monday in the first week of June. The former governor of Tennessee, Ray Blanton, had just been indicted for selling pardons, and one of my first byline stories for my new employer was a sidebar on the reaction of locals. Now, the pace at a daily newspaper is much faster than a weekly or bi-weekly, and it didn't take me long in the days and weeks that followed to figure out I would be working like a crazy man for that extra $10 per week. Probably the CIA would have been much lower-key, come to think of it. Initially, *The Leaf-Chronicle* editors had me covering the education beat, but it was only temporary and to replace the regular reporter who was on maternity leave. When she returned, I was immediately switched to police and courts, a natural for me since one of my college degrees was in police administration.

Someone who was most helpful to me on my first day on the job was the newspaper's veteran photographer, W.J. Souza. Nearing retirement, he was quite a legend for his photography skills. As a sideline, he also was a special deputy and routinely snapped crime scene photographs for the Clarksville Police Department and Montgomery County Sheriff's Department. Old W.J.—as Tim reminded me—also had another sideline. The wreck photos that didn't appear in the newspaper often were sold to insurance investigators. Nothing wrong with that ... back in those days. Anyway, as it turned out, because of my beat, Mr. Souza and I were joined at the hip most days at work.

It took several weeks for me to make the connection, but, ironically, I had met W.J. way back in 1973 when I was a paperboy for *The Leaf-Chronicle*, delivering to several neighborhoods on Fort Campbell, That year I was the co-recipient of the Meyer Brick Award for Newspaper Boy of the Year, and it was this grizzled World War II tank veteran who was sent out to take my photograph. Now, eight years later, we were colleagues. How cool is that?

W.J. Souza worked for *The Leaf-Chronicle* for 54 years, retiring in December 1983. He died at the age of 84 on Aug. 7, 2005. Interestingly, Mr. Souza snapped some of the last photographs ever taken of legendary Tennessee Sheriff Buford Pusser of "Walking Tall" fame, when the tough-as-nails lawman visited Clarksville in late July 1974, about three weeks before his mysterious death in a car crash. Bet Mr. Souza wished he'd made it to that crash site. Talk about big cash paydays.

I worked at *The Leaf-Chronicle* just short of two years, from June 1981 through April 1983. I don't know if it was because of too many full moons or because these were the Reagan years, but the pace was not for the faint-hearted. We hit the streets running, and we never stopped. We put out two editions—one for the racks and one for home delivery — Monday through Friday, and then had a Sunday morning newspaper. In April 1982, we added a Saturday morning newspaper, and exactly one year later, we converted from an afternoon publication to a morning newspaper delivered all seven days of the week.

There always seemed to be more news and sports than our small editorial staff of about 25 could humanly cover and get into the paper. It seemed like we had sensational trials just about every other week in our courts, and heinous crimes like the Nishiyama and Long slayings occurred far too often. Helicopters kept falling out of the sky at Fort Campbell, and dozens were getting killed each month in traffic accidents. Dirty politics plagued the school system and government bodies. News was everywhere, every single day. There was no rest for the weary. And, contrary to the view of management and bean-counters, gathering and writing up a story is not akin to stopping at a market to pick up a loaf of bread. It requires hard work, support, and sometimes cooperation and good timing.

In all newsrooms, the stress of the job takes a toll. It was no different at *The Leaf-Chronicle*. In the time I was there, more than 60 people came and went, with one new reporter working only one day — a slow one at that — and never returning to the office. Hell, to this day, I don't know what happened to her. She wasn't fired. She just looked around and didn't like what she saw. You have to have worked in a busy newsroom to understand the kind of frantic environment that exists at every newspaper.

The saga of the runaway reporter was somewhat matched later on, when *The News Brothers* raged. One day, after going out on a coffee run, Tim showed up in the office and found a young man sitting in his chair. The kid, it turns out, had all but accepted a job at the newspaper. He was waiting to talk to Tony Durr, the editor, to finalize things. Tim at first didn't say anything, simply nodded at the kid and took his scarf and fedora off and set them on the corner of the desk near his green ceramic ashtray. Then, he put his two packs of smokes next to the ashtray. Finally, he took off his Deerfield High School, Class of 1969 football letter jacket and prepared to put it over the back of the chair, where it belonged. The kid didn't move. So Tim, with a bright smile and his irrepressible charm, asked the kid: "What the hell you doing in my chair?" Actually, he probably used a stronger word than "hell." Regardless, it really was kind of a weeding out thing. If the kid couldn't take that kind of full-frontal jab, well, he wasn't cut out for what we were doing.

The kid laughed. But he never came to work at the paper.

So the bodies kept coming and going. But, no matter what they threw my way, I met the challenge and excelled. I took it as a personal challenge. That's not to say I didn't get ticked off on occasion and let the powers-that-be know I was not happy. Usually, my Days of Discontent involved "newspaperman" Wendell Wilson, the city editor.

Wendell's only real claim to fame occurred around the time I started working for *The Leaf-Chronicle*. He arrived at work at 5:30 one morning and noticed smoke coming out of the top part of the Montgomery County Courthouse, which was directly across the street from *The Leaf-Chronicle* building. Apparently, lightning from a thunderstorm had struck the clock-tower and started a fire. Wendell called in the fire, and firemen put it out. A brief in that day's newspaper reported the near disaster, including a graph that credited "newspaperman" Wendell Wilson with reporting the fire to authorities.

Tim, who had watched all of the action from his sports editor's desk next to the window, had written and edited that brief and the quotes around the "newspaperman" were his little joke to himself. It was subtle, but extremely mean-spirited, in a way that few, other than "Flap" and me, at times can pull off. I may have been the only one to get it at first. Like I said, compared to most people, we've both marched to the beat of a different drummer all our lives.

Now, Wendell, most of the time, appeared to be the only one in *The Leaf-Chronicle* newsroom who had any free time on his hands. I'm not going to say the man was never busy, but he sure had lots of time to bug his reporters about things that didn't matter, and always right on deadline…Here I was, struggling with a story like a one-legged man in an ass-kicking contest, when my telephone would ring minutes from deadline, and the voice on the other end — Wendell — would ask: "Do you have a minute?" That was Wendell Wilson, in a nutshell...The kind of guy you wanted to beat up because he thought he knew it all, and he wore the same kind of smirk on his face as George W. Bush and most fraternity boys.

On one occasion, Wendell summoned the entire reporting staff to his desk for a quick meeting — right on deadline, of course. In his matter-of-factly and superior way, he advised us that our publisher, "The Big Guy," was not very pleased because we were making too many mistakes that were showing up in the newspaper. Something needed to be done to make it better. Well, I lost it...Wendell's sorry attempt at constructive criticism launched me into the Mother of All Tirades. In no uncertain words, I advised him in a loud voice that no one — including the reporters — enjoyed making mistakes, and we were doing everything humanly possible, under the circumstances, to get things right.

I reminded him that people were working like dogs because *The Leaf-Chronicle*, as usual, was short-handed..."When are we going to get someone to sit at this desk? What about this desk, and this one?" I screamed, doing a little dance around several empty desks. "Maybe the management of this newspaper should try to determine whether the lack of help is the reason for all these mistakes."

During my two-minute tirade, the entire newsroom went dead silent. You could have heard a pin drop. At some point, I glanced over at Tim, across the room, just in time to catch a huge smile and thumbs-up. Wendell, not usually at a loss for words, was speechless. He might have even been shell-shocked. "Gee, Rob, I didn't mean to get you upset. We're just asking everyone to be more careful and try harder not to make any more mistakes," he said, with a stammer.

With that plea, Wendell's meeting was over. We were now past deadline, which probably resulted in more errors for that day's newspaper, not to mention a late press time. One of the other reporters, Bonnie Calhoun, came to my desk to express her appreciation for me going to the mat for everyone else. "I really admire you," she said.

In a very short time, I had cemented a reputation at *The Leaf-Chronicle* for being not only their ace reporter, but also a rebel with plenty of causes…all of them good, in my opinion.

What I liked most about being a newspaperman was the unexpected. One day I might be interviewing the garbage man and the next day I could be getting in the face of the former prime minister of Great Britain. Every day was different and could bring a surprise. Like the time I noticed one of my colleagues at a nearby desk interviewing a woman who looked very familiar to me. Turns out the mystery woman was one of my high school "crushes"—my favorite cheerleader, Linda McCormack. She had just returned home to Clarksville from a trip to California, where she had appeared on TV's "The Price is Right" and won a refrigerator and some other kitchen appliances.

As the newspaper's police reporter, I was always in the middle of the action, which kept my byline on the front page of the newspaper most days. It goes without saying that my job could be dangerous.

On one particular Saturday, I covered two shootings that occurred within hours of each other. The more serious of the two involved an elderly man who had wounded a next-door neighbor's son in the leg while the youth was raking leaves. The shooter then barricaded himself into his home. Arriving at the scene, I found a police car blocking the street, but no police officer in sight. So naturally, I started walking up the street to locate the scene of the crime. That's when I heard the newspaper's chief photographer, Larry McCormack, trying to get my attention with a half-yell or scream. He was crouched behind a vehicle a few feet away, taking cover with several policemen, who were trying to get the man to give up peacefully. And, here I was standing right in front of the suspect's house—out in the open, exposing myself to possible gunfire. Luckily, The Man Upstairs was looking out for me that day because I didn't get shot. I managed to take cover with everyone else until the deranged gunman finally surrendered to police. As he was handcuffed, he looked at the officer and remarked, "Who the hell do you think I am, John Dillinger?" It made great copy for the Sunday newspaper. The "Dillinger" line really thrilled our editor, Tony Durr, who liked colorful characters. Tony thought I had just hung the moon with that story.

The life of a reporter was not just about front-page bylines and plenty of adventure. If you were a good reporter and did your job the right way, you could count on being called every name in the book....even "murderer."

It happened to me, only months after I joined *The Leaf-Chronicle*. As a new reporter, I had inherited several high-profile stories. One involved an ongoing Vice Squad investigation that resulted in the arrests of a dozen or so men for lewd behavior at a local park. The story was winding its way through the court system so it was appearing quite frequently in the paper. Anyway, one of the suspects, a respected member of the Austin Peay State University community, turned up dead one day, apparently a suicide victim. A few days later, my telephone rang and it was someone from a national gay rights group in Chicago, accusing me—through my news stories—of causing the man to take his own life. "You're nothing but a murderer," the man told me. It was not a pleasant telephone conversation. And, I'll have to confess, it got me thinking about the unpleasant things I had to do in my job as a reporter covering the news.

But, with the bad, came the good. My work gained me respect in the community and sometimes it was even communicated to me.

The late Jack Hestle, a judge, served as the district attorney general, or chief prosecutor, during some of my time in Clarksville. I always suspected he was the inspiration for Tim's imaginary barrister, Court Agate. (That's a FACT, Jack!)

Anyway, when Jack lost his bid for re-election in late 1982, he wrote me a nice letter that I've treasured all these years.

It read, in part: *"I am very pleased with the way you handle yourself and feel that you have a bright future in journalism. In the ten years I have worked with* The Leaf-Chronicle *staff, you and one other reporter have stayed in my mind. I very much appreciate the fact that you were a person that could be told about any secret information and you always tried to see that the news was accurately reported."*

I'd like to think I earned the respect of Ed Patterson, too. When I was working in Clarksville, Patterson was the chief deputy for the Montgomery County Sheriff's Department, a job he still holds today, more than 30 years later.

Our first—and last—confrontation occurred over something I wrote in the paper that apparently had something to do with the Sheriff's Department. I have no memory of the story whatsoever, so it couldn't have been very important. If I had to bet, I'd probably guess it included a paragraph or two about a sheriff's deputy doing something stupid, or not doing what he was supposed to do.

Anyway, on a rare peaceful morning at the office, my telephone rang, and I answered it. On the other end was an irate Ed Patterson, who launched into a verbal assault on me as soon as I picked up the phone. I didn't get a chance to say, "Hello." The veteran lawman let me know, in no uncertain terms, that I was lowlife, and perhaps even Tim's favorite creature, a slug. It was, and remains to this day, the worst tongue-lashing of my life…After listening to Ed rail against me and tell me how sorry I was for two or three minutes, I snapped out of my stunned silence and started yelling back at him over the phone. Hell, I wasn't going to back down for doing my job.

When I started yelling, Ed got quiet. When I stopped, the chief deputy spoke in a calm, civilized voice. "Rob," he said. "I'm sorry if you took this the wrong way. It wasn't personal. We all have our roles to play. And, I was playing mine. I have to stand up for my deputies, no matter what." With that explanation, the disagreement was forgotten, and I'm sure Ed and I bought each other drinks the next time we ran into each other at The Camelot.

Ah yes…Just playing our roles in the Game of Life….Tim, too, once had to play his role when he went toe-to-toe with Ed.

He was checking out a tip from inside the Sheriff's Department about a major development in the Rodney Long case. The tip got him a face-to-face meeting with Chief Patterson that ultimately led to the infamous "Wallet Found: It's Rodney's" headline. When

Tim determined his tip about Rodney's wallet being found along the interstate near Knoxville was solid, he went down to "The Cop Shop" where he played the game, got in a shouting match with Ed—and came back with the story.

Now, Ed wasn't always yelling at reporters. He was responsible for plenty of good deeds over the years. He and some of his pals at the Clarksville Police Department "made my day" when they invited me—"Dirty Rob"—to shoot with local lawmen on one occasion out on the firing range. I got quite a bang out of that experience, which was the first—and only time—I ever fired a gun in my life.

And, then there was that unforgettable day when Ed's quick thinking probably "saved" Tim's life.

The incident involved a bomb scare during a high-profile murder trial at the Montgomery County Courthouse, just across the street from *The Leaf-Chronicle* building.

Anyway, Ed and a few sheriff's deputies discovered a suspicious briefcase in the main courtroom. They dragged it slowly outside onto Commerce Street. Meanwhile, Tim, not knowing what was going on, walked out the front door of the newspaper to investigate the situation... That's about the time he heard Ed Patterson yell, "Tim...DUCK!" just seconds before the briefcase, containing someone's lunch and probably a flask, was exploded by the Bomb Squad in the middle of the street.

All Tim got from the experience was an earache. But, the deputies got a pretty good laugh that day. Which brings me to the next point: Over the years, there were many lighter moments on the job, too.

Once, I was assigned to cover a banquet for a group involved in agriculture and soil conservation. Along with a good meal, everyone at the banquet had the opportunity to win several nice door prizes. I told the head honcho NOT to put my name in the hat because I was there to do a story and not win prizes. Freebies for reporters are frowned upon in my profession, I explained to him. After arguing with him for awhile, I told him to do what he wanted to do. Hell, I never win anything, anyway. There were 500 people at this dinner, and the chances of my name being drawn were slim to none, so I thought. The drawing went like I thought it would go, until they came to the last prize. It was for some ungodly amount of fertilizer. "Oh shit," I thought...I started praying....Please God, don't let them call my name. But, it was my name that was drawn. The crowd hooted and roared with laugher. The newspaper guy got the pile of fertilizer. How appropriate...I never picked up my prize...Of course, I had no use for it, living in an apartment in town. But, I will confess *The News Brothers* contemplated having it delivered and dumped on the lawn of someone we knew was most deserving of such a gesture. I won't mention his name, but he'll never know just how close he came to being up to his neck in highly regarded shit.

Another time, while running the police beat, I came across a report of a newspaper employee being assaulted at his home. Apparently, he was punched out after answering a knock at his door. The puncher accused the startled man of having an affair with his wife, who also worked at *The Leaf-Chronicle*.

As it turned out, it was a case of mistaken identity. The man who got punched out had the same first name as another guy at the paper who, it turned out, was having all the fun. Of course, I knew everyone involved in the sordid affair.

In fact, the wayward babe, in question, had once winked at me at The Camelot. But, *News Brothers* don't kiss and tell.

I'm damn glad my first name was Rob, instead of that other three-letter first name, or it might have been me who was accidentally beaten up. Those police reports could be so damn entertaining....

During my days at *The Leaf-Chronicle*, our newsroom staff worked hard, and we played hard...Sometimes harder...

On one occasion, our "youngsters"—Jim "Flash" Lindgren and his wife, Brenda Myers—got several of us together, and we went to a midnight showing of "The Rocky Horror Picture Show." We dressed up for the cult, classic movie and even mimicked the characters, throwing rice during the appropriate scenes and playing out other bit parts on the screen just like all the other strange people in the movie theater.

Another time, we decided to throw ourselves a Halloween party, where everyone dressed up in a costume that fit their character. The choices were quite interesting. I arrived in my sports car as "Magnum P.I.," while Tim was a hippie who didn't trust anyone over 30, including himself. It was very entertaining to see Max Moss dressed as a 2-year-old child, Frank Wm. White as General Douglas McArthur, and sports writer Jim Pickens as a cowboy. I think the cowboy outfit gave Jim, now at the Owensboro, Kentucky, daily newspaper, a nickname that has stuck with him all these years: "Slim" Pickens. Wendell Wilson failed to show for the party for some reason. Maybe, he didn't have a costume. But, if he had come, my guess is he would have pretended to be a "newspaperman."

When I wasn't out frolicking with *The News Brothers*, I was usually hanging out with Dennis "Denny" Adkins. Actually, I was trying to make a damn nice guy out of him. One of my regular running buddies, Denny was single like me, in his mid-20s, and he worked in the newspaper's Composing Room. He was thin, hard-headed in his thinking and always seemed to be nervous. My friend also was the spitting image in every way of Don Knotts, the actor who played Barney Fife on television's "The Andy Griffith Show."

A member of the *News Brothers* entourage, Denny could be a pest, without giving it much effort at all. It was part of his charm, I guess. He would ask you the same thing, again and again, wearing you down until he got the answer he wanted to hear. If Denny asked you for advice, you could bet your life he would do the exact opposite of what you just told him he should do. But that was just Denny....We put up with him because he was fun to have around...Every now and then, we also needed a butt for our jokes.

All kidding aside, Denny was, and still is, a nice guy. Yep. He's really a prince of a fellow. Thirty years later, we're still friends... One of us is lucky, I suppose...I'll never forget the time in October 1990, when we were on vacation, doing Europe, and Denny got us thrown out of a Gentleman's Club in the Soho District of London. I really don't want to embarrass anyone with the distasteful details. Anyway, Denny ran, like lightning, for his life, leaving me alone in a dark alley—with only my dignity and six very large and angry bouncers. "RUN…..Rob!" he shrieked, his scared-shitless voice echoing back to me from somewhere around Piccadilly Circus. I'm lucky to have lived to tell the story.

To be fair, I'll have to give Denny credit for rising to the occasion in his support role with *The News Brothers*. Back in the heyday, he was loyal and one of my biggest fans when it came to appreciating my "Michael Jackson" impersonation, which I liked to do quite frequently at The Camelot. I'd pull my coat up over my head, while spinning around and moving my neck from side to side. Yeah, I was "Bad," and Denny laughed even on an "off-night" when it wasn't really that funny.

In the early days, Denny, who had a college degree in English, wanted, in the worst way, to be a reporter. And Tim often told him he would have been a reporter in "the worst way." Not sure he ever got that one…

I think Denny reasoned being a reporter would help him get beautiful women. Often, he submitted freelance articles to the City Desk, looking for his big break. Years earlier, right after college, he had worked in the Advertising Department at the newspaper, but he got the boot because he was no salesman. Hell, he couldn't sell snowshoes to an Eskimo. Now, during the years when *The News Brothers* reigned, Denny was back at *The Leaf-Chronicle*, where he worked in the Composing Room and helped put together and paste up the newspaper pages before they were sent to the Camera Room.

The thing Denny liked best about working in the Composing Room was that nearly everyone there (except for him, of course) was a woman….And, several were damn, good-looking divorced gals, who often joked about "going on the prowl" after work. Denny spent most of his time on the job, trying to make time with these hot, single co-workers, none of whom, it turns out, even desired his casual attention. But, Denny didn't want to hear the "I like you as a friend" line (although he should have liked that considering how few people really liked him as a friend), and so he was persistent in his pursuit of the ladies.

He chased and chased one dark-haired beauty until she almost had a nervous breakdown. That can happen when someone won't leave you alone. Anyway, one day, after declining Denny's invitation to go out on a date for maybe the hundredth time, she decided she had had enough.

Staring him down with the evil eye, she said, "Denny. I want you to listen to me. We work together. There's no way in hell I'm ever going to (*do*) you. OK? Do you understand me?"

Now, in the interest of full disclosure, I guess I should confess I'm told a word much, much harsher than "do" actually came out of her sweet mouth. Try using your imagination...

Anyway, Denny got the message...finally. This babe was not interested in visiting The Love Palace.

Curiously, the same young woman, in November 1982, was the last one to leave the movie premiere after-party. When Tim, single in those days himself, in his yellow fedora, loaded up his old Duster, hauling a purple-hatted Tony Durr to the airport in Nashville at 5 a.m., she rode shotgun. Jerry "Chuckles" Manley, in his yellow aviator's cap, was passed out in the back seat of the car. No one ever told me how that story ended, other than that Tim made it to work the next day.

Even more curiously, the same young woman and I hooked up a few years after that crazy airport ride and spent some quality time in my sports car.

But, *News Brothers* don't kiss and tell.

Characters like Denny always seemed to find and attach themselves to *The News Brothers*. We loved people after all, and we loved making fun of them, and ourselves. Still do. Reagan was president during our time on top, and we were convinced the world probably would come to an end because of it. So, we made up our minds to make the best of the situation.

When *The News Brothers* roamed and reported in Clarksville, it was the best of times at *The Leaf-Chronicle*. It was the worst of times, too. Those who walked among the boys knew they could talk the talk, but also walk the walk. Damn nice guys to the end, they'll long be remembered for being tough, honest, and fair.

But, to tell the entire truth, *The News Brothers* also were, and remain today, a bunch of softies at heart...Real newsmen, if they're honest, aren't afraid to cry....There's no crime in having compassion.

Actions always speak louder than words, even for *The News Brothers*.

Once, while walking past The Royal York Hotel on the way to the *Leaf-Chronicle* offices, a young man who obviously had fallen on hard times in the Land of Reagan asked me for some spare change. I reached into my pocket and gave him a few nickels and dimes. As I started to walk away, I had second thoughts....I pulled out my wallet and took out a $5 bill—all I had—to hand to him. "Here," I said. "Take this and go get yourself something to eat...You need it more than me. I'm more than blessed — I'm a *News Brother*."

Hell, looking back...I think that bum may have been Denny....Just kidding.

As for Tim, anyone who knows him will tell you he's the kind of guy who would give a stranger the shirt off his back...But, as kind-hearted as he is, I'm not so sure that generosity would extend to his autographed, Lone Ranger mask...

In the late 1980s, when old "Flapjacks" was the last *News Brother* still standing at *The Leaf-Chronicle*, he proved with a good deed that he would never abandon his humanity.

One night, long after his comrades had departed, he was wandering from the newspaper offices toward his car. Never in a hurry, he smoked and smiled, enjoying the sights and sounds of the city he loved so much. Yes, he missed his pals, but he still was teaching the younger folks, cussing at management, visiting "The Big Guy" and tilting at windmills. Hell, Tim tilted—hard to the left—in general.

Anyway, on this cold 2 a.m. late night/early morning on South Third Street, Tim passed The Royal York Hotel, where a bunch of fellows so tough their spit could bounce were watching whatever cowboy show was on *The Late, Late Show*. A pretty good-sized dog, some sort of Airedale mutt, was standing outside the doors to the hotel and barking, apparently seeking shelter from the brutal cold.

Tim couldn't resist coming to the rescue. First he asked his friends in the lobby if they knew the dog that he let in the hotel and that they all petted. Nope, they said. Then he decided he really didn't need a dog, that this nice-looking canine had to belong to somebody. He tried to lose the dog by going in one door of the nearby Post Office and coming out the other side. The dog sat there at the other door…waiting.

Well, to make a long story short, the dog—looking for a friend and a home—ended up chasing Tim's car down the middle of Madison Street. So, old "Flapjacks" rolled to a stop and opened the passenger door for the mutt to jump in…

The dog—who also took the name, "Flapjacks"—died long ago, but lived a happy life, off the street, thanks to a damn nice guy.

Rob Dollar pulls his MG into the driveway of his parents' home during a visit to Hopkinsville, Kentucky, in the early 1980s

Tim Ghianni takes a smoke break outside *The Leaf-Chronicle* building in the early 1980s.

Chapter 6
(Tim)

HIGH PROOF NEWS COVERAGE

Alcohol in the newsroom is a myth now when reporters operate in cubicles and dress like insurance executives on casual Friday.

But it wasn't a myth back in the days when I began my career on Sept. 12, 1974, when I stepped into a cloud of smoke on my first day of work at *The Leaf-Chronicle*.

By the time I grabbed my pica pole and wax pencil from the top drawer and rolled a double-sheet of newsprint—always use two so you don't damage the carriage—into the old Underwood, I had to reverse some of my personal health policies.

I had quit smoking by the time I went to work for the newspaper. People around me had died and respiratory woes plagued my family, so I had put away the "snarfers" as my "Uncle Moose"—Steve Mainquist—dubbed them when he and I were in college at Iowa State University. I have no idea why Moose called cigarettes "snarfers." Probably funny at the time. I'd ask him, but he's dead. One of my many close friends, in and out of the news business, who have gone ahead to set up the record player and get things ready for my arrival, I hope, in the distant future.

A lot of things were funny back in college, as I'd been a free-range hippie, so I enjoyed combustibles in general while hanging out with guys nicknamed Captain Kirk, Jocko, Wizard, Coach, Nardholm, Uncle Moose and Carpy. But, for awhile at least, I decided I didn't want to die before I got old, so I snuffed the snarfers.

Didn't last five minutes into my first long day as the new kid in the newsroom, the curly-haired guy with the bow tie and the bell bottoms, a bit different from the rest.

The fellow who had the task of training me was Max Moss. Hell, I thought he was 50, but I suppose he was 35. He was a Winstons man. And in addition to sharing his wisdom—and he did know the professorial basics, skills and ethics of community journalism (traits which later did him in when such skills were not called for by the corporate beasts)—Max shared his cigarette smoke with me while telling me what to do.

"Smoke doesn't bother you, does it?" he asked, that first day, as he fired one up without waiting for an answer.

Hell, how could I exist in that room if smoke bothered me?

Richard Worden, the city editor, had a square ashtray with four corner indentions for cigarettes. He had one burning in each one. He'd fire one up, answer the phone, fire another one up, edit some copy, fire another one up....

But he wasn't the only one. Others had at least two going in an ashtray at the same time. They were asking questions in boozy breath. Even Big Jim Monday, the city's beloved religion writer and a truly sweet and genuine mountain of a man with the voice of an angel when he sang (and he did occasionally, on deadline), smoked back then, though he quit soon thereafter. Big Jim is retired now, after almost 50 years in the business, but he still writes an occasional column for *The Leaf-Chronicle*.

News stories were clattered out on the old manual typewriters and then rolled up into those pneumatic little missiles like those that now go to the deposit windows at banks. Back then these little missiles carried rolled-up news copy and photos the length and height of the building, en route to the Composing Room.

In addition to the frenzied smoke and banter that set the pattern for the newsroom, the teletype machines clattered with the latest news from *The Associated Press* and the *United Press International.*

Something big happened, the bells would chime.

Different numbers of chimes, as I recall, depending on how important the news.

Say there was a new Miss America, perhaps a bell or two.

A new war, perhaps three or four chimes.

Elvis found dead hugging his commode? Hell's bells.

This copy was ripped off the machine by using a pica pole as a sort of "razor" to give the torn sheet a straight edge. Then the same pica pole was used to measure the copy on the page—the depth of the actual type on the page helped determine the column inches. I can't remember the formula.

Also wire photos came in, wet and stinking of chemicals. If we had time to let them dry, fine. If not, they were "sized" for column width with a scale wheel, rolled up in the pneumatic tubes, just like the copy and sent to composing and the Camera Room.

One of my duties, as I often was the first one to arrive at work, was to go into a closet upstairs and pull back the big lever that started the vacuum system so the pneumatic tubes could function. I always enjoyed that, even though it was one more case where a task was added onto my slate simply because I was conscientious. When I pulled that 3-foot-long lever to start the process, I could feel the floor shake, hear the hack-hack-hack of the massive machine sucking into life for another day.

Ah, but we were talking about smoke, weren't we?

On my first day, as Max burned his Winstons and Worden his Camel straights, as all flavors of Kools, Salems and Marlboros turned the air thick and blue, I realized I had no real choice.

It was a sort of a join them or join them thing.

I could have been a holdout, but I'd still have stunk like cigarettes and my lungs would be coated with tar and nicotine. Without the smooth, long-lasting pleasure.

So, I went to the machine in the cafeteria, plunked in a couple of quarters and got some Winstons.

Later switched a few times, Camel Lights for a long while and then Merit 100s, but from the second day or so I was at the newspaper and for perhaps the next 30 years, I was a dedicated smoker. Smoke 'em if you got 'em, with the first cigarette of the day lighted while I drove to work and the last one before taking my evening shower. One, two, three packs in between.

Story pressure? I didn't really ever show it. Except that I would suck harder and more frequently, the smokes would disintegrate.

Back then, even football coaches smoked and in my first year, when I was a prep sports writer, I'd often be asked by a coach for a smoke during the games. Hell, even the team doctor used to bum off me. I once went to visit him in the hospital when he was coughing up blood. I'm not sure if he quit after that.

Later, talking to a source or cussing at a cop who had told me a lie, I would punctuate my monologues by throwing a smoke hard, into the gutter, delighting in seeing it explode into ashes and sparks.

I loved to smoke.

Made me feel like a journalist, right up until I snuffed the last one to have surgery to remove a tumor on my neck.

"Hey, Flap, if you smoke for the next six weeks, this surgery won't heal properly," said the friendly doctor.

That had something to do with my quitting. Also, by the time I'd quit, I'd adopted two kids from Romania who would look out the back window of the house and holler at me for using those "fire sticks."

"We don't want you to die, Daddy," said Emily. She's probably changed her mind a few times since then, as teenagers do, but even though there were the doctors' warnings, the real reason I quit smoking was that I love my kids.

Without them, well...

Gotta admit, still would like to light one up as I write this story of how and why *The News Brothers* came to be....You know, let it burn in the ashtray...

Man, fill all four corners of Richard Worden's old ash tray. Well, I can't do that anymore. I had his ashtray, the green ceramic one Rob and I mentioned earlier, right up until the late spring of 2010 when I broke it while trying to save my belongings from The Great Nashville Flood, a massive disaster that claimed half my house.

I hadn't been using it since the tumor. It just reminded me of Richard and newspapering, how it was when newspapers mattered.

Naah. You're done, Timothy. At least until they give you a death sentence for something else. Besides that "newspapermen" don't smoke any more. They eat tofu and Thai food and wash it down with bottled water or designer local brews.

No whiskey and cigarettes allowed in today's Information Centers.

Anyway, smoking was fun. It was a part of the business. Like I said, it was a smoke 'em if you got 'em world. And we all had them.

More than one journalist died because of this attitude. Of course, perhaps if we hadn't smoked, we could have had strokes from the stress.

And what would we have done with our extra hands while we were drinking, anyway?

Especially if Glover Williams, the Composing Room foreman, happened to add a dose of his magic from Kentucky's backwoods into our 5:30 a.m. bottles of 7Up.

Tim Ghianni sits at his desk in the *Leaf-Chronicle* newsroom sometime in the early 1980s, plotting out the coverage for that Sunday's newspaper.

Chapter 7
(Tim)

The Royal screw job

I mention earlier the Charlets. It should be noted and highlighted that while they were splendid people, they also enjoyed being treated royally.

Every Christmas, they would tell those of us who worked at the newspaper what they wanted. The latest Philco or Westinghouse, or perhaps a new lawnmower.

We were given price and model and then everyone was "asked" to contribute their share for the new color set, the washing machine or one of those new-fangled microwave machines. Your "gift" donation was outlined and based on salary, so generally it was only $5 or so for me. Can you imagine what the poor guys who were making top wages, $160 or so a week, may have "decided" to donate?

When it was presented to them at the holiday party, they acted surprised. We didn't care. By the time that mid-afternoon present was awarded—usually by Camera Room Superintendent Ronnie Kendrick, a wonderful man and beloved friend who also was their "darkie" (his term, not mine) when it came time to clean the home—we had been drinking since before dawn.

Let them have their TV, man. Where's the bourbon? Where in the hell is Glover? Napping on his desk, a half-empty bottle of help-yourself by his right hand, a cigarette's ashes covering his index finger.

Custodian John Spurlin, a great guy with a boisterous laugh who had an indentation in his forehead from the bullet to the brain he took during a late-night incident, was always too busy to be at the party. He was cleaning up all the empty bottles and cigarettes smashed into the cement floor. He may have made an occasional visit to Glover's office, though.

As for Ronnie, while he won't appear much if any in the rest of this tale, he was there every step of the way, photographing our pages on the big camera, copying our pictures of covered corpses so he could strip them onto the negatives.

He may have been the nicest guy I ever met in Clarksville. I don't see him or talk to him, but I think about him and his kind honor every day. And I loved his Mom, who liked me well enough to occasionally send one of her caramel pies to me, via her son.

Ronnie, if you are reading this, I still love you like a blood brother. Nothing's changed, man. We just got old. And I appreciate your greatest advice to me in a time of personal turmoil: "Ain't nothing to it once you do it."

Max Moss not only trained Tim Ghianni when he first showed up to work as a sports writer,
he also set an example for all staffers by practicing decent and ethical journalism.
A few years after this 1970s photo was taken, Max also was the man who interviewed reporter candidate Rob Dollar.

Leaf-Chronicle staffers who brought home Tennessee *Associated Press* Managing Editors photography honors in 1979 included, from left, Max Moss, Tim Ghianni, Kathy Cobble and W.J. Souza. Tim earned one of his plaques for best sports photo, in recognition of a Special Olympics picture that later was used by the national organization and earned him a citation from Eunice Kennedy Shriver and the Joseph P. Kennedy Jr. Foundation.

In the late 1970s, *Leaf-Chronicle* newsroom staffers assembled for a portrait. Among those in this picture are Max Moss (front left), Tim Ghianni (second from left), Larry Schmidt (fourth from left), Wendell Wilson (next to Larry), Jerry Manley (sixth from right), Richard Worden (fifth from right), Paula Casey (fourth from right), Ron Taylor (third from right) and Jim Monday (foreground, center).

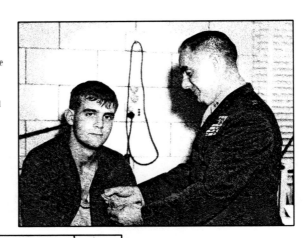

Richard Worden getting his Marine Corps physical before going to Vietnam. After the war, Worden became one of Tim Ghianni's first and best newspaper friends.

An exhausted Richard Worden works on his headache as he listens to the complaint of some official or other crackpot.

Leaf-Chronicle City Editor Richard Worden works two phones to get both sides of the story as news breaks sometime in the 1970s.

Chapter 8
(Tim)

MY PAL THE DEER HUNTER

In setting up this tale, I ought to talk a little bit more about Richard Worden.

As I mentioned, he was the city editor when I began work in Clarksville in the 1970s.

He had been a Marine in Vietnam, got part of one of his legs filled with shrapnel by a mine.

He always wore cowboy boots to cover that injury. Hell, I had him over with the rest of the newsroom to the pool at the Malibu Apartments where I lived a decade or so, and while everyone was cavorting and mostly in their bathing suits, he kept his boots on and smoked.

Richard was a great newspaperman. He also had demons. And he shared them with me.

Many Friday evenings were spent on the deck of his house out in the country, in a community called Sango outside of Clarksville. A herd of bison roamed a farm field up at the end of his road, which always gave us a destination if we wanted to go for a midnight ramble.

Mostly, though, we would march, drink for drink, through a bottle of Scotch and laugh. Time to drink from another one? Hell, throw the first one off the deck and hear it shatter in the yard, the same place where the cigarettes landed while we howled at the moon.

The toughest day we had together was when we went to see "The Deer Hunter" one afternoon after the paper rolled.

He and I had gone to see movies together many afternoons. No big deal. But there was hesitancy in his voice when he asked me if I'd go to see "The Deer Hunter" with him. He needed to see it, he said. But not alone.

No need to go through the plot here, but Michael Cimino's dark and daring motion picture of Vietnam's effects had Richard in need of talking long into that night, telling me of his horrors, perhaps why he drank so much, why he smoked so much, why he could keep up with me.

In addition to being among my greatest friends, Richard taught me much about newspapering. He also taught me some about heartache. He took a weekend off to get married once and by the time he came back to work he was divorced. Nice woman. Way to treat a damned war hero, lady.

He never said a bad word about her. He just came into work, no wedding ring, shrugged and fired up his Marlboros and kept working.

"She decided it wasn't right," he said, by simple explanation to all who would listen. And that was it. Soon he was editing copy and smokes burned in every corner of that green ceramic ashtray.

He left the paper in Clarksville long before the teenagers were murdered, although he did call me to talk about the stories. I think he was envious that I was covering such potentially gripping news stories.

He went off to Memphis, where for a long time he rode a bicycle around town and stopped in parks to read books. I had turned him on to hard-boiled detective novels, Chandler and Hammett and the like. But for all I know, this very special guy read poetry while looking out at the Overton Park band shell.

His second wife, Paula Casey, was a Memphis journalist of some sort. They'd met in Clarksville, where she spent a couple stints as features editor. I can't remember what she did in Memphis, other than, I hope and I'm sure, make Richard happy.

Anyway, he eventually got on with the newspapers in Memphis. He wore his boots to work every day and diligently made sure the right questions were answered, that there was humanity served in the stories.

One holiday, he and Paula went to his favorite place, the Outer Banks, for a week.

The night they got back, he lay in his bed and died. I'd like to say he died with his boots on, but I'm not sure.

The coroner said that a blood clot in his leg, remnant from the long-ago Vietnam wound that caused him to hide his legs in those boots, had broken loose and killed him.

Another victim of that damned war. Richard would have made a helluva *News Brother*.

Rob Dollar was a back-up quarterback for the Fort Campbell Falcons football team in the early 1970s.

Tim Ghianni, who was a sports writer and then sports editor for *The Leaf-Chronicle* in the 1970s, always chose the sidelines over press boxes while covering football games.

Chapter 9
(Tim)

"C'MON ALL YOU BIG STRONG MEN"

I mention the military a lot because they are an ever-present part of Clarksville and the surrounding area. And, I have an expert on the military helping me fill in some of the blanks in the amazing story of *The News Brothers*. Of course, I'm talking about my best friend and comrade in arms, Rob Dollar.

He's a few years younger than me. He's also an Army Brat, having lived all over the world with his career Army officer father, his mother and his three sisters.

But he settled in for high school at Fort Campbell, the home, as I mentioned before, of the 101st Airborne Division (Air Assault).

Interestingly, Rob was named in honor of his great-uncle, Robert Stanley Dollar, who fought in World War II with the Navy, surviving the sneak attack on Pearl Harbor and the Battle of Midway. His luck finally ran out in mid-October 1942 when the USS Meredith was sunk off Guadalcanal. Japanese bombs and sharks killed a total of 237 American sailors in the incident, including Robert Stanley Dollar, of Fitzgerald, Ga.

As fate and irony would have it, I wrote about the younger Robert Stanley Dollar long before I met him and we began tilting at windmills. One of the high school teams I covered regularly during my first couple of years in Clarksville was the Fort Campbell High School Falcons.

The guys on this team faced a disadvantage because their families moved so frequently, keeping the team from developing long-term leadership.

One year the Falcons were expected to make a championship run, largely because Rob, one of two veteran quarterbacks on the team, and some of the other guys—including Roger Richardson, Preston Owens, Mike Hellums, David George, Alan Garcia, Brian Yuhas, Donnie Thomas and Mike Rose—were returning for their senior years. Having veteran players at Fort Campbell "was about as rare as pink parachutes," I wrote one Saturday morning in praising that squad, coached by the legendary Marshall Patterson. I should probably note here that I did have one strange encounter involving Coach Patterson. In a story I wrote after one of the games, I mentioned that the iconic football (and wrestling) coach "chuckled." The next morning, his wife called me: "My husband never chuckles. I've never heard him chuckle," said the angry Mrs. Coach P. I gulped for a second and then said: "I wonder whose fault that is?" She hung up on me, but Marshall always liked to chuckle when recounting that tale. At least I like to recall it that way.

Being a newspaperman in Clarksville had a lot of benefits. Over the years, I covered a lot of stories involving the military and learned a lot about what they do, their experiences, their high-stress lives.

It also was great to be able to drive out to Fort Campbell and roll through Gate 4—back then there was no real security and all you had to do was wave at the guard and keep rolling.

That changed after 9/11, of course, as did we all.

But this was still a time of relative peace, other than the occasional little skirmish here and there.

So, a newsman got the opportunity to see some of the stuff everybody else wished they could see.

For example, probably not many of you have witnessed a full airborne assault, helicopters chopping, missiles exploding, live artillery blasting …. But I was welcome to personally witness this stuff most of you only saw in movies.

The same goes for Rob and many other reporters who worked for *The Leaf-Chronicle* over the years. Rob, a real rough-and-tumble newspaper reporter, once even rappelled down the 34-foot tower at the post's Sabalauski Air Assault School—when he was well past his 40th birthday…HOOAH!

And then, of course, there are the helicopters, always on the skyline in Clarksville if not flying right over downtown.

The most popular Army helicopter—the successor to the Vietnam-era UH-1 "Huey" and now used so frequently in those other wars we won't debate here—is, and was, the UH-60 Blackhawk.

The primary delivery mode for the 101st's Screaming Eagles into the battle zone, I'd long admired them as they flew over.

One day, sometime during 1981, the post spokesman—the late Bill Harralson, a retired Army officer and longtime employee of the Fort Campbell Public Affairs Office—asked me if I wanted to go for a ride in a Blackhawk.

Seems some journalists—cameraman and TV broadcaster—were visiting from Japan. And Fort Campbell wanted to give them a show. The spokesman thought I might enjoy meeting my fellow journalists from the land they called The Rising Sun.

So, Chief Photographer Larry McCormack and I were on post one early summer's day and after shuffling through a big field of tall grass, whipped into a frenzy by the beating rotors, we climbed aboard a Blackhawk. We went on the ride of a lifetime, a tree-topping, roller-coaster that made about everyone except me sick and some feel like they might toss their cookies.

Larry may not have lost his cookies, but he lost his wallet. Deep onto the post, as we were flying over the dense woods and Larry was leaning out to shoot pictures, his wallet fell to earth.

Well, he didn't know it fell immediately, but he missed it and figured it was gone. Course he was a newsman, so there wasn't much money in it, but it did have his license, his Captain Kangaroo Club card and other collectibles.

Now Fort Campbell is the size of a small state (the military reservation is a bit more than 102,000 acres), so the chances of ever finding the wallet were not even slim.

But, against all odds, one day, about a week later, Larry got a call from the Public Affairs Office. Seems a soldier out on maneuvers, deep in the woods, pretending he was killing Grenadian terrorists or some such enemy, had found the wallet and carted it back to the Public Affairs Office.

Nothing was missing.

At the time, Rob and I had contemplated putting together a fake newspaper page to preserve this most amazing story for posterity. But that was one project—maybe the only one—we never completed. Ironically, the headline planned for the fake front page—"Wallet Found: It's Larry's"—was saved in our heads and used on a very dark day the following year when a college football star's disappearance was in the news.

Now let's talk some more about Fort Campbell. The sprawling military reservation was constructed and opened in the early 1940s. Not surprisingly, it's THE major draw in the area for everything, and anyone, looking for a world stage. Over the years, presidents (Lyndon Johnson, Ronald Reagan, George H.W. Bush, Bill Clinton, George W. Bush, and Barack Obama) have visited the post along with such celebrities as Joe Louis, Bo Derek, Larry King, Danny Glover, Don King, Wynonna Judd, Buzz Aldrin, Oliver North, Al Gore, Donald Rumsfeld, Gary Sinise and his "Lt. Dan Band," Dick Cheney and Joe Biden. And that's just a partial list of the "who's who" of visitors over the years. We're not even counting the notorious *News Brothers*.

Retired Army Gen. Colin Powell, a former chairman of the Joint Chiefs of Staff and George W. Bush's secretary of state, served at Fort Campbell as an Army colonel in the mid-1970s, commanding the 2nd Brigade.

In the early 1990s, he returned to the area as America's top military man for an event at Austin Peay State University in Clarksville. Powell met with the media and commented that Clarksville had grown and changed a lot since his days at Fort Campbell. But, he joked, he was happy to see one of his favorite shopping places still very much alive and thriving—Grandpa's, the iconic department store on U.S. 41A in the north part of town.

Tim Ghianni covers a basketball game during the mid-1970s.
Ghianni started his newspaper career as a prep writer for *The Leaf-Chronicle*.
He later became sports editor and held other jobs before eventually becoming associate editor/columnist.

Actor/playwright Sam Shepard watches the filming of a scene from the movie, "Sweet Dreams," while visiting the Fort Campbell Army Post in December 1984.

Hollywood is a frequent visitor to the Army post, which still has many World War II-era barracks in fairly good condition. Late in 1984, several scenes from "Sweet Dreams—the movie about the life of country music star Patsy Cline—were filmed at Fort Campbell, with stars Jessica Lange and Ed Harris. (Probably ought to note here that Harris was playing Patsy's husband Charlie Dick, who actually became one of my first friends in the music business when I moved to Nashville. It was after visiting with Charlie that I met Bill Monroe at a gas station off Dickerson Road. But that's a story for another book.)

Working—not acting—in the role of a reporter, Rob hung around the "Sweet Dreams" movie set one day and got to pal around with Jessica Lange's significant other at that time in her life—playwright/actor Sam Shepard, who was showing everyone the new coat he had just bought at some place in the Mojave Desert.

Heck it was even at Fort Campbell in the early 1960s that a young paratrooper on the verge of washing out of the Army, a skinny kid from Seattle named Jimi Hendrix, began playing his guitar with bass-playing pal Billy Cox. Interestingly, there's a bar on Franklin Street in downtown Clarksville, The Front Page Deli, that has a lasting reminder of Jimi Hendrix's ties to the area—a framed pawn shop ticket from a day long ago when the great musician put up his guitar for some cash.

Jimi later left the Army to conquer the world, but eventually he and Cox reunited to help form Hendrix's post-Experience outfit, Band of Gypsys. Of course, Jimi's long gone, but Billy is still alive and living in North Nashville. And, he's a buddy of mine now.

Rob's military family moved to Fort Campbell in November 1969, just after his father completed the first of his two tours in Vietnam. At the time, Rob was in junior high school. Less than two years after their arrival on post, Fort Campbell was the target of a major protest against the Vietnam War. The anti-war rally was held in what is now Patriots Park, across from Gate 3, and the celebrity who showed up to lead "The Fish Cheer" was none other than Country Joe McDonald of the rock music group, Country Joe & The Fish.

It's funny now, but Rob and some of his buddies, curious to see the "hippies," pedaled over to the protest on their bicycles. Poor Rob had the misfortune of being in the background while a television reporter from Nashville interviewed one of the protesters. He spent the rest of that day praying his father would be too busy that evening to catch the 6 o'clock news...Because if CW2 Dollar had seen his son with those long-hairs...well, there would have been hell to pay.

Now, if I had been around at the time of the Fort Campbell protest, I probably would have fit in rather nicely. I had actually met Country Joe and joined him on stage a few years earlier, when I was known as "The Dancing Bear" while growing my hair long and attending Iowa State University and in my spare time rambling across the Great Plains. "Give me an F!" ... "Gimme a U!" ... well you know how "The Fish Cheer" goes.

About four years after Country Joe's visit, and only a few weeks before Rob graduated from high school, Fort Campbell was the site of the first-ever rock festival on a military base. The concert—called "Music You're My Mother"—was held at Fryar Stadium on Thursday, May 22, 1975, with a crowd estimated as high as 40,000. The event, which was to be filmed and shown to military audiences worldwide, starred Joe Cocker, Barbi Benton, Rufus, Chaka Khan, Pure Prairie League and the Earl Scruggs Revue. (I am fortunate, by the way, that in my later and calmer life I have had many opportunities to interview Earl, one of Nashville's kindest gentlemen.)

Now, Rob still can't remember why he missed the infamous concert, but it may have been a blessing in disguise....Chaos reigned hard, making the event a public relations nightmare for the Army. There were some stabbings, drug overdoses and dozens of soldiers and civilians arrested for drunkenness and disorderly conduct.

Unless his memory is playing tricks on him, Rob said there was some "scuttlebutt" at the time that one of the "headliners"—I won't mention a name, but you can probably guess it wasn't Earl

Scruggs—had overdosed prior to the concert and refused to perform. A high-ranking post official, maybe a general, knowing the show had to go on, ordered the entertainer in question taken to the post hospital, where his stomach supposedly was pumped and he was revived to his senses or at least close enough to his senses to actually perform...."That son-of-a-bitch is going to get on that stage and sing," the commander declared, according to the narrative of the legend, as passed down over the years.

The whole truth or an unfounded rumor? Well, if it actually happened, it's certainly one secret—maybe the only one—that's ever been kept at Fort Campbell.

Since Joe Cocker was at the concert, I guess I should share another of my own secrets from my youth as the omnipresent "Dancing Bear" at parties and concerts in and around Ames, Iowa. Yep, get me in the right mood and I don't usually fight or even cuss much. But I do like the smell of the greasepaint and the roar of the crowd.

Mr. Cocker—as I'm sure you know if you've gotten this far in the story—has a style of performance that I enjoyed mimicking at parties and on the occasional stage. Well, during one stop in Ames, I actually climbed up on his stage. I think he was singing his version of "A Little Help From My Friends," and I participated in the twitching and grooving on the edge of the stage.

Some of my college chums bragged that old Joe even took a lesson from me. Can't do that kind of stuff nowadays, of course. Post 9/11 security keeps guys like the old "Dancing Bear" away from the stage.

I was in Clarksville at the time of the Fort Campbell concert, and a fairly regular visitor to the post ...Remember, I covered old Rob when he was playing football for the FCHS Falcons at Fryar Stadium.

The only reason I missed the big event was I was working that day and night at the newspaper, which even at that tender age had begun consuming my life.

I guess I wouldn't have fit in anyway. It was a violent and mean night ... and I was to see enough of those soon enough. Fortunately, I made it through, with a little help from my friends.

But, can you imagine what the post commander would have said if the "Dancing Bear" had made it on stage at Fryar Stadium?

One thing is for sure, though. Since that near-riot at Fort Campbell in May 1975, I don't remember any other Army posts or military bases having a rock concert.

Back to the importance of Fort Campbell. Without question, the Army plays a key role in the type of people who make their homes in the civilian communities surrounding the post. Yes, there were and still are a lot of retired military stabilizing the economy. Hopkinsville became home to Rob, when his father, preparing for retirement, bought the family house in that nearby Kentucky city back in 1974.

Retirees, of course, are only the tip of the iceberg. About 30,400 active-duty soldiers, with nice paychecks, make the military very desirable tenants in the largest cities closest to the post— Clarksville, Hopkinsville and Oak Grove.

In fact, Fort Campbell ranks as the largest employer in two states—Kentucky and Tennessee. In addition to active-duty soldiers, there are more than 5,100 civilian employees at the post, and about 3,000 contract employees. The most recent financial figures put the annual payroll disbursement for Fort Campbell at $1.67 billion.

The post also has a world-class hospital named in honor of the late Army Col. Florence A. Blanchfield, who was superintendent of the Army Nurse Corps from 1943 to 1947.

Blanchfield Army Community Hospital opened in September 1982, and it was at the dedication ceremony that Rob first met someone who would become a colleague and good friend at his next newspaper—Mary D. Ferguson of the *Kentucky New Era*.

"Mary D." covered Fort Campbell for the Hopkinsville newspaper. Early in her journalism career, she worked for The Charlets at *The Leaf-Chronicle* before becoming the *New Era*'s first female staff writer/reporter. She knew Fort Campbell like the back of her hand, and was on a first-name basis with every general who had ever commanded the post—including legendary Gen. William C. Westmoreland.

Well into her sixth decade of newspapering, "Mary D." continues to work part-time at the *New Era*, writing her weekly "Inquiring Reporter" column, which began on Rob's watch at the Hopkinsville paper.

Her husband, retired state Trooper R.N. Ferguson, is probably the most interviewed person in Kentucky since he was among the first lawmen on the scene to investigate the alleged alien landing at nearby Kelly, Kentucky, on the night of Aug. 21, 1955. The so-called "Little Green Men" incident was the basis for the huge 1982 Steven Spielberg movie, "E.T."

As neighbors, the military folks from Fort Campbell bring much to the table. They worship in the local churches. They help out at the schools. They serve as coaches. And, they're heavily involved in such activities as Boy Scouts and Girl Scouts.

But for all the good the military does, there also is a bad side, which most often is reflected in the crime reports.

Not that the soldiers are bad. Remember, there are rotten apples in every barrel, including—and perhaps especially—in 21st Century journalism.

Most of the military I met are good guys, including "Sarge" an obese fellow who lived across the hall from me in my first flop in Clarksville. Fattest Army guy I ever knew. He would eat two frozen meat loafs for dinner.

He would ask me to join him, but, well, I literally couldn't stomach gluttony. Still, I liked the guy, and we sat outside in the evenings while I smoked cigarettes and he drank quarts of malt liquor mixed with root beer. And we counted the train cars as they moved through our yard.

Rob Dollar stands in front of an MH-47 Chinook helicopter after a flight over a backwoods area of the Fort Campbell Army Post. Dollar and several other journalists spent an entire day as guests of the secretive 160th Special Operations Aviation Regiment (Airborne) back in April 2002.

Chapter 10
(Tim)

...TH WAITS IN THE DARK'

...wadays the 160th Special Operations Aviation Regiment (Airborne), known as "The Night Stalkers," are considered a part of the Fort Campbell community just like the 5th Special Forces Group (Airborne), or Green Berets. Both elite units found their way to Fort Campbell in the 1980s, further enhancing the reputation of the Army post as a place where the best of the best serve their country.

Retired and active duty Green Berets even have a "Safe House," off post, near Campbell Army Airfield, where they drink and tell war stories and likely cheer the warmongering of guys like George W. Bush and, unfortunately, my pal Barack Obama.

After all, while these are nice and honorable men, they also are warriors. They love to fight. Like it better when they are allowed to kill.

No, they aren't Robert Duvall, loving the smell of napalm in the morning. But I'll bet they got their share of fun chasing and shooting Saddam's "forces" when Baghdad fell in April 2003.

Rob and I got to visit the "Safe House" in the summer of 2006, while I was working for *The Tennessean*, on a story about Robin Moore, author of the best-selling book, "The Green Berets." Moore, a good friend of John Wayne and Bobby Kennedy, had moved to Hopkinsville, Kentucky, to be close to the 5th Special Forces Group while writing his memoirs.

We became good friends with the literary legend, his wife, Helen, and some of the retired Green Berets, who cared for the old man until his death in late February 2008. Rob even was afforded the privilege of having a drink from "Dave's" special $10,000-bottle of Scotch Whiskey.

But, let's get back to the subject of "The Night." In the heyday of *The News Brothers*, the 160th did not exist, according to Fort Campbell and Army officials. It was the blackest of America's black operations, maybe second to Area 51.

Of course, we—the newspaper guys at *The Leaf-Chronicle*—knew the secret unit was there at the Army post, training at "The Bird Cage," beginning sometime in late 1981...maybe earlier.

This back area of Fort Campbell had once been known as Clarksville Base, a Naval installation, and it was where America had stored some of her nuclear weapons for a time in the 1950s and 1960s.

In 1981 and 1982, there were several fatal helicopter crashes involving personnel from Fort Campbell. It didn't take a genius to figure out the Army's best aviators were pushing the envelope and experimenting with Night Vision Goggles. So, there was no doubt in our minds "The Night Stalkers" were real, even if the Army told us otherwise.

The newspaper's military reporter, Frank Wm. White, who had once been in the Army, at some point investigated and wrote an outstanding front-page story, suggesting the 160th was the newest secret of the secretive Bird Cage. Damn...Frank's take-no-prisoners, filled with facts, story royally pissed off Army officials at Fort Campbell. I was damn proud of old Frankie. So was Rob, who spent a day or two doing his "Happy Dance" since he enjoyed it thoroughly whenever people got angry with us for being "in the right." I even think he taught old Frankie that dance.

In December 1984, just more than three years after Frank's article was published, Rob, too, wrote a controversial story about those same 160th Night Stalkers. Now, this story *really* ticked off the Army. At the time, Rob was working for the *Kentucky New Era*, the daily newspaper in Hopkinsville, Kentucky, with the multimillion-dollar military contract to print the *Fort Campbell Courier* newspaper. So how unhappy was Fort Campbell's top brass? Well, the post's commanding general was part of a delegation that paid a visit to *New Era* Publisher Bob Carter soon after Rob's story hit the streets. The brass demanded satisfaction *or else*....But, as it turned out, loyalty meant everything to Bob Carter, a member of the Kentucky Journalism Hall of Fame who died at age 77 of lung cancer on Dec. 31, 2011, at his home in Hopkinsville. He backed Rob on that story, and many others, to the very end...The hell with the consequences. Rob never forgot Mr. Carter's act of courage under extreme fire and possibly even heavy artillery.

Only a few months later, Rob was smiling...in a photograph snapped in the *New Era's* Photography Department studios. It had been taken, in jest, by *New Era* Graphics Editor David Riley, a longtime pal of Rob's who died 20 years later after a courageous fight against cancer. I guess Rob was taking his victory lap in the photograph. Anyway, the photo showed him wearing sunglasses and a "Night Stalker" T-shirt, while reading a copy of the *New Era* that had his Night Stalker story at the top of the front page...The very story that—at some newspapers run by publishers without spines— could have cost him his job. And not because it wasn't true.

The funny part about the photo was the "Death Waits in the Dark" T-shirt. It had been borrowed from "The Lady Night Stalkers," the wives and wives-to-be of 160th personnel. The group of military spouses actually published a monthly newsletter that David Riley helped them put out as a courtesy and as part of the *Fort Campbell Courier* contract. So much for keeping secrets, huh?

Now, if nothing else, "The Night Stalkers" sometimes brought about their own publicity. They could be their worst enemies. Personnel from the outfit often were active participants of the nightly beer-fueled, high-speed frivolity along Fort Campbell Boulevard, and we also had female employees in *The Leaf-Chronicle* building who claimed to be married or going out with these daring pilots from the top secret unit.

But were they there? Prove it...Well, journalists tried hard to get stories, on the record. Yet no one would budge, and the unit stayed in the shadows.

Until a photograph appeared in *Newsweek* or *Time* of an American helicopter pilot killed in the wake of the "safe" invasion of Grenada, the Gipper's chip-shot war back in October 1983.

Tim Ghianni (right) and Rob Dollar visit with author Robin Moore and his wife, Helen, at their Hopkinsville, Kentucky, home in August 2006. Moore wrote several best-selling books, including "The Green Berets" and "The French Connection." He died in February 2008.

With his book, "The Green Berets," Robin Moore helped create the legend of the Special Forces. The Massachusetts native went to college with Robert F. Kennedy and was best friends with the rogue actor Errol Flynn.

The problem of how to reveal the fact "The Night Stalkers" even existed was solved with a phone call.

The widow of that fallen soldier—Capt. Keith Lucas—had become something of a fan of my writing and she wanted to know if I'd come out to the post to talk.

I had to get the proper military escort from the Public Affairs Office to her family quarters. But once inside her home, the Army couldn't stop her from talking about her husband's proud duty with "The Night Stalkers" and why she was tired of the government not telling the truth.

News Brothers did some damn good work.

Even, with this breakthrough, the Army continued to try and minimize the publicity surrounding this classified unit. They even started playing mind games. Fort Campbell officials, for a time, continued to insist there was no 160th aviation unit assigned to Fort Campbell. Then, finally, someone let it slip that the 160th, although based at Fort Campbell, actually was assigned to the Special Operations Command at Fort Bragg, N.C. So technically, the Army wasn't really lying to the media.

Ten years later, The Night Stalkers had no choice but to emerge from the shadows forever. And, it was their dangerous work, not the media, that exposed them.

In October 1993, Chief Warrant Officer Mike Durant was shot down in his helicopter and taken prisoner in Mogadishu, Somalia. "The Blackhawk Down" incident—chronicled in a grisly and gripping motion picture—put Durant's face on the cover of every national magazine in the country.

The secret unit with the motto, "Death Waits in the Dark," was a secret no more.

Less than 10 years later, in April 2002, Rob was smiling again. The 160th wanted to tell its story to the public in order to enhance the chances to gain more money from Congress for aircraft and other equipment to fight the War on Terror. As a result, about 10 journalists—including Rob and one of his *New Era* staffers, Jennifer P. Brown, *The Leaf-Chronicle's* Chantal Escoto, and a few reporters from the national media—were invited to visit the top-secret Night Stalker Compound on post. The daylong event included a flight on one of the 160th's souped-up and bullet-riddled MH-47 Chinook helicopters just back from Afghanistan.

Rob said the once-in-a-lifetime experience was *real* neat, especially since his hosts were Special Operations soldiers the Army once claimed weren't *real*...

NSDQ means "Night Stalkers Don't Quit." Neither do *News Brothers*.

Yes folks, it's true: He who smiles last, smiles best.

And a little footnote here about the secrets of Fort Campbell. After SEAL Team Six killed Osama Bin Laden... finally ... President Obama came to the post ostensibly on a regular presidential visit in early May 2011, just days after the successful kill mission in Pakistan. However, the president and Vice President Joe Biden took time out to take a side trip to visit with and salute the daring men involved in that mission. Night Stalkers? For sure. But was SEAL Team Six also at the Night Stalker Compound that day, maybe finishing up a post-mission debriefing? You can bet on it.

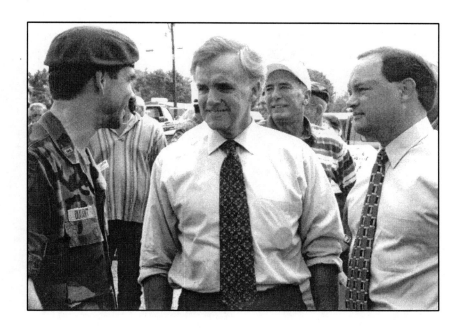

"Night Stalker" Mike Durant (left) talks with former Nebraska Sen. Bob Kerrey (center) and Steve Henry, the former lieutenant governor of Kentucky, during a public event in Hopkinsville in the summer of 1995. Kerrey, as a SEAL during the Vietnam War, won the Medal of Honor.

Tim Ghianni, then the sports editor of *The Leaf-Chronicle*, interviews football great O.J. Simpson at the Clarksville Country Club in the late 1970s or early 1980s. "The Juice" is now serving time at a Nevada prison for a robbery conviction.

Chapter 11
(Tim)

FORE AND 30 YEARS AGO
WITH A FEW SPORTS LEGENDS

I may have mentioned that Tony Durr liked golf. He wasn't good at it. He just liked it. He liked any excuse not to work, really.

Little guy. Big dreams. Lack of ambition and dedication. But I loved the guy. Still do. Course he's dead. Love him more if I could pick up the phone and talk to him.

Every day in the nice weather, it seemed he would summon the aforementioned lard-ass reporter into his office and they'd leave to go play nine holes at Mason Rudolph Municipal Golf Course. (That reporter, by the way, tells me he'd prefer to be referred to in this book as the "sweet, jovial fellow everyone loved," but assures me "lard-ass" is likely more accurate of his physical state at the time. Both are true, of course.)

Mason Rudolph, the fellow for whom the little municipal course was named, was a friend of mine. One of Clarksville's favorite sons, he was a PGA star in the early Palmer/Player days. He even went head-to-head with "Slammin' Sammy" Snead once. And while Mason, who died in 2011, never got a green jacket at the Masters, he did his fair share of damage out there. I walked with him and his family the last time he made the cut in a PGA event.

I don't remember the year, but it was in the mid-1970s. He was playing in what was then called the Danny Thomas Memphis Open, played at the Colonial in Germantown, outside Memphis.

As sports editor, I went to cover the event.

I actually had some pretty good times and met some good people when I was sports editor.

Well, not all of them were good. I spent a couple of afternoons with O.J. Simpson, the great college and professional football running back, when he was spokesman for the local Acme Boot Company. Actually, I kinda liked the guy.

Best interview I did with O.J. was when he was the first black person to play tennis at the Clarksville Country Club. The boot company held their national gathering there and "The Juice" was there to play tennis with the big shots.

He thought it was interesting that people of his color had only previously come onto the club property as laborers, cooks, caddies and the like. But it didn't bother him much. Still I focused a part of my story on that fact.

The best afternoon we spent together included an interview at the country club and dessert afterward at one of my favorite downtown restaurants, Austin's, owned by my good friend Jerry Uetz.

Interesting thing, though. O.J. had ordered ice cream ... and he kept fingering the steak knife that was on the table while we talked.

Later, in June 1994, when he was the prime suspect in the murders of his ex-wife and her friend, I thought a lot about that knife-wielding good guy. By the way, when they charged him in the case and he took off for the low-speed chase on the interstate in Los Angeles, well, I was the only *Nashville Banner* ranking editor around—I never took lunch—who could authorize going late for news. So while my staff put together a new front page, streaming about O.J. on the run, I ran downstairs to the press room and shouted "Stop the Presses!"

Yep they used to really do that stuff. I'd done it before. But this was the last time

On a more memorable note, I got to spend a fair amount of time with Muhammad Ali during the course of my career, even swinging press credentials and enough company dough for a cheap Garden District hotel room for a week out of *The Leaf-*

Chronicle management. I swapped my Master's credentials and the budgeted money for that trip in exchange for the OK to cover the Leon Spinks-Ali fight in the Superdome in New Orleans. Ali claimed the title for the third time that night, Sept. 15, 1978.

Afterward, I did the typical interview stuff and met Larry Holmes, Floyd Patterson, both Spinks brothers, Kenny Norton, Joe Frazier, Bundini Brown, Don King and more guys I was proud to meet.

But it was Angelo Dundee, Ali's corner man, who gave me a bit of information that the next morning, at 8, Ali would be receiving press in his room.

I got there, as scheduled. But only two other journalists showed up. The rest of the sports writers had doubtless done all their reporting from Bourbon Street the night before.

Anyway, I spent the morning with one of my heroes, one of the greatest men of the 20th Century and found him proud, brave ... and he had incredibly sore hands and softly asked me to take it easy with the handshake. He will always be the champ.

As I left Ali's room, I ran into Howard Cosell, who began ordering the champ around so he could get his interview for *ABC's Wide World of Sports*. For those who want to know, Howard Cosell was an arrogant turd. And I'm being, as usual, very kind here.

There were a lot of other sports legends I got to interview over the years.

First of all there is Wilma Rudolph, the heroic Olympics track star who was a Clarksville native and a cousin of my friend, Ole Steve Pettus, a great pork shoulder barbecue genius and a gospel-singing legend. I was invited to Pettus family reunions and the long and lean and lovely Wilma was always there. Of course I interviewed her professionally as well and was a guest at the screening of her biopic. Sitting nearby in the theater? Muhammad Ali.

Mickey Mantle, Whitey Ford, Brooks Robinson ... great ballplayers. John Wooden, The Wizard of Westwood. And Magic Johnson, who remains the best basketball player ever. Bob Knight even answered questions from me without getting mad and throwing a chair.

Then, there was Al McGuire, who I once interviewed while we were at adjoining urinals during an NCAA tourney. I liked the guy and got a good column out of that odd encounter. Although it was sanitized for a family newspaper.

Few of the people I've met while chasing news left as strong an image in my brain as Henry Aaron. I love baseball and in my youth had met some great players. Like Al Kaline, Ernie Banks, Fergie Jenkins, Willie Mays, Ron Santo, Jim Bunning, Luis Aparicio, Pete Rose—just to name a few.

But, of course, Henry Louis Aaron was a class above them all and he kind of demonstrated that during the time I interviewed him.

I remember him as kind of surly, at least on first meeting.

Of course, I guess I didn't blame him for coming off that way. After all, here was the greatest ballplayer of all time having to pimp himself out to sell Magnavox televisions in a small Southern city.

And anyone who knows anything about Henry Aaron knows this son of Mobile, Alabama, had less-than-wondrous times in Southern cities … including, of course, Atlanta.

I think our encounter was the autumn of 1976, after he finished up his short "homecoming" stint with the Milwaukee Brewers.

The new Magnavox dealer, out on the south end of Clarksville, called to say "Hank" was coming to sign autographs, I believe for a grand-opening ceremony at the store.

Of course, the great home run king was getting paid by Magnavox. Still, it was kind of disconcerting to me, as a guy who went to Atlanta to watch his last game in Fulton County Stadium a couple years prior, to see this rather unassuming fellow in a sport coat standing over glistening ebony cabinets containing the best TVs on the planet … or at least the best ones he was hawking.

Still, it was Henry Aaron, and I called him "Mr. Aaron," when I approached.

While I couldn't allow myself the privilege of being a "normal fan," I wasn't going to miss an opportunity of a lifetime. I had a poster—with its illustration of him arm-in-arm with Babe Ruth, the words "Brotherhood of Excellence" written beneath it—out in the car that I hoped he would sign for me.

His surliness went away as my old smile and interest in humans, particularly home run kings, gained on him. At least while he was talking to me, he could ignore the fawning line of autograph seekers and local corporate hotshots who wanted to call him "Hammering Hank."

I realized he liked that I was providing a nice, curly-haired diversion and making "The Man" wait for him. Anyway, after I wrapped up my 45 minutes or so with him, I asked "Mr. Aaron" if I could go out and get the poster in my car for him to sign.

"They gave these out at Henry Aaron Appreciation Day down in Atlanta," I said, offering the poster that on this day hangs in my son's room.

"They didn't appreciate me in Atlanta," he said, or words to that effect. "I don't remember that day."

Still he signed it, simply: "Best Wishes, Henry Aaron."

He rolled it up and handed it back to me.

"Thanks, Mr. Aaron," I said.

At which point the great baseball player smiled, nodded and said words I'll never forget:

"My name's Henry, Tim."

On a different level—as he was a reporter to the bone rather than a superstar of the diamond, gridiron or boxing ring—Joe Caldwell was a sports legend who had a big impact on my life. He didn't play anything. But, boy, could he write...

I guess he's my fondest memory of my time on the desk at *The Tennessean*, my first stop after the *Nashville Banner* folded. It was there I spent many late nights with Joe, who had also worked for the *Kentucky New Era* very early in his career.

A great sportswriter, especially when it came to NASCAR, Joe and I had been friends since I was a young sportswriter in Clarksville and he covered the Ohio Valley Conference—

including Clarksville's Austin Peay State University—for the *Banner*.

Like me, he was hired by the Nashville morning paper—after the *Banner* was killed by greed—to work the night news desk, editing copy and laying out pages. He should have been in sports. He and I also were the "last two"—the two guys who stayed the latest every night, me checking off pages in the composing room, him waiting in the newsroom for the final copies of the last editions. It was our "punishment" for being the "new kids," I suppose.

I didn't mind, really. Because I got to know my old friend much better. Late at night, we'd talk about what we should be doing. He'd tell me I was the best writer ever to hit Nashville and I should be out doing my people stories, the chronicles of lovable losers, society's castoffs, injustices and the like, the types of stories I loved doing and which had gained me national recognition.

At the same time, I knew Joe should be covering NASCAR. He was among the best in the business and had been honored as such around the circuit back during his *Banner* days.

One night, as we walked out of the building, from which all *Nashville Banner* signage had been stripped from the "Gannett" building at 1100 Broadway, he told me that it looked like he was finally going to get moved over to sports, to work the copy desk, but at least he'd be in the area he loved, where he belonged.

He never reported for work again. He was victim of a massive heart attack, dying in the late spring of 1998, just 78 days after the *Banner* was shut down. For several more months I had the late duty to myself. And damn I missed Joe and his sometimes ribald tales as well as his constant health complaints. Turns out he wasn't such a hypochondriac after all.

Joe was, by the way, brother-in-law ... or something like that ... to great college football coach James "Boots" Donnelly, who Joe and I both covered when Boots won the OVC for The Peay.

Boots, who left APSU to coach at Middle Tennessee for decades, gave a masterful eulogy, while *Tennessean* brass glared at me, apparently wondering what I was doing at a funeral when I should be working the copy desk. Of course they should be excused for their ignorance, as they didn't realize that my work day didn't begin until 4 p.m., just as they probably had been unaware—until Boots' eulogy— that Joe had been a great and greatly admired sports writer.

But this segment is about golf and the Colonial Country Club and drunk Danny Thomas. Did I say Danny was drunk? And mean? Oh well, I was just a kid. I suppose the big nose must have made him angry. Bless him for his work for St. Jude, where he helped so many children. But, well sorry Marlo, he was something of an ass, at least to this writer.

Anyway, actually covering the tourney was special. I loved Mason Rudolph and also the adventure.

It was one of the more fun assignments. You know that the big shot journalists just sit up in the press tent and wait for the golfers there, while consuming beer and shrimp cocktails and pulled-pork barbecue.

Me, well, I like the action. I never liked press row or press boxes. I liked to roam. And since I was there to cover Mason, I walked the course with him for two days. I got to joke around with his friends like Gary Player, Lee Trevino, Chi Chi Rodriguez and the lot.

Even drank a beer from an on-course vendor while Player told me what a great man Mason Rudolph was. And he had no need to stop and talk to a kid from Clarksville. Player was one of the greatest golfers ever and he had time for me. Wonder if Danny Thomas liked him?

Anyway, Mason made the cut. But as I called in to file my story that day, I was told I couldn't stay in Memphis for the last two rounds.

I can't remember why. I think someone was hung over and I had to go back and run the paper that Saturday night. For all I know, maybe that was the weekend Richard Worden got married that first time and nobody had remembered to have someone to fill the editor's job for the Sunday paper.

So on the third day of the tourney, Saturday morning, I checked out of my room. On my way out, I said goodbye to the nice young golfer who had been in the next room—a young

Spaniard named Severiano Ballesteros, who was just starting his eventual conquest of America—and went back to the course to walk a few holes of Mason's third round before heading back to Clarksville.

When Seve—as he asked me and just about anyone else to call him—died not long ago from his brain tumor, I thought a lot about our brief chats in the elevator and the hallway and by his room. He was a charming and kind guy and we both were just in the beginnings of our careers. I was glad to see him remembered not only as a golfer but as a world-class nice guy.

Anyway, that's an aside.

Mason Rudolph loved Clarksville and that nine-hole public golf course named after him.

For someone who took golf as a pass-fail class in college in order to fill out my P.E. requirement (I also took fencing and tennis), I was really no good. So I didn't play.

But one day, in the hot summer after the murders, *The News Brothers* decided to have a Tony Durr Invitational Golf Tournament at Mason Rudolph Golf Course.

Since we usually got off work at about 2 p.m. (we got in at 4 or 5 in the morning, remember), we just went over to the course, stopping first to buy large quantities of tall boy (16-ounce) beers at the store next to Pal's Package.

While Tony and the previously mentioned lovable large fellow—Billy Fields, now a government and Democratic party hotshot in Nashville and some say a future mayor of Music City—started out, the rest of us went in and rented enough clubs between us to play.

I think we shared a couple of bags. And while we warmed up, the beer-drinking began.

The players: Tony and Billy, Jerry Manley, me and Rob, John Staed, Jim Lindgren, Ricky G. Moore, Neesa Perry and Sandy Smith. Sandy was Tony's secretary, and Neesa was the paper's TV writer.

The prize was a candy-striped red jacket we bought at The Mustard Seed—a used clothing place—on the day of the tournament.

Someplace out there, I think high-ranking in the U.S. military now, is Lars Braun. At the time, he was a summer intern. A good kid who came to us to learn about journalism and covering the big story so he could finish up his journalism degree before going off to kill in the name of God and country. Or something like that.

For Lars, we rented a cart, so he could drive around with the beer. He never was allowed to stray far from me and Rob and Jerry. He was a damn good intern. Wonder if he'll ever be chairman of the Joint Chiefs of Staff and instead of allowing some sort of "Dr. Strangelove" world calamity to occur, he'll calm all of his comrades down by detailing his days with *The News Brothers*.

Come to think about it, it could end up like that—The *News Brothers* saving the world...by accident and beer. God bless us.

Anyway, it was a strange tournament. Balls were flying like missiles, driving respectable people out of our way.

Sometimes we let people play through—after all, I really like the people of Clarksville and they liked me too, even when I was "happy." Other times, the locals watched in awe to see us even standing up after the consumption on a hot early summer afternoon became virtually one beer per stroke.

Rob was playing golf for the first time in his life. The funny thing is the more beer he drank, the closer he came to making a hole-in-one. Not always on the right green, but what the heck. He probably would have had a few holes in one by the end of the day, if we had played 18 holes instead of nine.

I really don't remember how well everyone played or didn't play. I know we all finished all nine. And we had an awards banquet at the local Pizza Hut that night.

All the beer and pizza we could consume was on the newspaper, thanks to Tony. And I had the honor of putting the winning jacket on the lovely Sandy.

I always liked her. I wonder if she still has that jacket today? Probably framed in her living room and hanging next to a vintage Johnny Unitas jersey.

I played golf twice more in my career in Clarksville. One night, Tony and Billy and I made a course up in downtown Clarksville.

Back then, a lot of the city was just abandoned. All the store fronts were shattered glass and pigeons. It's since been renovated not once but twice, because of a tornado in January 1999.

The F3 tornado occurred at 4:15 a.m. on Friday, Jan. 22, 1999. On the ground for about five minutes, with a width of 880 yards, the tornado traveled 4.3 miles, ripping apart a five-block area of downtown Clarksville. Five people were injured, and the property damage was estimated at $72.7 million.

In all 124 buildings were destroyed—including the Montgomery County Courthouse. *The Leaf-Chronicle* building was severely damaged along with about 500 other structures. Austin Peay State University reported damage to 22 buildings.

Richard Stevens, the night editor at *The Tennessean*, had just been named the new editor at *The Leaf-Chronicle*, with plans to take over that job in the near future. But the tornado speeded up his transition. The editor at the morning daily in Nashville called Richard and directed him to get on up to Clarksville immediately. I know, because I was in the room at the time.

My own request to participate in coverage—a request echoed by my colleagues who knew of my own love for the Queen City—fell on deaf ears. Truly, it was as if nothing had been said. The only thing the editor did was show me a wire photo of the demolished *L-C* building, adding, with a laugh, "Here's your newspaper." He wasn't being any more of a jerk than normal. It was just a "newspaperman'" being cynical.

I was told I needed to be in Nashville, where I was entertainment editor. I have to admit to some anger at the time, although I wished Richard well on his first day as the editor of *The Leaf-Chronicle*, as he had been my immediate supervisor back when I was on the night copy desk and he treated me well and with respect.

The disaster forced *The L-C* to call on one of its neighbors, the *Kentucky New Era,* for assistance in putting out its paper.

For several days, *The L-C* staff worked from the *New Era* facility in Hopkinsville, Kentucky. Rob, then the *New Era*'s copy desk chief and associate editor, acted as the liaison, facilitating cooperation between the two newspapers.

Because of the disaster, Rob got to see some of his old *L-C* buddies—like Ronnie Kendrick and Tom Drumheller, the mailroom superintendent—for the first time in more than 15 years.

Within a week, *The Leaf-Chronicle* had set up shop in a vacant Clarksville building that at one time was home to a supermarket. It operated from the facility until its building on Commerce Street was rebuilt.

Anyway, let's get back to playing golf in an abandoned downtown Clarksville. One night after work, beginning at about midnight, we played 18 holes of golf through the streets of downtown. Extra points if you went through a window. And of course, playing it where it landed sometimes was difficult if you were inside an abandoned storefront. You'd just bash out enough of the already broken window so you could properly address your ball and hope a rat didn't bite you in the butt.

No, this isn't a confession of anything illegal. Clarksville cops drove by, told us not to hurt ourselves. And we toasted them with our beers.

The last time I played the actual game of golf was years later, long after *The News Brothers* had gone their separate ways, at least temporarily.

Tony flew back into town to visit. I did love the guy and he was known to drop in on me, as he knew I always had a spare bed for a friend and that I loved listening to his lies. And he called to see if Billy, then in P.R. at some podunk college in Kentucky, wanted to drive down.

We played golf, with the stakes being the set of used clubs Tony had bought for the occasion.

I won. Still have one or two of the clubs in the garage. Use them in case of burglars or other terrorists.

I have one club that's a wooden "midgelet" or something. If someone wants to buy it from me, well it's for sale. Not the memories, though.

Tim Ghianni gets a bird's-eye view of the City of Clarksville from a vantage point atop a downtown building. For years, in the 1970s and 1980s, the city declared war on pigeons for one Saturday a year. On those days, no journalists — not even Tim — dared to climb onto downtown roofs.

Chapter 12
(Tim)

BACK ON THE SUBJECT OF PIGEONS

In the just concluded golfing anecdote, I mention that pigeons were kings of downtown Clarksville.

Twice a year, the powers-that-be tried to fix that problem.

There'd be a Saturday pigeon hunt in downtown Clarksville.

Men, bankers and doctors and pedophiles, would tote their shotguns downtown and plant their wide rumps on top of buildings or simply march down Franklin Street at dawn, shotguns cocked and loaded.

Very Ramboish, really, these fat, polyestered guys with their blunderbusses.

Explosions would rocket through the atmosphere all morning.

It was the one Saturday you'd get to work early and stay inside the building. Out of range. We'd look out on downtown, for we faced the Courthouse Square, and hope some of these hearty souls realized that their daylong beer consumption probably didn't improve their aim.

I can remember clearly the late Bob Goodwin, then the job shop boss (he and his crew printed posters and the like on the old, out-dated hot-lead presses), and I standing at the window and watching the gunplay. Glover Williams, who also has gone on to his just reward, was probably there too, wagering on the total kill for the day.

Of course we covered it as well, interviewing the guy who killed the most pigeons, photographing his kill as if he was Bungalow Bill, standing there with pigeons and his gun.

The men, assisted by the friendly coppers who refereed the bloodbath, were supposed to clean up after themselves.

Still, every year, every pigeon-kill Saturday, by the time we left the office, late at night, pigeon carcasses littered the landscape and the feathers blew down Commerce Street.

The Montgomery County Courthouse, located across from *The Leaf-Chronicle* building in downtown Clarksville, was rebuilt after it was destroyed in the January 1999 tornado.

Tim Ghianni and Okey "Skipper" Stepp model the official *News Brothers* T-shirt. Produced in the weeks before the November 1982 premiere of the "Flapjacks" movie, the T-shirts are now a collector's item.

Jim "Flash" Lindgren, wearing his *News Brothers* T-shirt, strikes a Frank Sinatra pose for the camera during a 1982 publicity event.

Chapter 13
(Rob)

BEEN THERE, DONE THAT, GOT THE T-SHIRT

The News Brothers spent most of the summer of 1982 on a labor of love, filming our special movie, "Flapjacks: The Motion Picture," the masterpiece that was going to get us an Oscar and also make tons of money to help the needy of Clarksville.

Most of the time, the "shoots" for the movie occurred at locations around town on a Saturday morning, in the hours just before we reported for work to put out the Sunday newspaper.

Saturdays (not "SATURDAZE"), Tim and I would meet up at The Royal York Hotel's Coffee Shop at about 7 a.m. to go over the day's "script." Well, there really wasn't one. We just had ideas, sometimes sketched out on a sheet of paper during our "preproduction" coffee breaks on Fridays.

If any of the other *News Brothers* wanted to participate, we'd use them. Sometimes they even showed up.

Of course there was the occasional Friday afternoon when we solicited extras, fellow newsroom denizens or residents of the Royal York or even members of "Clarksville's Finest" if we thought we would do a special scene, filled with all the special effects you could do with Super 8 film.

Hell, we even got a Vice Squad cop we liked, but who had a trigger-happy reputation, to slap leather for a scene that eventually had as its soundtrack The Beatles' "Happiness is a Warm Gun."

We were skewering, but not screwing, everybody. Especially ourselves.

Remember: This was before the advent of home video. No digital tricks here. Just, what Tim liked to call "Weird Scenes Inside the Goldmine" and point at his obviously afflicted brain.

Fortunately for all involved, I was similarly afflicted. It was our escape from depression, from the realities of the news coverage. But man, I'll have to say, Tim and I had the time of our lives.

We filmed everywhere…Downtown…The airport…On the roof of *The Leaf-Chronicle* building…At the old freight train depot near the Cumberland River…On a golf course…On the campus of Austin Peay State University.

On one occasion, we filmed in a local cemetery, pretending to search for a friend who no longer was around. It was the same cemetery, where the famous actor, Frank Sutton, who portrayed Marine Gunnery Sgt. Vince Carter on the 1960s television series "Gomer Pyle, U.S.M.C.," was buried. Sutton was a native of the area, and his parents, Frank Sims Sutton and Thelma Spencer, actually had met while both were working at *The Leaf-Chronicle* in the 1920s. While *The News Brothers* danced around the cemetery, I'm pretty sure we stopped long enough to pay our respects to Sgt. Carter.

I vaguely recall us kneeling at his grave and saying a few words: "I can't hear you," we piped in unison, although softly and very respectfully, as we are classy fellows.

The next time I delivered the line, away from the cemetery and in the newsroom at *The Leaf-Chronicle*, it wasn't soft…It was the full Sgt Carter voice, now among my favorite impressions. Damn. I couldn't get enough practice. I also used it sometimes to stir daydreaming reporters out of their idleness.

But it really paid off … in laughs… weeks after the cemetery visit, when actor George Lindsey came to town to visit with participants and fans attending the 17th annual U.S. Jaycees/Daisy International BB Gun Championships at Austin Peay State University. Lindsey played Gomer Pyle's cousin, "Goober," on "The Andy Griffith Show," if you remember your TV history. He also was a regular on "Hee Haw." Anyway, I got to pal around with the TV funnyman while I interviewed him. Turns out, Goober laughed more at me, especially my now perfect Sgt. Carter impersonation… "I CAN'T HEAR YOU!!!!!!!!"

Rob Dollar and Tim Ghianni map out the strategy for filming one of their movie scenes at the Montgomery County Fair in the late summer of 1982. (right)

In a scene from the movie, "Flapjacks: The Motion Picture," Tim Ghianni and Rob Dollar battle it out during a pie fight. They both were left with pie in their faces. (below)

Rob Dollar interviews actor George "Goober" Lindsey on the campus of Austin Peay State University in Clarksville, Tennessee, on July 10, 1982. In addition to his role on "The Andy Griffith Show," Lindsey also appeared as a regular cast member on "Hee Haw."

Now, when it was time to go out on location with *The News Brothers*, there was no script to work from.... As I previously explained, there was no *real* script to actually hold and thumb through the pages. Tim and I would talk about things the day before and then one of us would offer up a suggestion: "Let's go to the county fair and shoot." And once we got there, well, we improvised. Every scene, every subtlety immortalized on film came instantly out of my head or Tim's head...Some of our work was quite brilliant, and some of it represented good examples of two wild and crazy guys taking advantage of an opportunity......."Hey, look at that sign that says 'Handicapped Parking.' Why don't we sit down over there under the sign and point at our brains? That might be funny."

And then, that's what we'd do, as we pieced the movie together, scene by scene. Maybe it was the nutty part of our brains spitting out the ideas for the scenes. Anyway, whatever dumb thing popped into our heads, we improvised and put it on film right then and there—and in only one take! Hell, not only were we creative geniuses, but we were pretty damn efficient filmmakers with the $19.82 budget I recall us having to make The Movie of all Movies. Well, it may have cost a bit more, but money wasn't the issue here. It was all about sanity and charity.

For some reason, Tim keeps reminding me we spent $200,000 making the film. Hold it ... that's three zeroes too many...probably four. That of course includes film, processing and the occasional prop, like a squirt gun or an emergency pair of replacement shades if one pair got damaged in a gunfight or a pie fight or by angry, red-eyed Secret Service agents.

Larry McCormack, chief photographer for *The Leaf-Chronicle*, served as our official cameraman on the movie project. I think Larry's dad owned the Super 8 movie camera we were using, and he didn't want anyone else to touch it...You know how that is...But, Larry ended up doing a decent enough job that we even gave him a cameo appearance in the movie as a completely worthless "bum" whose nap inside a boxcar is short-circuited by a face full of pie thrown at him, point blank, by *The News Brothers*.

We also need to mention Robert Smith, at the time the No. 2 photographer at *The Leaf-Chronicle* and a helluva guy. Back when Tim was a young man (long, long ago in a galaxy far, far away, so far that he can hardly remember), he would have to cover Montgomery Central High School ballgames. Robert, then a sophomore at MCHS, would walk the sidelines with the future "Flapjacks." When Robert got on at the newspaper—something that resulted in large part from Tim's lobbying, urging and loyalty—it was a great day for all involved. Robert's still there at *The Leaf-Chronicle* now, having survived and thrived. But during the summer of *The News Brothers*, he was our backup cameraman. He also sometimes came to the set to shoot publicity stills of me and Tim doing something serious. And, when it came time for the editing, Robert had the keys to a photo shop on Riverside Drive, and we'd meet him there for all-night sessions to view "dailies" and piece together the movie.

Tim considers Robert as being among his favorite people, an under-rated contributor to *News Brothers* lore. We hope the mention in this book is seen as an act of love rather than a setback in his journalism career, as he is among the last ones left still practicing that dying art, more or less—if you don't count Ricky G. "Dumbo" Moore. But, hell, look at "Dumbo"! How could you *not* count him? Here's a guy who, in our movie, put two pies in his own face.

While making the movie, our new friend, Okey "Skipper" Stepp, an old merchant marine and ex-carny, was with us most of the summer since he had key roles in several scenes—including a pivotal moment when he, Tim and I sit on a bench in front of his home at The Royal York Hotel. Old Skipper really enjoyed himself while on location, mugging for the camera and hobbling around the set just like his favorite television character—"Chester." (Marshal Dillon's reliable deputy in the "Gunsmoke" reruns.)

"Flapjacks" was about 40 minutes in length, due to our short attention span or maybe our ability as true journalists to focus—and get to the point. Well, actually, we also were short on time, and Tim and I were running a little light on financial resources for the movie, as our application for help from Hollywood moguls Steven Spielberg and Ron Howard had not yet yielded a response. Just kidding...

With friends looking on, Rob Dollar (left) and Tim Ghianni strike a pose for a photograph that was to have promoted education on the official 1983 *News Brothers* Calendar. The project was one of the few that never got completed.

This was the front artwork for the official *News Brothers* T-shirt created in the summer of 1982.

The film had an accompanying rock 'n' roll soundtrack. A comedy, the story-line was simple: It was about a bunch of outlaw newspapermen—*The News Brothers*—who go on a search for their missing editor, Tony Durr, who coincidentally had just been fired by *The Leaf-Chronicle* in early July. Turnover can be brutal in the newspaper profession.

The movie actually was roughly patterned after our own pursuit of the truth in the Nishiyama and Long murder cases, right down to a bogus headline or gravestone. More than that, of course, the two dead teens inspired us to live for the day.

During our search for Tony, "Wallet Found: It's Not Tony's" was the headline we put on a fake front page. We took some pot shots at popular culture, with improvised bits borrowed from "Rocky," "The Spirit of St. Louis," "Mission Impossible," "The Monkees," "Easy Rider," John Belushi and Dan Aykroyd's "Blues Brothers," "Hill Street Blues," and the Spaghetti Westerns, while paying tribute to The Doors, The Beatles, Kris Kristofferson, Steppenwolf, The Rolling Stones, Willie Nelson and Joe Cocker.

Nobody ever can recover from Tim's Joe Cocker impersonation. I'm not saying it's great. It's just…well, impossible to forget. Hell, he's 60 now and doesn't drink. And he'll still do it if asked. He claims to have perfected it during his numerous "study breaks" when he attended college. Or at least when he was living on a college campus "somewhere in the Midwest." I've never seen an actual diploma, though he swears he remembers walking in some sort of graduation parade "back around 1973."

Now, before I continue with this most amazing tale, I must emphasize in the strongest of terms that the crazy side of *The News Brothers* never, in no way whatsoever, affected our performance on the job. We were true professionals and award-winning journalists, putting out the best of the best in newspapers on a consistent basis.

The movie simply was a way to escape the pressures of our jobs and blow off some steam. None of us could sing or dance or had hobbies to take our minds off our jobs so we could keep our sanity. There aren't many things of leisure to do that can accommodate the crazy work schedule of a journalist. So, all we really had was the movie.....and damn....we needed the laughs to keep us going. Take it from me, 1982 was the Year from Hell...

Anyway, the loose plot basically helped us work off and sweat out some of the tension from the hard months of covering the stories about the two dead teenagers.

It ought to be noted that, other than our elaborate title credits, the opening action scene showed *The News Brothers,* including Tony Durr and Billy Fields, dancing like drunken derelicts or Baryshnikov up a ramp from an alley in downtown Clarksville.

It actually was one of the few scenes in which Tony and Billy appear in the movie. For Tony's farewell party, Tim had asked his friend, Jerry Uetz—who owned Austin's, the restaurant where Tennessee Williams sought refuge and "Flap" had admired O.J.'s use of steak knives—to stay open for an after-work party, beginning at midnight, after Tony finished his last shift and hours before he fled to Texas.

Not only did Jerry allow the joint to stay open, as soon as Tim got to the back door, Jerry gave him the keys and told him to lock up when we left. At dawn, we rolled out of Austin's, Tim locking the door. Tony had left around 3 and supposedly was en route to San Antonio. The rest of us showed up around noon to clean up Jerry's restaurant and bar, only to be greeted by this kind gent, who had already cleaned it up and was eating what had been left of our potato salad.

"I like this," he said. "We'll call it even." Jerry, a great gentleman, and Tim crossed paths again when Tim later visited in San Antonio to interview for a job on Tony's staff, only to be greeted by Jerry Uetz, who at that time was opening a restaurant in that Texas city. Jerry insisted on taking the whole crew out to dinner. Eventually, he returned to Clarksville to reopen his restaurant there for a few years.

By the way, Tim turned down the San Antonio job, partly because he can't stand bad mariachi music but mostly because, well, he knew Tony.

Anyway, as noted, Tony left in the middle of the party and began his drive to "San Antone," we think by using the gear shifter instead of the windshield wipers. Billy Fields also left around this same time, mainly because he had no one to take him golfing when he should have been working. But we didn't throw him a party. Refused to, in fact. Most of us didn't even know he was gone until someone asked, "What happened to Billy Fields? Wasn't he around here when we began our movie?" Everyone looked at the almost-busted desk chair that Billy had occupied, shrugged and got back to work. (Billy reminded Tim recently that when he left for P.R. in Podunk, Kentucky, everyone simply applauded and called the lovably large fella "a hack and a whore." I personally don't remember Tim and I applauding, but I gotta admit it does sound like us.)

That first scene is just a short setup in the film, introducing some of the characters, but it has a lot of heart in it.

But it didn't compare with the heart Tim and I put into every scene—whether we planned it out or made it up on the spot.

As summer turned to fall, and the movie was close to being finished, those damn wheels in our heads started spinning again. You know, I hate when that happens...When we started, the movie was about saving ourselves, at least that was the point for Tim and me.

It had worked. None of us had been committed to the loony bin. Now, Tim was pitching a mission of mercy for the less fortunate. Soon, a damn good idea was hatched... We would stage a world premiere of our movie in Clarksville, charge admission and raise money for several local charities.

With our big hearts beating wildly, Tim and I got busy over the next several weeks, using our connections around town to plan and make into reality a party that no one would ever forget. Remember, our budget was pretty pitiful. We prayed hard that there would be other big hearts out there in the Queen City willing to help us for free...And, we weren't disappointed, when push came to shove.

George Terrell, the co-owner of The Roxy on Franklin Street, gave us a place to host the festivities. We had full use of the old, stately theater, which at the time was shut down. The heating system also was broken, which meant people were going to have to dress warmly for the big event scheduled for Friday, Nov. 12, 1982. In addition to the theater, George provided *The News*

Brothers and their entourage with fancy duds to wear that night for the Red Carpet Ceremony.

George also gave us the keys to the theater, and all we had to do was scrub the dirty floors and urinals, chase out the rats and run a vacuum cleaner over the carpet. Some of the brotherhood showed up to help, although one night Tim and I actually worked around the clock, even sleeping in the lobby for a few hours before manning our scrub brushes and Lysol again. "Chuckles" and "Flash," I believe, were home making popcorn.

Before I forget, it should be noted that at the time of our premiere, The Roxy was targeted for demolition to make room for a multi-level downtown parking lot. Because we cleaned and polished the old theater and then let in adoring people — including the mayor, "Old Wild Turkey" himself, Ted Crozier— some took notice of the treasure that stood abandoned in the city. What with marble floors and statues and neon lights, this was a splendid Art Deco building. We have been told by credible sources that our movie premiere may have stalled the demolition talks long enough for a pair of energetic theater fellows to come in and save the old Roxy. Now it's a landmark, a point of civic pride and those fellows keep staging prize-winning theater there to this day. They keep a picture of *The News Brothers* among their historic paraphernalia chronicling the history of the building.

We don't really believe it, but there has been talk that The Roxy hopes to one day do a play called, "How *The News Brothers* Saved Clarksville." Actually, I think I heard that from Tim…So, consider the source.

Anyway, back to 1982 and the days leading up to the Greatest Show on Earth.

Several community groups also stepped forward, volunteering to provide music and entertainment at our world premiere. Mayor Crozier promised a personal appearance and a proclamation. The Clarksville Fire Department OK'd a request to ferry *The News Brothers* to the theater aboard their best fire engine. And finally, the Clarksville Police Department agreed to rush into the theater after the movie ended and pretend to arrest us for the crime of offending the public by showing a bad movie. It was our way of getting the fairly decent sum of money out of the old theater in what was then a basically derelict section of Clarksville.

"Clarksville's Finest" had many featured roles in the "Flapjacks" film itself, including the pivotal "slow-speed" chase near the train depot that leads to the climactic pie fight.

In another memorable scene, we're confronted by cops who actually think we're drinking whiskey from a bottle that we'd filled with Coke for a celebratory one-truck parade through the streets of the city.

"You can't do that kind of thing in Clarksville, boys," said a less-than-friendly copper who dumped our Coke in the sewer, giving us a stern warning instead of jail after realizing we didn't have any liquor on us. He said he was disappointed because he always had hoped to arrest a *News Brother* ... and here he had a whole damned truck filled with them. And he had to let us go.

It should be noted the proceeds from the movie premiere were earmarked for the Fire Department's Christmas Toy Drive, Cops for Christ and The Mustard Seed, a sort of locally owned Goodwill store that sold second-hand clothing and used the proceeds to help the poor and homeless. Many of our fine duds for the filming of the movie came from The Mustard Seed.

Finally, we had reached the point where everything was set in stone for our big day. Now it was time to get out the word and do some marketing. Make no mistake about it, *The News Brothers* were visionaries, far ahead of their times. Hell, we were multi-tasking way back in the early 1980s when there wasn't even a word for what we were doing.

One of our first tasks was to design and make posters and T-shirts celebrating *The News Brothers*, this Band of Brothers with hearts of gold.

Tim and I, as usual, ended up fronting the money to get the posters and mustard yellow "*News Brothers*" T-shirts done and into circulation. We were in charge of sales, and sold the products for more than they cost to make. But, being damn nice guys, we donated the profits to the local charities.

Jerry "Chuckles" Manley, wearing his yellow aviator's hat, mugs for the camera at the world premiere of the "Flapjacks" movie.

Jim "Flash" Lindgren and *The News Brothers* arrive at the theater aboard a fire engine for the world premiere of their movie on Nov. 12, 1982.

Fans and loved ones of *The News Brothers* dance in the streets prior to the world premiere of "Flapjacks: The Motion Picture." The happy people in this photograph included the parents of Tim Ghianni

Ted Crozier (center), at the time the mayor of Clarksville, Tennessee, reads a proclamation that declared Nov. 12, 1982, as "*News Brothers* Day" in the Queen City.

George Terrell (center), a former co-owner of The Roxy, shares the spotlight with *The News Brothers* at the world premiere of their movie.

Clarksville, Tennessee police officers, in on the joke, assist *The News Brothers* in their escape from fans following the midnight showing of their movie. The "give what you can" admission proceeds — collected in the garbage can being carried by Tim Ghianni — went to local charities.

Most of the T-shirts were very large in size, and many gals were having a hard time finding one small enough that they could wear with their tight jeans. Not having any more money to make some smaller T-shirts, we had to come up with a way to appeal to the women so we could sell everything we had in stock.

"Ladies," I said, putting on the charm. "You can wear these T-shirts to bed." Then, I added, with a big wink, "*News Brothers* don't kiss and tell."

So, with those words, *The News Brothers* launched the very successful "Sleep With *The News Brothers*" marketing campaign. Damn. Those T-shirts were as hot as flapjacks on a griddle. (Not Flapjacks, the *News Brother*; flapjacks, the hotcakes.)

Thirty years later, the T-shirts are still around. Again, like most *News Brothers* memorabilia, the T-shirts, available on e-Bay, are collector's items. In October 2010, while I was at a high school reunion, a former classmate, Dennis Fendler, surprised me. He walked up to me with his *News Brothers* T-shirt in hand, seeking an autograph. Dennis, who now lives in Arizona, worked in *The Leaf-Chronicle's* Press Room back in those bawdy 1980s.

In the weeks leading up to the world premiere, Tim and the rest of us did what we could to publicize the event. There were radio plugs and even a story in the newspaper's weekly entertainment section.

I even made a mid-October trip up to Richmond, Kentucky, to drum up publicity for *The News Brothers* and promote our movie in the Bluegrass State. It was homecoming weekend at Eastern Kentucky University so I thought I'd be able to sell *News Brothers* T-shirts to old college pals like Brian Blair, Dean Holt, Mark Turner, Ginny Blackson, Libby Fraas, Jim "The Duke" Renfrow, Brian Keith, Mike Behler and Don "Gringo" McNay.

I probably would have sold a lot more T-shirts than I did if I hadn't taken Denny Adkins along with me on the publicity road trip. During our visit to "The Campus Beautiful," Denny snuck out of a party with one of Gringo's lady friends and ended up in "The Ravine"—a notorious spot on campus known for romantic interludes. He apparently was trying to play doctor with a woman who wanted to become a doctor one day…Maybe she realized her dream and today is saving lives somewhere in the world...I don't believe she saved Denny's life or even his evening....Anyway, Gringo was not amused by Denny's behavior (who is, after all?), and I don't remember him buying a T-shirt. My old friend did sell me a modified life insurance policy before I left town, which had me wondering if there was a hidden message in our business transaction. Just joking....

Occasionally, during *The News Brothers'* push for publicity, we even gave away free T-shirts, particularly to celebrities. The governor of Tennessee at the time, Lamar Alexander, was running for re-election in 1982 and stopped by *The Leaf-Chronicle* for a quick interview during a campaign swing through town. I don't remember who interviewed him, but I do remember *The News Brothers* ambushing him in the Photography Department, where he was having his portrait made for the upcoming story. Tim, Jerry Manley, Jim Lindgren and I used the opportunity to present him with a *News Brothers* T-shirt. And then, miracle of miracles, we conned him into posing for a photo with *The News Brothers*. Don't you just love it when a politician is running for re-election? Hell, they'll do anything... By the way, that photo of us and Alexander, now serving as the senior senator from Tennessee in the U.S. Senate, later was used on the front page of a newsletter put out by *The Leaf-Chronicle's* then corporate owner, Multimedia Inc.

Many months later, we found out what the good governor did with the T-shirt given to him by *The News Brothers*. Tim's mom was shopping in the Kroger store in Brentwood, Tennessee, just outside of Nashville, when she walked into a young woman wearing a T-shirt with her son's face on it...The girl was Lamar Alexander's daughter. It makes me happy she liked our T-shirt enough to wear it out in public. Unlike her old man, at least, she thought *The News Brothers* were cool.

Now, although the governor-turned-senator, apparently never wore our T-shirt, he apparently had not forgotten his Close Encounter of *The News Brothers* Kind.

Then-Tennessee Gov. Lamar Alexander accepts a T-shirt from *The News Brothers* during a visit to Clarksville, Tennessee, in the fall of 1982.

Rob Dollar presents actor/comedian Eddie Murphy with a *News Brothers* T-shirt and poster prior to his performance at Austin Peay State University in Clarksville, Tennessee, on November 5, 1982.

In the late 1990s, when I was working at the *Kentucky New Era* in Hopkinsville, Kentucky, U.S. Sen. Lamar Alexander of Tennessee made an official visit to the nearby city of Elkton, Kentucky, to talk about some government issue. I sent a reporter, David Blackburn, to cover the event and gave him a copy of the 1982 photograph of Alexander and four damn nice guys wearing shades. I told him to see if the senator would be so kind as to autograph it for me…Well, he did—and with a great big grin on his face. At least that was the word from my reporter.

Maybe the senator was thinking to himself: "Hey…Here's a picture of that funky T-shirt my daughter likes to wear."

Eddie Murphy, the world-famous actor, also has a *News Brothers* T-shirt, unless he gave it away or tossed it into the trash long ago. Perhaps he lost it in a divorce proceeding. Who knows? Murphy came to Clarksville on Nov. 5, 1982, to perform at Austin Peay State University's Homecoming. Before his comedy routine, the comedian and actor met with the news media, and I was lucky enough to draw this particular Friday night assignment. Scott Shelton, a *News Brother*-to-be at the time, also was at the news conference, working for WJZM Radio.

Anyway, it was one week to the day until the world premiere of our movie, and we were still drumming up publicity. So, I decided to present Eddie Murphy with a poster and T-shirt and tell him *The News Brothers* were a bunch of damn nice guys. At the time, Eddie, then the star of TV's "Saturday Night Live," had just finished his first big-screen movie ("48 Hrs."), with Nick Nolte. Of course, let's be honest here: We, *The News Brothers*, wanted Eddie Murphy to have one of our T-shirts because we were hoping he'd wear it on "Saturday Night Live." No such luck. But I did get a nice photo, taken by Scott, out of the experience—of me giving Mr. Murphy his *News Brothers* stuff.

Eddie thanked me for the poster and T-shirt, but looked at me like I was kind of crazy. Closely examining the poster and T-shirt, he asked me, "Why do you all have sunglasses on? This is what I was doing in the hotel room, (wearing sunglasses) and doing my impression of me after the show."

I told him a little about *The News Brothers*, and our charity movie planned for the following week, which would be attended by the mayor of the city. "Mayor Ted," he laughed, pointing at the poster photo of Mayor Ted Crozier, wearing sunglasses.

After our meeting, Eddie went to work and performed quite a bawdy show. I think APSU was expecting him to do his famed Buckwheat or Gumby bits. Not quite. I'm told the president of the university and some other VIPs left very early, embarrassed by the profanity and other antics of the young comic. The late George Carlin, another genius in the World of Comedy, once put out a record about the seven dirty words you can't use on TV…Eddie used them all that night at Austin Peay State University and added a few more…The APSU staffer who booked him as the entertainment was lucky he got to keep his job. (By the way, *The News Brothers*, in later years, had an odd encounter with Carlin, who kind of liked old "Flap," then entertainment editor at one of his Nashville stops. Carlin told Tim he could have all the time he wanted for an interview, as long as it was recorded. "I hate to be misquoted," he said. Tim agreed, but much of what Carlin said couldn't be used in a newspaper. And Tim told George he already knew the seven words, anyway.)

Three decades later, as I've already mentioned, there are still plenty of *News Brothers* T-shirts floating around. I have a couple. But, like on most of *The News Brothers*, the T-shirts no longer fit. No problem with the jock straps, though.

Tim Ghianni, wearing one of his trademark Hawaiian shirts,
works on his column in *The Leaf-Chronicle* newsroom during the summer of 1982.

Chapter 14
(Rob)

MONKEY SEE, MONKEY DO

In the days of *The News Brothers*, Clarksvillians couldn't wait to get their hands on the Sunday edition of *The Leaf-Chronicle*. In fact, it was not unusual for the most loyal of our readers to actually wait in front of their houses, at the crack of dawn, for their carrier to arrive with the paper. We know that because sometimes we drove around to see the deliveries in person after a long night telling lies at The Camelot. Or other monkey business....as you'll soon find out.

Sure, the Sunday paper was bigger, and it had more of everything in it. But what really made it special was it always seemed to have *The News Brothers'* fingerprints all over it. They were the ones, after all, who most often worked on Saturdays, the day when most of the Sunday paper was put together. The big bosses and white collar employees of the paper always had the day off to play golf or get drunk at the lake. The two elder statesmen of the "Shaded Fab Four"—Tim, the associate editor, and Jerry Manley, the news editor/copy desk chief—were in charge of the weekend operation. Tim actually was in charge, but his longtime pal, Jerry, was a great technician and perhaps the world's best line editor, a guy who knew when to ask questions and when to let creativity flow. So basically, Tim would hand out assignments and give a first edit to the copy and smoke and Jerry would execute, to perfection and more. And smoke.

Folks, ever hear about what happens when you put foxes in charge of a hen house? (Just kidding. Of course, the answer is you get dead chickens.... or was that monkeys?) But these two 30-year-old seasoned newsmen did know how to take risks for the benefit of the reading public.

And, of course, their main "reporter," the guy who helped them in their mission of informing the public, was, well, a somewhat younger guy and almost-CIA agent. We're talking about me, of course. Tim always tells me I'm the best cops reporter he ever worked with ... as well as "the best damned monkey reporter since Clarence Darrow." Oops, tipping my hand here.

Anyway, you never knew just what you might read about in the Sunday paper. But, you could count on one thing: *The News Brothers* were going to make sure the paper was a "must-read" and it sold out in the racks all around town.

Who doesn't remember the Sunday, Aug. 15, 1982, edition of *The Leaf-Chronicle*? Someone told me a copy might actually be on display at The Smithsonian or Newseum in Washington, D.C. Tim is not shy to tell you that Richard Nixon actually asked for a copy to be sent to his retirement home in Saddle River, New Jersey.

"Deputies Go Bananas: 'Monkey At Large!'" screamed the six-column, banner headline at the top of the front page. It was in 72-point type, too. People nowadays don't really know about point size, but if a president dies, you probably go with 90 or 100 point.

If family members are murdered in their sleep in your town, you're probably looking at 60 point. So a 72-point headline promises importance...Hell, it guarantees it....

The importance of an attention-grabbing headline—whether intentional or not—should never be underestimated. It's the headline, after all, that draws people to a story. One of my old *Kentucky New Era* colleagues, Sonny Allen, was responsible for a screaming headline that announced the death of the leader of the former Soviet Union, Leonid Breznev, back in the early 1980s.

Sonny's headline read, "Breznev Laid in Red Square: Soviets Mourn." Now, when Sonny was writing that funny—and memorable—headline, he wasn't seeing what readers would eventually read...That's the funny thing about newspapers...You never see an error or miscue until you start reading the paper after it's long off the press...Then, it jumps off the page at you...But, of course, by then, it's too late to do anything about it.

Tim tells of the day he had to use a short filler story on an inside sports page back in 1975. Whitey Ford had just been presented on that Saturday night the Judge Emil Fuchs Memorial Award "for long and meritorious service to baseball." Tim wrote a quick headline that read: "Whitey Ford Fuchs Winner." OK, read that again. Now, think about the very religious and conservative copy editor who asked Tim: "What did Whitey do to the loser?"

Anyway, if you remember the monkey incident, as a reader of *The Leaf-Chronicle*, tell me you didn't smile, and tell me you didn't read every single word of the story. OK. I rest my case that this piece of journalism certainly was no case of monkey business.

Granted, the news was slow in Clarksville that mid-August weekend, but give *The News Brothers* credit for taking nothing and turning it into a truly wonderful little story that brought some laughter to the breakfast tables of thousands of Clarksvillians at a time when such chuckles were definitely needed.

The story had my byline on it, because I was the one who discovered it while going through the police and sheriff's department reports in the media basket at the Criminal Justice Complex. Details were lacking on the report, but I recognized immediately that an incident involving a runaway monkey was, well ...pretty unusual. I made several telephone calls over the next hour or two, got my scoop and then wrote up the story—using a bit of creativity and more than a few puns.

While I worked on it, Tim had the office police scanner cranked full blast, and we continued to follow the desperate situation.

By the time Tim and Jerry read and punched up the story, working their magic on it, we had quite the gem...The reader could just picture, in their heads, sheriff's deputies and residents, scrambling around in a frenzy, trying to catch a small African-breed Spider monkey on the loose in a county neighborhood.

The story began: *"It was a routine night of patrolling the highways and byways of the county. Check on a drunk here...a fight there...a report of vandalism...typical Saturday night tasks for the county sheriff's department.*

An unusual complaint at about 7 p.m. threw a monkey wrench into that routine. There was a monkey at large.

Sheriff's Deputy Freddie Maxwell said a resident of Rossview Road called the Criminal Justice Complex to tell authorities that a monkey was on the loose in the neighborhood.

The report had to be something of a first for those manning the weekend shift, who had very little knowledge of Tennessee's monkey law. While the critter wasn't terrorizing anyone, it was causing quite a spectacle for bewildered residents who were apparently going bananas..."

What most news organizations would have overlooked as a simple lost pet story became a well-deserved tale of hope, life, death and bananas.

When the paper was put to bed for the night, The News Brothers, proud of their work, ventured over to The Camelot to toss down a few and make jokes about the monkey that was terrorizing the Queen City and suburbs. Of course, most of the drunken clientele, listening to our strange tale, hadn't yet seen the paper. So, I imagine they probably thought we were pulling their leg. Remember, we were the guys who went kangaroo-hunting with Willie Nelson, after all.

One cluster of police officers—guys who had spent much of the preceding year dealing with deaths of beautiful young people—knew all about the folks going ape over the missing primate, but they didn't believe we'd followed through on Tim's decision to play it up like a lunar landing.

I wish I could have seen some of their faces the next morning when they picked up their Sunday papers.

The first thing on Monday, Tim got to see a face, the face of "The Big Guy"—Luther Thigpen, publisher of The Leaf-Chronicle. He kind of got into Tim's face about the coverage given to the runaway monkey.

The Big Guy had no words for me—the writer of the story. I guess I always left him speechless. It was strange that, in the two years I worked at The Leaf-Chronicle, I can't remember one conversation I ever had with him. At best, he might have muttered a "Good Morning" to me once or twice when we passed each other in the hallway. He definitely was not a warm and fuzzy guy to me.

Tim, who had kind of grown accustomed to his dealings with The Big Guy, actually expected the summons. But he had figured it was worth it.

When he arrived in The Big Guy's office, Tim was told to be seated as the publisher rocked back and forth in his leather chair and continued to peruse the Sunday front page.

Then he turned it around and held it up for Tim to look at.

"Great story, boss," Tim said, using the old "best defense is a good offense" strategy. "Everybody's talking about it."

The Big Guy, our publisher, wasn't amused.

"I wouldn't have played the story quite that way," he said, making a face and scratching his head. But, Tim wasn't in a mood to monkey around. He wasn't going to let a stubborn publisher drive him bananas. He stood his ground and defended the decision to lead with the story, particularly since nothing else of significance had occurred in the news cycle.

"I wouldn't have done it that way," said The Big Guy, obviously having trouble with expanding on his earlier sentiment.

"We'll just have to agree to disagree on that one, then," said Tim, not worrying about having a monkey on his back. "Given what else was going on, I'd do it again. It's a helluva story."

The Big Guy couldn't think of anything else to say, so he nodded and pointed to his office door. Tim did his best to ape the nod as he left to climb the stairs to the newsroom.

An office assistant later told me that she witnessed the events—everyone kinda grew silent whenever Tim was in The Big Guy's office. She said that after Tim left, Luther stood up at his desk and started jingling the change in his pocket, whispering under his breath… *"News Brothers….News Brothers…News Brothers…"*

Maybe The Big Guy disagreed—frequently—with the associate editor's choice and story play. But circulation figures spoke for themselves. Sunday morning newspapers had become the city's "must-read." And Luther knew it.

Down deep, he may even have been proud to be a part of it all and that's why, for a time at least, he didn't monkey with the Sunday morning team. But I doubt it.

By the way, it was three months later before we heard anything more about the monkey who helped *The News Brothers* entertain Clarksville that Sunday.

Turns out the little guy's name was Chico, and he was someone's pet that had run away from home. He apparently stayed on the run until Nov. 26, not long after the first hard frost of the year, when his body was found in a wooded area off Rossview Road. He had been attacked and killed by another larger animal, probably a dog, according to authorities.

Chico The Monkey was dead.

So, why was this monkey so important to *The News Brothers?*

Many years later, with the benefit of hindsight, I think I can offer an explanation that makes sense, at least to me. Chico The Monkey, during his short life, came to symbolize everything that was good and important to *The News Brothers*...Like Freedom...Hope...Love for your fellow man and monkey.

But poor little Chico had a far more important purpose for being sent to this earth by a higher power. It was to teach *The News Brothers* a valuable lesson about trust...a lesson they, unfortunately, learned too late in life for it to do any good in saving their careers.

Chico trusted dogs, and that trust proved to be his undoing. *The News Brothers* trusted the owners of America's newspapers to do right by their readers, and when they didn't, it led to our fall from grace and exile into a wilderness where good journalism now is rare in this country.

Sometimes, if I sit here long enough and dwell on it, what's happened to newspapers in recent years is something that makes me go bananas.

Chapter 15
(Rob)

THE RIGHT STUFF

By now, if you've learned anything about *The News Brothers*, you know we were a bunch of damn nice guys with The Right Stuff. We weren't American Heroes…yet. But, we sure as hell had some high hopes.

For starters, we tried to live our lives every day by The Lone Ranger Creed:

"I BELIEVE…That to have a friend, a man must be one. That all men are created equal and that everyone has within himself the power to make this a better world. That God put the firewood there, but that every man must gather and light it himself. In being prepared physically, mentally, and morally to fight when necessary for that which is right. That a man should make the most of what equipment he has. That 'This government of the people, by the people and for the people' shall live always. That men should live by the rule of what is best for the greatest number. That sooner or later, somewhere, somehow…we must settle with the world and make payment for what we have taken. That all things change but truth, and that truth alone lives forever. In my Creator, my country, my fellow man."

The Masked Man, the late Clayton Moore, was one of our heroes and someone who we actually got to meet in mid-January 1983 in Hopkinsville, Kentucky Tim ended up writing a powerful column for the newspaper about how Korporate Amerika had kicked our hero to the curb and taken away his mask because he was old and fat. The only good thing was now he got to wear sunglasses just like us.

John Glenn was another hero to *The News Brothers*. So, imagine our excitement when we learned in the late summer of 1982 that he was coming to Clarksville for a visit. Far out! At the time, we were still in the middle of filming our charity movie. There was no arguing about it. *The News Brothers* were going to shake hands with one of the original Mercury Seven astronauts and the first American to orbit the Earth.

"Damn. Let's see if we can film this and put it in the movie," Tim said. A damn fine idea. The rest of us replied, "Sounds reasonable," which was Max Moss' standard response to just about anything a person said to him.

Because our hero was arriving in town on a Saturday, when *The News Brothers* both filmed and worked, it looked like the stars were lining up perfectly for us.

In 1982, John Glenn was a U.S. senator, representing the state of Ohio.

At the time, he also was testing the waters, contemplating a run for the presidency two years later. His trip to Clarksville was made to promote his White House ambitions as well as to campaign for Randy Tyree, the Democratic mayor of Knoxville, who was running for governor that November in the general election against the incumbent Republican, Lamar Alexander (our T-shirt pal).

After scrutinizing the press release and John Glenn's itinerary, we decided the best place for us to catch our hero would be right after his airplane landed at Outlaw Field in North Clarksville.

Harold "The Stranger" Lynch, our government reporter, had been assigned to cover the Glenn visit, so he already was at the airport that Saturday morning, waiting on the plane, when four out-of-breath *News Brothers*—Tim, Jerry Manley, John Staed and I—sprinted onto the tarmac. We were in all of our "Saturday-Dressed-for-Work Glory"—long hair, stubble, sunglasses, Hawaiian shirts, football jerseys and jeans. The contrast was sharp, when compared to the appearance of the few other people there. They were neat, and dressed in coat-and-tie, including our working reporter, "The Stranger," and Clarksville Mayor Ted Crozier.

Anyway, the plane soon landed and John Glenn and his entourage got off and started walking toward the waiting crowd. *The News Brothers*, quick on their feet, got to the front of the receiving line. There, with Secret Service agents staring us down suspiciously, *The News Brothers* shook hands with John Glenn, an American hero and presidential candidate, and welcomed him to their town.

The historic scene was captured in living color on film and is my favorite part of our now infamous movie. The looks on everyone's faces are really priceless.

Mayor Crozier, who probably put up with *The News Brothers* only because he was a politician who wanted to get re-elected, played along with us as we filmed the event. While Harold Lynch interviewed him for a legitimate story to appear in Sunday's edition of *The Leaf-Chronicle*, "Hizzoner" wore a campaign button we had made that proclaimed, "Tim Ghianni for Mayor."

As the historic meeting unfolded, Tim and I, as usual, were at the front of the pack, running out to meet the great astronaut and American hero. If you never get a chance to see the movie, well, just try to imagine the craziness of this airport scene that lasted all of two minutes at the most...

Picture these images in your mind: The Secret Service agents, responsible for protecting John Glenn, staring us down, suspicious of our intent. All the while, we appear anxious that they are about to reach for their weapons.

John Glenn, after all, was not supposed to greet any visitors until he got off the tarmac and through the gate to the parking lot that had somehow become unlocked.

And yet, here is this horde of guys in sunglasses on a gloomy Saturday. "The senator doesn't have time for this crap," one of the agents barked. Or glowered. I can't really remember, because to tell you the truth, I was so damned excited.

Anyway, as the guys with the guns told us it was time to leave, John Glenn uttered words that are ever etched into my All-American heart. "I'd like to meet these young guys," he said.

Meet, perhaps, but the agents nevertheless tried to get the great American into his waiting Lincoln, or whatever it was, and off the tarmac so he could go greet and solicit help and money from local political bigwigs, as is the basic political process.

Tim and I, never really knowing boundaries and also encouraged by the senator's bright smile, moved forward. Tim stepped into the open doorway of the vehicle, preventing John Glenn from getting in, while I tried to get a few more words of advice and also bask in the moment.

Eventually, he told us he had to go, but it was good meeting us. Damn. An astronaut who was proud of meeting me and Tim … and the other, perhaps more timid (and sane, some say) *News Brothers* who didn't risk getting in the way of possible gunfire by security.

Tim and I told our hero, almost in unison, that we were behind him, that we wanted him to become president, that it was time to put a real hero in the White House. Of course, it's true we were fond of Ronald Reagan, not because we liked his politics, but because we liked his old movies, and he reminded us of our grandfathers.

But Ronnie's heroism was in film. John Glenn was the real deal, as big a hero, I believe, as we ever met. Except perhaps The Lone Ranger.

John Glenn never got elected president. Instead he lost the 1984 Democratic nomination to U.S. Sen. Walter Mondale of Minnesota, who then was clobbered by "The Gipper" in that year's general election.

It took 20 years before the Federal Election Commission agreed to relieve the Ohio senator of a $3 million campaign debt accumulated during his failed presidential run.

The day our hero, John Glenn, met *The News Brothers*, he was wearing an out-of-this-world smile on his face. I can still see it to this day.

He wouldn't smile like that again until October 29, 1998— when he basked in the glory of becoming the oldest person, at age 77, to fly in space, after rocketing into the wild blue yonder aboard the Space Shuttle Discovery.

Chapter 16
(Rob)

MIRACLE ON COMMERCE STREET

Every December, I fondly recall my "Christmas to Remember." Everyone has one in their life. It's that special Christmas, where the magic and true meaning of the holiday season hits home like a ton of bricks. And, you might even tingle a little bit. Glow, too. For us old *News Brothers*, well, it just proves that George Bailey was right. It is a wonderful life. Damn wonderful, I tell you.

It should come as no surprise to anyone that my favorite Christmas would somehow involve *The News Brothers,* those damn nice guys who loved making merry and making people laugh. It was December 1982, just four weeks after the triumphant world premiere of our charity movie at The Roxy. Now, movie stars, at least in our own scrambled minds, it was time for the next project. Our fan base virtually demanded it.

After little or no thought, we decided the timing was perfect for us to take on Hallmark, the greeting card giant, and produce our own special Christmas card. Hell, we were feeling pretty good. We were on top of the world...People loved our movie...They loved us...We had made money for charity and made people laugh...We even thought at the time that we were the toast of management at the old *L-C* ... There was no stopping us now. *The News Brothers* were ready to tingle it up with the holiday.

What better way to tingle and say "thank you" to everyone for loving us than with a one-of-a-kind Christmas card? Tim was really gung-ho on the idea. He was an "idea man," after all, and could see the potential. In his mind, he could envision *The News*

Brothers running down Commerce Street in downtown Clarksville— just like George Bailey's run through Bedford Falls in the Jimmy Stewart film, "It's A Wonderful Life," but without the snow—handing out Christmas cards.

"Yeah...Ho. Ho. Ho," I laughed, seeing those same happy visions dancing around in my head. "And, like old George Bailey, we'll shout: 'Yay! Hello, Clarksville....Merry Christmas...Merry Christmas Roxy...Merry Christmas Austin's...Merry Christmas, you wonderful old *Leaf-Chronicle*...Hey, Merry Christmas, Big Guy.'"

Tim smiled...Yep. We both knew where this was going....

Making a Christmas card was much easier than we thought. It wasn't going to be anything real fancy, anyway. None of that glitter and fake sentiment. Just a simple, one-sided post card with a photograph and our very own holiday greeting. A local printer agreed to print up a couple hundred at a special rate...It was Christmas, after all...And, of course, Tim and I would be doing all the paying...We were either the only *News Brothers* who had any money, or the only ones who weren't cheap. If it was for a good cause or for fun, we spent money. If it helped widows and orphans, we spent money. If our friends wanted coffee, well, we spent money. If a loose-lipped cop needed a drink, well, as previously noted, we spent money.

When it came time to take the photo for our Christmas card in *The Leaf-Chronicle* newsroom, somehow we found the Christmas magic missing. *The News Brothers* were there, dressed to kill in their world premiere movie best, some of us wearing the same hats and tuxedoes borrowed and still not returned to George Terrell. We also had a wreath or two, but we really needed something that screamed out, "Christmas." Looking around the newsroom, I quickly spotted a vision of beauty. There, working hard at her desk to make deadline for the TV section, was Neesa Perry, a very curvy and most attractive woman with damn nice legs. Single, too. And, so nice. It was time for some sweet-talking, and no one can talk sweeter than a *News Brother* who wants something. With a straight face, and plenty of charm (nerve, too), I begged Neesa to take off her clothes, put on a Santa Claus suit and get photographed with us for our special Christmas card. I might have winked at her, too. The blond bombshell smiled and agreed, without giving my strange request a second thought. She might have winked at me, too. Tim insists she winked at him, and he winked back.

News Brothers have that kind of effect on people—especially women. But, *News Brothers* don't kiss and tell.

Jerry Manley and Jim Lindgren—the two married *News Brothers* at the time, winked, too, but they will deny that to this day. Not out of any sense of propriety, but because— and Tim swears this is true—Neesa didn't wink back at them. She rolled her eyes and looked nauseous.

With her "Yes"— it always made my day when Neesa told me "Yes"—I sprinted outside to my sports car to retrieve my authentic Santa Claus suit.

I always carried one with me around Christmas. Still do—just in case I come across any widows, orphans, nuns or unappreciated journalists getting glum at the holiday.

It happens, you know…In fact, many years later, during the Damn Nice Christmas of 1996, I had to put on the Santa suit at the *Kentucky New Era* in Hopkinsville, Kentucky, where I handed out presents to my stressed-out colleagues in an attempt to boost newsroom morale. Damn nice guys tend to do those kinds of things.

But let's get back to the Damn Nice Christmas of 1982 in Clarksville.

Well, Neesa went into the ladies' room and got undressed and into the top half of the Santa suit, and a mighty fine Mrs. Claus she turned out to be…What a trouper! The photo was made and a week or so before Christmas, the printer had our order ready. Now a collector's item and available on e-Bay, *The News Brothers* Official Christmas Card proudly proclaims in large boldface letters, with all of the spirit of the holiday season: **HAVE A DAMN NICE CHRISTMAS!** *The News Brothers*.

When we finally got those cards in hand, I thought Tim was going to cry. He was so damn happy. Hell, I had to make sure he didn't have a breakdown. Silly sentimental bastard.

Our first order of business was to go down to the Royal York, where we slid a card beneath each door on each floor. Then we filled up the mailboxes down behind the front desk and handed cards in person to the guys watching "Gunsmoke" reruns in the lobby.

This was the official Christmas card of *The News Brothers* during the 1982 holiday season. Hundreds were handed out to friends and strangers in the Queen City.

Later, during Christmas week, we started giving the cards out to friends and colleagues at *The Leaf-Chronicle*...Even to complete strangers on the street.... We even slid them beneath doors of most of the downtown lawyers' offices. It was Christmas after all, and maybe, just maybe, the world was not all bad, like most of the news of 1982.

Of course, there's always a Scrooge every Christmas, somewhere. We didn't have to look out of *The Leaf-Chronicle* building to find the one that was going to shake *The News Brothers'* Christmas tree that particular year. "The Big Guy," Luther Thigpen, our publisher, was not very happy or amused. Tim had slipped a card underneath his office door, not wanting him to miss the joy. It was Christmas, after all...Tim was summoned to the publisher's office to take some lumps for *The News Brothers* and pick up our stockings of coal....Mr. Thigpen, it seemed, decided our Christmas card was sacrilegious and he wanted the distribution to cease immediately...Bah Humbug!!!

Tim smiled and told him we had already given out all the cards, spreading good will and holiday cheer all across Clarksville. The Big Guy stood up, looked at him, and started jingling the change in his pocket... "*News Brothers...News Brothers...News Brothers*," he whispered under his breath. Anyway, that's the way I remember hearing the replay from the publisher's office. Luther may remember it differently, which is, of course, his right as the former and much-ballyhooed "Big Guy" of *The Leaf-Chronicle*.

Everybody else in town liked our Christmas card. Thirty years later, I know people who received that card and still put it up over their fireplace every year when they celebrate Christmas. We sent one to the White House, and have been told that President Reagan "got it" and used it as a smile-triggering decoration even up into his final, sad years in California. The card was nice, and thoughtful, and I got a pretty good tingle out of it, but little did I know the Mother of All Tingles was still to come for me that Christmas season of 1982.

Rob Dollar, posing as Santa Claus, surprises copy editor Laura Field and other newsroom staffers at the *Kentucky New Era* in December 1996. Santa's visit, in addition to spreading good will, was part of a campaign to boost morale at the Hopkinsville newspaper.

The Editorial Staff of the *Kentucky New Era* poses for a holiday portrait in December 1996. From left, in the front row, are: Mike Herndon, Pete Wright, Tonya Grace, Cathy Kanaday, Tracy Sherrill, and Laura Field. In the back row, from left, are: Rob Dollar, Mary D. Ferguson, David Riley, Ray Duckworth, Tracey Lewis, LaMar Bryan, Joe Wilson, David S. Jennings, David Blackburn and E.L. Gold. Missing from the photograph are Jennifer P. Brown and Ken Litchfield.

Christmas Eve and Christmas Day were designated holidays, but the newspaper still had to be put out for its readers A bachelor, I volunteered to work the weekend holiday shift, Friday and Saturday, so that my married co-workers could spend Christmas Eve and Christmas Day at home with their children. I was the only *News Brother* working Christmas Eve, but most of the others planned to come into the office on Saturday. Tim always volunteered for Christmas Day duty throughout his career, and he had gone on down to Nashville to spend Christmas Eve with his critically ill mother. He's a damn nice guy, after all.

That Christmas Eve started out quiet in the near deserted newsroom of *The Leaf-Chronicle*. There wasn't much news for me to report and write that night. It's funny, but even criminals and evil-doers tend to take Christmas off and act like regular human beings, giving prettily wrapped boxes filled with stolen flashlights and summer sausage to their wives and children. With only a few hours left before I could call it a night—we had early deadlines not out of Ho-Ho spirit but so the company wouldn't have to pay extra holiday overtime to the press crew—everything changed, and for the worst.

The police scanner went crazy with the excited chatter of First Responders dispatched to a house fire on Commerce Street. The boss, Managing Editor Max Moss, told me to keep an ear on the scanner and make some calls to find out what had happened. It might be something big that would be nice to get into the Christmas Day edition of the paper, Max the Mentor explained, as he sucked on a Winston. Sounds reasonable, doesn't it?

So, that's what I did for once—I listened to Max. I managed to track down the assistant fire chief, Carl Perry, who informed me that an elderly disabled woman had been rescued from her burning house at 1202 Commerce St. by an unidentified passerby dressed in a Santa Claus suit. "He ran up to the house, kicked the door down, dragged her out and saved her life. She would have burned up if it hadn't been for him," Perry said, talking a mile-a-minute.

Now, when authorities arrived at the fire scene, they found the injured woman, Mabel Marshall, on the ground, outside the burning home, being given aid by some in a crowd of onlookers.

Santa and another person who was his helper were nowhere to be found, though. The pair had slipped away into the night. It was a heck of a story…particularly since the Santa rescuer had vanished without giving anyone his name. Damn, Max was right, and we had a great story to tell our readers. He smiled, between deep draws on his smokes, as he read my incredible story. "Sounds reasonable," he said, with a nod. "We'll lead with it."

Clarksvillians awoke on Christmas morning to the news of a true Christmas miracle: "Santa Claus" had rescued a woman in a house fire and then stole away into the night, headed for parts unknown…The story made *The Associated Press* wire and was carried by newspapers around the world…People had to be scratching their heads. So, there's no such person as Santa Claus? Well, then, who rescued Mabel Marshall? No one could say.

The answer came later that Christmas Day when the hero, prompted by radio and television appeals, stepped from the darkness and into the spotlight. Santa was David Rodriguez, a high school choral teacher in Clarksville. He and a friend, Mike Abernathy, had been delivering toys to underprivileged children on Christmas Eve when they made a wrong turn in their route and stumbled upon Mabel Marshall's burning home. Rodriguez kicked in the front door, and crawled into the house, locating Mrs. Marshall and carrying her to safety. With the arrival of the Fire Department, the two men left the scene to finish their toy route.

Rodriguez and Abernathy paid a visit to *The Leaf-Chronicle* Newsroom to recount to me the details of the harrowing Christmas Eve rescue. All of *The News Brothers*, dressed in their tuxedoes, were there that day to rejoice in the follow-up, a most amazing story that topped the front page of our Sunday edition. "God led me…" Santa Rodriguez confessed. We smiled a lot that special day. Life was good.

But, we weren't going to let ourselves get fooled. Darkness often was just around the corner in our lives. Sadly, Mrs. Marshall, after a few months in the hospital, died from the burns she sustained in the house fire.

Chapter 17
(Tim)

HAVE A DAMN NICE CHRISTMAS

"Have a Damn Nice Christmas!"

Makes you feel like breaking out the hot chocolate and singing about that Wenceslaus fellow feasting on Stephen or whatever. That Damn Nice holiday sentiment nearly cost me my job back in the winter of 1982.

Fortunately, I was able to make our publisher at *The Leaf-Chronicle*—"The Big Guy"—blink. Perhaps the dollar signs I'd help him earn blinded him temporarily, long enough for me to back out his door, put on my yellow fedora and fire up a smoke.

Now, Rob gave a pretty good account of that Damn Nice Christmas of 1982. But, he left out a few things.....That happens, even to *News Brothers*, when you get old...Sometimes you forget things...And, sometimes you remember things that might not even have happened...

Well, I do remember the Christmas card...

Hell, for all I remember, and sometimes that isn't much, The Big Guy maybe even smiled. At the very least he jingled the change in his pockets and nodded, blankly, thinking "How in the world can I get back to Carolina and out of this institution?..." He was from that state populated by basketball and Biltmore and his prize, upon retirement, was to get back to the mountains and feast on Cream of Wheat.

Call me naive or innocent (few do, you know), but I was surprised by the fuming anger of The Big Guy, as I didn't understand what was so wrong with this sentimental greeting. I even sent one of the cards to my mom, and she didn't object. She was willing always to have a Damn Nice Christmas right up til she died. I think she hung the card on the Christmas tree. Still she had been a journalist, so I suppose she got it.

That greeting that was broadcast around Clarksville came during the heady early days of *The News Brothers*. Yeah. We were blue-collar journalists, telling blue-collar stories to a blue-collar (and Army-drab-collar) town.

 Most people liked it when we wished them a "Damn Nice Christmas" more than 29 years ago. After all, wasn't that the last line from "It's A Wonderful Life"? Jimmy Stewart looks into the camera, eyes twinkle as the bell tinkles and he whispers: "Attaboy, Clarence: Have a Damn Nice Christmas!"

Listen closer next time, as that part of the line gets drowned out by all the joyous singing.

As the readers of this book know by now, in the weeks and months leading up to delivering the holiday greeting to The Big Guy, I'd been helping to guide what came to be prize-winning coverage involving the deaths of two beautiful and innocent young people. Of course, we weren't looking for recognition. We just were looking for the truth. And justice. And, when the adrenaline and nicotine wore off, perhaps some sleep.

Kathy Jane Nishiyama and Rodney Wayne Long were still children, really. Promise extinguished. Forever frozen as "mug shots" that ran daily on the front page with eerily parallel dispatches about the mysteries, searches, chases, savagery and mourning.

 The newspaper wasn't large in staff, but the staff was large in heart. We were pretty young ourselves, though our own innocence had been washed away by years of covering trailer-trash murders and gunfights involving prostitutes, transvestites, serial killers and soldiers.

Suffice it to say that for the most part, we worked around the clock to tell those stories, to cover the deaths and to get to know the families of the teenage victims and the killers.

But let's get back to Christmas 1982 and the card. You remember the Christmas card, don't you?

It actually seemed like a great idea, guaranteed to raise a smile, in the wake of all that had gone on in the news. And besides that, Rob and I were coming off the success of the movie we'd produced and directed, written, whatever the word might be, and even starred in ... along with "Flash" and "Chuckles" as co-stars and others who occasionally dropped in to take part. Half the town's police force and firefighters and charitable organizations were involved to some extent. Even the mayor and the first American to circle the globe participated.

"Flapjacks: The Motion Picture"—with its intricate plot revolving around news events, along with its slapstick and satire poking fun at journalism (we didn't realize we were the last generation of practitioners of that profession at the time), law enforcement, pop culture and current events—holds up to this day.

Even the newspaper hierarchy was pleased by the movie that came a month before Christmas ... some young staffers, after all, had done this on their own time, made headlines in Clarksville and in the corporation for raising money for charity ... and at the same time won journalism awards.

Of course, with all this holiday cheer floating around, Rob and I decided the best thing a group of guys can do is put together a Christmas card to thank our friends and to express our belief in peace on earth and goodwill to all mankind.

There was nothing complex about the Christmas card. We'd wear our *News Brothers'* best—bits and pieces of the tuxedoes we'd worn in the days of the "Flapjacks" premiere. Rob, "Chuckles," "Flash" and I showed up in our finery. Our newsroom clerk, a pretty woman named Neesa Perry, was good enough sport to show up to don the top half of a Santa costume and expose what were and likely still are damn nice legs.

Fresh from the photo shoot, Rob and I dashed to our favorite printer and ordered a few dozen postcard-sized copies of that picture, with the phrase "Have a Damn Nice Christmas!" printed below the picture.

Delighted by the result, Rob, in his white top-hat and I in my yellow fedora immediately distributed these cards around town.

We started out in the old Royal York Hotel, that high-rise former swank joint that had degenerated into a flop for widows, widowers, lovable losers, liars and murderous drifters. Many of them were our closest friends.

We went up the elevator—remember, it was one of those you drove yourself—and stopped at each floor, sliding a card beneath each door. "Gunsmoke" reruns blared from the TV sets in 90 percent of those rooms.

We then left a stack at the desk to be distributed in the lobby. In the next hours, we wandered the streets of the city, handing them out, sliding them into the mail slots for county and city officials. It was sort of a Charlie Dickens scene we were creating in the cold, snowy Clarksville night. (If it wasn't snowing, it should have been.)

We even saved one in case Chico The Monkey ever came back from the dead. I still have that one. Just in case.

Then, spreading Christmas cheer, we went to the newspaper complex, going from the press room to the advertising offices, to the camera room, to the job shop, sliding cards beneath doors and leaving them on desks.

The last one, and we didn't hesitate, went beneath the office door of The Big Guy.

"He'll like this," said Rob.

"Yeah," I said. We didn't really think he'd mind one way or another, as long as he could jingle the change in his pockets as loudly as possible.

Perhaps he was still angry over the Chico coverage. Maybe it was my long interview with a drifter named W. Robert Cameron. I'd caught him while he was resting along a railroad siding, taking a breather from his secret mission of hitchhiking to Austria to see the chancellor about world peace.

Maybe it was Rob's steady stream of stories about death and destruction. Not good for the Chamber image, I suppose, in hindsight. Especially at Christmastime.

"Tim, uhh, this is The Big Guy, uhhhh," was the voice the next morning when I picked up the Flap phone, one of those blue plastic contraptions that I kept next to the Mr. Potato Head collection on my desk. "Could you come down here and see me?"

I still didn't know what was going on. He didn't sound angry. Just self-important.

"Uhh, Tim, uhh, could you close the door and, uhh, sit down." I noticed he was jingling his change harder and faster. I wondered if I should offer him a loaded cigarette.

He held up the card. "This is wrong," he said, sounding like a sinister Bobby Knight. "You do not put 'Damn' and 'Christmas' in the same sentence. You guys have gone too far. Do not give any more of these out."

Once I explained that half the town had them, he stood up and walked across the room. He was jingling wildly. The rosewater scent of his hair spritz filled the tiny confines.

"Tim, uhh, you are a great newspaperman, uhh, but this is too much. Do you have any of them left?"

I nodded. "Sure. How many more do you want? And I can order more."

He stood there, in silence, nodded to the door and then said "Don't do this again."

I looked at him and smiled.

"What?" he said, in a benign bark.

"Big Guy, Have a Damn Nice Christmas."

He shook his head. "You too," he muttered. "You too."

I ambled back upstairs to the newsroom, where Rob greeted me. He put on his top-hat, fired up a Kool and we went for some coffee. Later, Rob reported back to the newspaper for Christmas Eve duty.

It was no Silent Night.

Of course, as luck, and the magic of Christmas would have it, Rob was the reporter who got to write the fabulous story of Santa's miracle rescue in the house fire that night on Commerce Street.

All I know is it was a great lead story on a holiday that should revolve around generosity, love and peace. I spent Christmas Eve with my parents in Nashville, but returned to town early the next morning as the papers rolled off the press, I carried one outside, onto Third Street, where a little snow was falling. (Again, if it wasn't, it should have been.)

Rob was standing out there, with our old friend, Skipper, the old carny and merchant marine who once served spaghetti to Al Capone. Rob had rousted him from his room at the old hotel.

It was cold. Boy was it cold.

We shared nips of cheap brandy and wished each other a great holiday: "Have a Damn Nice Christmas!"

As Skipper began telling some of his stories, Jerry Manley and Jim Lindgren arrived on the scene. He handed them the bottle of cheap brandy.

Skipper, who wasn't wearing his teeth, looked up to the sky and began singing "Silent Night" in his amazing Irish tenor.

With that beautiful voice echoing off the old buildings around us, I looked to Rob and the others and smiled. "God Bless us every one."

Chapter 18
(Rob)

'THE BIRDS SHIT ON ME'

The News Brothers were the darlings of the Queen City in the months after the world premiere of our charity film. It hadn't taken very long for our reputation as outlaws and advocates for truth and justice—for all—to take root. Some, as Tim says frequently, called us "nuts." Speaking of which, they were mighty big ones. No one, and I mean no one, could carry our jock straps, let alone wear them.

The love shown to us had some definite benefits for guys who made their livings at a newspaper. If someone was wronged, or had a good cause to promote to the world, who did they call? Not Ghost Busters, but *The News Brothers!* I couldn't even begin to count the number of great stories that just fell into our laps.

Most went to Tim, who wrote an award-winning human interest column, or yours truly, the newspaper's muckraker. We were getting telephone calls on a daily basis from tipsters. Some of the victims of wrong even took the time to come to our offices to plead their case with us and maybe even kiss the secret *News Brothers* ring that Tim wore on his *"Right"* forefinger.

A guy named Delmar Harrison was one of the wronged who walked into *The Leaf-Chronicle* newsroom one day in late January of 1983, looking for "one of those good guys who wear sunglasses and help people." Actually, Delmar might have contacted me earlier by telephone to arrange an interview. Anyway, he was directed to my desk, shook my hand, and then started telling me his story of woe. It would have made a great country music song, if he had put it to music.

Delmar, a native Clarksvillian, was big, bearded and had a chip on his shoulder. He was in town visiting relatives. For the past decade, he had been living in exile in Morgan City, La., where he worked as a tugboat captain.

The thrust of his story was that he had been forced to live hundreds of miles from his family for more than a decade because he was run out of town by a miscarriage of justice.

Delmar said that, in 1970, while he was working for the Clarksville Fire Department, he was "framed" by corrupt policemen who planted marijuana in his sports car and then arrested him. Politics or a dispute the night before with another city employee may have been the reason for what happened to him, he said. Soon after his arrest, the powers-that-be in the Queen City let him know through back channels that the marijuana possession charge, then a serious felony, would go away if he resigned from the department and left town quietly, Delmar claimed during my interview with him.

So, he left town with his tail between his legs and without asking any questions…A few months later, when grand jurors reviewed the case, they declined to indict Delmar because they were very suspicious about the circumstances of the traffic stop—including the fact an anonymous caller, only minutes before the drug arrest, supposedly tipped off police and told them where the marijuana would be found in Delmar's car.

Apparently, while a few in authority believed Delmar had been set up from the very beginning, no one had ever communicated that vote of confidence to the firefighter now down in hot, miserable Louisiana, toiling hard and stinking of sweat and dead fish on a tugboat.

Delmar thought the charge disappeared only because he had taken someone's advice to get out of town. Years went by, and he remained in the dark. Making matters even worse, it seemed a court clerk failed to update Delmar's police record, after the grand jury cleared him, and the serious drug arrest kept showing up in background checks until 1977, costing him several jobs.

When Delmar came to see me, he said he just wanted to come home. But, he said it wasn't possible without him first finding a way to clear his name.

"Whenever I hear anybody talk about liberty and justice for all, I want to kick a hole in the TV," he said to me, with tears in his eyes. Learning I drove an MG, similar to the sports car he had at the time of his arrest in 1970, he joked that he hoped I was a luckier person than him whenever I took the top down. "The birds sing for some people. They shit on me," Delmar said.

Before Delmar left, I asked him to step outside with me so I could photograph him. I decided the perfect photo would be one of him sitting in my sports car. I told Delmar I would check out his story, and if everything seemed on the level, I would make a pitch with my editors to write something for the newspaper.

Delmar thanked me and also warned me, telling me that anytime anyone had ever tried to help him in the past, bad things happened to that person. The comment kind of caught me off guard and made the hair on my neck stand up.

"Rob, I know you're probably not going to do a story. The powers-that-be in this town won't be too keen on a story in the newspaper about what happened to me almost 13 years ago," he said. "It's OK. I really appreciate you at least taking the time to listen to me. Getting it off my chest felt good, anyway."

Over the next several days, I started making telephone calls and doing interviews to try and determine the accuracy of Delmar's tale about the wheels of local justice going awry. It might be hard for you to believe, but sometimes people lie, exaggerate and even leave out parts of a story. Delmar's story turned out to be a big challenge, and I had to be very careful in my investigation because it involved now-retired police officers and prosecutors, politicians and quite a few pillars of the community. Tim told me I could get killed if I wasn't careful. "Man, they'll turn you into Cumberland River catfish bait." He wasn't joking, either.

From the moment I started asking questions, it became pretty clear to me that Delmar wasn't pulling my leg about what had happened to him. Everyone I talked to remembered the case, some vaguely, and no one really disputed Delmar's claim that he was set up. Not surprisingly, everyone I interviewed denied involvement in any kind of conspiracy to railroad poor Delmar and run him out of town.

Once I determined I had a great story on my hands, I asked for and got a green light from my bosses to go forward and get something ready for publication. After looking at all the stuff I had gathered, I decided to write five or six stories and run it as a series.

Now usually, when a reporter writes something on a subject that's sensitive or controversial, the shit hits the fan only after the newspaper goes to press and the story is out there for everyone in the world to read. But, with the Delmar story, the flak started before I was even done with my series of stories. I had been grilling a few of the "beautiful people" of Clarksville about ruining a man's life, and someone—possibly a Country Club or golfing buddy—may have been taking their concerns about what I was doing directly to the "The Big Guy" at our newspaper. I don't know for sure, but that's what I figured. Perhaps someone even threatened to pull an ad or even drop the paper.

All I know is I turned in a series of five or six stories—damn good stories. Later, someone on the City Desk told me the managing editor, Max Moss, was ordered to go through my work with a fine-toothed comb and consolidate everything into just one story. I was a little ticked off, at first, but I must admit Max (the guy Tim called "The Silver Hammer") performed quite an editing miracle. In the finished piece, Delmar's story was getting told and the most interesting details of the case were still there. If my memory is correct, the only thing missing from the article were the names of a few "beautiful people," who don't like negative publicity and know the right people.

As a courtesy, and to give him advance notice, I called Delmar the day before his story was to be published in the paper. He said it was too good to be true. "Something's going to happen," he predicted. "I'll believe it when I see it."

On Sunday, Feb. 13, 1983, Delmar's story appeared in that day's edition of *The Leaf-Chronicle*. It was in the lower part of the front page, a nice photo-and-story package, with the headline, "Delmar Wants To Come Home."

The next day, at the office, my phone rang and it was Delmar. The man was crying like a baby, tears of happiness. "Thank you, Rob. Thank you," he said. "I'll never forget what you did for me."

I replied, "Delmar, I was just doing my job. But, I'm real happy it worked out for you. I'm glad the birds are singing for you. You're a damn nice guy."

When I asked him if he had any plans for his future, he said he hadn't had time to give it much thought. He was concentrating, for the moment, on the present. "After the newspaper came out yesterday, I went around town, buying up as many copies as I could find in the racks," Delmar said. "I might even come up to the newspaper offices this week and see if there are more for sale. I want to give a newspaper to everyone in Clarksville so they can read my story."

I never checked, but it wouldn't surprise me if *The Leaf-Chronicle* set a circulation record for sales that Sunday in February 1983.

Of course, Delmar could have just put 50 cents in each rack and taken the whole stack. But, as I said, he was a damn nice guy.

I don't think Delmar ever drove a convertible again. Fact is, I started keeping my top up most of the time from then on, whenever I tooled around town in my sports car. But that was then, and this is now. To tell you the truth, I haven't driven that MG in 16 years. I parked it on my carport in 1996, where it sat all these years, reminding me of Delmar and his sad story. Finally, I sold it last year to my youngest sister, Dede, who hopes her boyfriend can get the darn thing running again one of these days.

I had thought about reaching out to see if old Delmar might want it, but, you know, it's a convertible.

Tim Ghianni, Rob Dollar and Scott Shelton were serious when it came to *The News Brothers* and their mission of playing the fool to make people laugh at them and themselves.

Chapter 19
(Rob)

ALWAYS THE FOOLS

> *"The first of April is the day we remember what we are the other 364 days of the year."*
> **-- Mark Twain**

April Fools' Day always was special for *The News Brothers*. You see, we just loved making fools out of everybody on April Fools' Day—or any other day of the year for that matter—even if there might be a price to pay for the misdeeds.

Our need to spread happiness in the world through laughter amounted to a sacred duty for this bunch of damn nice guys who didn't mind acting the fool. For us, of course, it really wasn't always that much of an act.

Now, not everyone enjoys a good prank or joke. I'm serious…There actually are people out there in the world who need a really good push before they'll let loose and have any fun. If you were one of those people, *The News Brothers* were always looking for you…

Every April 1st, April Fools' Day, we knew we pretty much had a free pass around the office, Even the dullest of dull dullards would put up with our tomfoolery…The *Leaf-Chronicle* employees expected…. Hell, they demanded we entertain them that special day with an outrageous prank that fittingly showed our mastery of the fine art of merrymaking. It was a task made to order for *The News Brothers*.

Not ones to disappoint, we planned to make April 1, 1983, a day that no one would ever forget. Perpetrating the ultimate April Fools' Day joke at *The Leaf-Chronicle* newspaper would be a two-man mission undertaken by me and Tim —the two sneakiest *News Brothers*, the ones who had absolutely no shame. We knew where the jugular was, and didn't mind going for it.

A few days before D-Day, our plan of deception got under way. We pretended to take colleagues into our confidence, discreetly and one by one, throughout the building, revealing to them what we promised would be an unforgettable April Fools' Day joke. The Mother of All Jokes. Everything was hush-hush…Top-Secret.

We told each one, that this was how it was going to go down: At precisely 2 p.m. on April 1st, Tim and I would stop work, without explanation, rise from our desks in the newsroom and walk across the hall and into the Photography Department. There, we would undress, taking every stitch of clothing off other than our boxer shorts, neckties and sunglasses. We then would return to the newsroom, head for our desks and resume working—without uttering a single word.

Everyone was told not to tell anyone else about the prank and to make sure they were in the newsroom a few minutes early so that they would not miss the revealing event. No one, and I mean no one, doubted the dirty deed would get done. Remember, *The News Brothers* had a well-earned reputation for daring misadventures, and they were known to appreciate and promote The Naked Truth.

The build-up was almost too much to bear. Tim and I kept on whispering to a few select friends. And, of course, they, with loose lips, continued to pass the word. As expected. Some suspected this would be our eventual undoing, that we were pushing the freedom thing just a bit too far. Others hoped that would be the case. The rest, well, they just admired us and wanted to see us in our naked sense of adventure.

But, finally, April 1st arrived, starting out just like any other Friday. Just before the witching hour of 2 p.m., there was a flurry of movement in the entire building. The mild and meek, looking for some adventure, slowly began filtering into the newsroom, joining the perverts who got there early for a good seat... Before long, there were more people in the newsroom than had ever been in it at any time in the history of the newspaper...I'm talking people up the ying-yang, many of them *Leaf-Chronicle* employees from other departments with no business to be in with the news staff whatsoever.

Remember, back then, advertising folks and news folks didn't really mingle. This was before advertising and news became the same thing. So, whenever the flirty, short-skirted beauties from the Advertising Department—Lee Harrison and Kathy Ziolkowski—entered our male-dominated domain, there was no happy talk. The world simply came to a stop. No one ever said a word. We just watched them strut their stuff, and we dreamed what probably was The Impossible Dream...

But it took *The News Brothers* to unite our newspaper as one—at least on this relatively balmy April day.

There everyone was, standing around, looking at each other and many looking as stupid as they really were. Most of the people there believed he or she was special and among the CHOSEN FEW who got advance notice of the joke to take place. Damn if I know what they thought of the growing congregation.

At precisely 2 p.m., two very smug *News Brothers*—Tim and I—jumped up from our desks, strutted across the newsroom and then disappeared into the nearby Photography Department. It consisted of a large studio, a darkroom and some office space. The clock of anticipation began to tick in the crowded newsroom...One minute. Two minutes. Three minutes. Four minutes. Five minutes. The suspense was too much for some of those waiting for their peek...But, I don't think anyone fainted....

Finally, after what seemed like an eternity, the door to the Photography Department opened, and two FULLY DRESSED *News Brothers* walked into the newsroom, went to their desks and started working. No words were said to anyone. After a few minutes of bewilderment, with everyone looking at everyone else for some kind of explanation, a female reporter who obviously had been looking for love in all the wrong places decided that the boys needed a good dressing-down. "You lied. You didn't take your clothes off!" she shrieked, shaking her finger in our faces. "What happened to your April Fools' Day joke? I'm not laughing."

Tim gave me a look, a look that only another *News Brother* could understand, and we let out a hearty laugh. Then, we looked over at our roomful of admirers, and with great, big smiles on our faces, shouted, "APRIL FOOLS!" "That was the joke," I explained. "That there is no joke." Tim added, "Never Trust a *News Brother.*"

Laughing like lunatics in what in less politically correct times would be called "a lunatic asylum," we congratulated ourselves for our silly masterpiece of manipulation. Let's see anyone top that one...Yes, life was good, and *The News Brothers* ruled... Of course, after our prank, the day was still young, and there was always the possibility there might be other fools out there in need of cheering up. I could think of one guy who was ripe for the picking and had already put a large bull's-eye on his back—secretly, of course.

Well, the other shoe dropped on my target, with a thud, about 20 minutes later when a stern-looking officer with the Clarksville Police Department walked into the newsroom and headed directly for Tim's desk. The policeman, with a warrant in hand, advised the startled, and very nervous-looking, merrymaker that he, Mr. Timothy Champ Ghianni, was under arrest and would be going to jail on the charge of... "playing a bad joke in a public place." Another crazy laugh echoed from across the newsroom. The laugh came from me, the sometimes quiet police and courts reporter and master jokester... Sitting at my desk, with a large smirk on my face, I yelled over to Tim, "Gotcha!"

I had just pulled off a joke within a joke—and on another *News Brother*...Oh, how clever I was...Tim took it in stride and just smiled at his partner in crime. But, it was a knowing kind of smile, a sneaky smile, one that made me very nervous. As it turned out, there was good reason for me to be nervous. At about 11 that night, I was hammering out a story on a tight, writing deadline. Fearing the possibility of a reprisal, and constantly looking over my shoulder, I was having quite a tough time. So tough, that I needed a smoke to get a grip on the stress. I grabbed one from a pack on my desk and put it into my mouth. As I lit the cigarette, it exploded, with a huge boom, right in my face, knocking me completely out of my chair. Oh, yes...The old, exploding cigarette trick...Don't get mad, get even.

"April Fools!" a gleeful Tim yelled from across the newsroom. He had been waiting for the big bang all night. "Never Trust a *News Brother*," he reminded me, very matter-of-factly. Lesson learned.

No prank even came close to the success of *the News Brothers'* legendary April Fools' Day joke until 13 years later when I was at the *Kentucky New Era* and decided to teach our eccentric wire editor, Ken Litchfield, a lesson in humility.

Ken, who passed away at age 79 in September 2008, was a Scotch-drinking, old-school journalist who worked at the *New Era* for 48 years. He walked to and from work, a total distance of about eight miles—seven days a week, 365 days a year—wearing a hard hat that had been given to him by fellow employees after he was mugged and nearly beaten to death near his Hopkinsville home.

To call Ken "legendary" would be an understatement. As a cub reporter on June 29, 1957, Ken rushed off to Guthrie, Kentucky, to cover one of the biggest stories ever to occur in this part of the country. A Memphis-bound L&N freight train collided with a passenger train—the Chicago-to-Miami Dixieland Flyer. In all, seven people were killed and 60 injured in the Todd County train wreck. Arriving at the disaster scene, Ken began looking for someone to interview when he fell into a ditch and hurt himself. Rescuers, after giving him medical attention, believed for a time that Ken had been one of the passengers on the train—until he convinced them he was a reporter.

For years, Ken, the veteran newsman, took great delight in badgering newsroom staffers during Pulitzer Prize Week. The day before the big announcement, he loved taking a dig at the young reporters and editors during the afternoon staff meeting. "Be sure to stay by your telephones tomorrow so you don't miss your call," he'd tell us. "They're giving out the Pulitzers, you know." And then, he would chuckle, insinuating, of course, how ridiculous the idea was that someone at the little old *Kentucky New Era* could ever win the Pulitzer Prize. Ken's annual "Pulitzer routine" had become somewhat of a tradition at the newspaper.

In April of 1996, City Editor LaMar Bryan and I decided the time had finally come for Ken to win a special Pulitzer Prize for his 40 years of City Hall reporting. Man, talk about the "Mother of All Punks".....Ken finally got what was coming to him...Our elaborate prank included the delivery of a fruit basket and champagne to Ken's office, congratulatory telephone calls and visits from well-wishers and even a television crew showing up for an interview with Hopkinsville's first-ever Pulitzer Prize winner.

Poor Ken actually believed he had won journalism's most prestigious award. Dazed, he shuffled from desk to desk in the newsroom, muttering, "I won a Pulitzer...I won a Pulitzer." We thought for sure he would catch on early during the ruse and start laughing after realizing he had been the victim of a pretty good joke.

In the end, LaMar and I, pressured by some of our newspaper colleagues with guilty consciences, were forced to break the sad news to our friend: There was no need to clear off any space on the mantle at the Litchfield house. The Pulitzer Prize would not be coming in the mail.

Ken looked at us and laughed. "No Pulitzer, huh? Well, at least I got a bottle of champagne out of it," he said.

But, you know, I always wondered in the back of my mind whether Ken was crazy like a fox and pulled a reverse punk on his pranksters.

Ken Litchfield, wire editor at the *Kentucky New Era*, answers a question from Hopkinsville television reporter Tim Golden during an interview in April 1996. At the time, Litchfield didn't know the interview was part of a prank being played on him by some of his colleagues at the Hopkinsville newspaper.

The News Brothers recreate The Beatles' Abbey Road album cover at a crosswalk on South Third Street in downtown Clarksville, Tennessee, in early 1983. From left are Jerry Manley, Rob Dollar, Scott Shelton and Tim Ghianni. That's Okey "Skipper" Stepp in the background.

Chapter 20
(Rob)

FIRED UP AND FIRED

Delmar Harrison warned me back in mid-February of 1983, after I helped him clear his name, that I'd better watch my back because it now had a large bull's-eye on it, making me a prime target for the powers-that-be in Clarksville. Looking back, I guess I should have taken his warning more seriously.

Anyway, I hadn't seen him in more than two months when our paths crossed again in late April at the Nashville law offices of one of Tennessee's most prominent lawyers, Lionel R. Barrett Jr. At the time we ran into each other, we both had business with the famous barrister. I had just been fired from my job at *The Leaf-Chronicle* and Delmar was hell-bent on suing everybody in Clarksville for ruining his life 13 years earlier.

I didn't have time to say "hello" before Delmar grabbed me in a bear hug, and exclaimed, "See, Rob. I told you they were going to get you."

"You were right, Delmar." I responded. "The birds sing for some people. But, they shit on me, too—just like you."

So, how in the world did I get to this low point in the story of *The News Brothers*? Sit back and allow me to plead my case for innocence.

If 1982 was the Year from Hell, then 1983 started out on a grueling pace to equal, or surpass, it in terms of misery and fatigue.

I spent the first two weeks of January putting in 12-hour days, driving back and forth to the nearby city of Springfield, where the two suspects in the Rodney Long slaying—Stephen Drake and David Frey—were standing trial. It was a big story across the state and there were hoards of media there, including Scott Shelton, the News Director for WJZM Radio.

With the departure of Jim "Flash" Lindgren, who left town a month or so earlier for a new job, Scott, or "Badger," had become the newest member of *The News Brothers*.

Now, Scott was a natural for acting the fool, jumping right into the middle of our fun. Already, in mid-January, Scott, Tim, Tim's brother (Eric Ghianni, who is widely considered more sane than his little brother, but still a damn nice guy) and I had hung out with The Lone Ranger—actor Clayton Moore—at an event in Hopkinsville, Kentucky We also had shot several photographs of the new *News Brothers*, including one of us walking along a crosswalk in downtown Clarksville, imitating The Beatles and their Abbey Road album cover.

The murder trial, which forced everyone to relive all the terrible memories of the prior year, was a slam dunk for the prosecution. Frey, the trigger-man in the slaying, had told investigators after his arrest in New Jersey that he was not afraid of dying in the electric chair. "Nobody's got any guts down in Tennessee to pull the switch," he remarked to a deputy on the ride back to Tennessee. Turns out his prediction of his fate rang true. Convicted of first-degree murder by a six-man, six-woman jury on Jan. 11, Frey was sentenced instead to a life term in the Tennessee State Penitentiary. He remains in prison to this day.

Drake, with Lionel R. Barrett Jr. as one of his court-appointed attorneys, was convicted of second-degree murder and got 40 years in prison. Several years later, Drake was shot and killed in prison during an incident with another inmate.

Scott organized a pool of all the reporters covering the trial to see who could come closest to predicting how long the jury would remain out before returning a verdict of innocent or guilty. I was the big winner, even beating out Nashville television reporter John Seigenthaler Jr., who in the years to come would work as an anchorman for NBC News in New York City. I don't remember what I won. But, considering how poor reporters are, it couldn't

The Lone Ranger (second from right), actor Clayton Moore, poses with *The News Brothers* on Jan. 15, 1983, in Hopkinsville, Kentucky. From left are Rob Dollar, Scott Shelton and Tim Ghianni.

Baseball great Brooks Robinson gets some pointers from *The News Brothers* during a 1983 appearance at Camera World in Clarksville, Tennessee. From left are Tim Ghianni, Scott Shelton and Rob Dollar.

have been much...Probably something like a free lunch, with everyone in the pool chipping in some spare change.

On a side note, Rodney Long's mother, Barbara Mack, upset with the results of the sentencing, got in a car wreck shortly after leaving the courthouse, only five miles from Springfield. She suffered minor injuries in the accident caused, in part, by ice on the road. I came across the wreck on my way home, and called Tim, who rushed off to the hospital to do a sidebar story on the never-ending woes of the Long family.

After the Long trial was over, it was business as usual for *The News Brothers*—for a short time, anyway. In the weeks after the world premiere of our movie in November 1982, Tim had written up a short article on the charity project and submitted it to the newspaper's corporate owner, Multimedia Inc., of Greenville, S.C. Every month, Multimedia put out a "good news" newsletter called "Interlink," and Tim thought, as any reasonable person might, that what we had just done was perfect for this publication.

Anyway, when the January issue of Interlink came out, there on the front-page was the story about *The News Brothers*, complete with a photo of us with Tennessee Gov. Lamar Alexander. The headline read: "Let's make a movie, they said, and did."

Unfortunately, I guess someone in the Ivory Tower actually read the story (that's unusual), which detailed the future projects of *The News Brothers*. With a movie, T-shirts, several posters and a Christmas card already under our belts, we were now promising a sequel to the movie, a picture calendar and a *News Brothers* Invitational Basketball Tournament (in which everyone must wear shades) for 1983. *The News Brothers* also were thinking about getting deeper into the greeting card business. There was serious talk about putting out a very special Mother's Day card for the male assholes of the world. (*Happy Muther's Day! But, I'm not a mother...YES you are.*)

At some point, someone probably high up in the organization, I'm sure, decided enough was enough and sent down the order from the top: *The News Brothers* have to go...

It's been said to kill a snake, you cut off its head....And so, Korporate, without looking into the facts, apparently decided that

Max Moss, the top editor at *The Leaf-Chronicle* since Tony Durr's unceremonious departure the previous July, had lost control of the asylum, and the patients were now running it. Boy, were they ever off base when they went looking for their sacrificial scapegoat. I suppose to them, it sounded reasonable.

Max was, and is, a great newspaperman and damn nice guy who was loved and respected by the entire staff of the newspaper and the Clarksville community. His downfall was he just wasn't a corporate flak or micro-manager. He believed in the finished product and in the young men and women who worked for him. This was back in the days when some thought loyalty still mattered. Max, a hard-working guy who eventually gave up cigarettes for heaping bowls of ice cream—was among the first victims of the misconception.

When Tony was escorted to the state line, "The Big Guy" called a news meeting to announce the departure ... supposedly on good terms. "Tony's got a great opportunity in Texas," he said. "But for all of you who are worried about it, there's no reason for me to look any farther for newsroom leadership. Max is my man."

I don't know if The Big Guy had been fooled or if he thought we were fools, but it clearly came down from up the corporate ladder to bring aboard an executive editor—Max retained his title of managing editor—to take the reins from Max at *The Leaf-Chronicle*.

And so, Korporate announced in a front-page story in the Feb. 27, 1983, edition of *The Leaf-Chronicle*, a new sheriff was in town....The new editor, Dee Bryant, was part of Multimedia's Middle Tennessee Newspapers Division.

A week or so before Dee's arrival—her first day on the job was Tuesday, March 1, 1983—I had been spending most of my time at Fort Campbell, covering the court-martial of a Fort Campbell soldier, Sgt. Randolph Artis, who was accused of beating his wife to death with a baseball bat on post five months earlier. The case ended in a death sentence for the soldier. Covering the court-martial with me was Lisa Human McCormack, who was Larry McCormack's wife and a correspondent for *The Tennessean*, and Lowell Atchley, of the *Kentucky New Era* in Hopkinsville,

Kentucky I didn't know it at the time, but in less than a year, I'd be working alongside Lowell in Hopkinsville, starting a friendship that has endured to this day.

Now, as soon as Dee reported for work, it seemed like the shit really hit the fan. News started breaking all over the place, and even with a change at the top, we never skipped a beat. On just her second day on the job, a Montgomery County school bus crashed while taking students on a field trip. At the time, I was out at Fort Campbell, interviewing the post's new garrison commander, Army Col. Bob Freeman. On my way back to Clarksville at mid-morning, I stumbled upon the overturned school bus in the median of U.S. 41A. The crash had left eight children with minor injuries. A Johnny-on-the-spot, I scored a major coup with a great front-page photo and a decent story that made both editions that day. I believe I even got a pat on the back from our new editor.

Just a week later, on Wednesday, March 9, 1983, a grenade exploded at an office in Public Square, slightly injuring three or four people. Tim and I were on that story like a duck on a junebug, rushing to the scene within minutes of the explosion, which shook much of downtown Clarksville. Hell, we even could be seen in a front-page photograph, looking sad and concerned as an injured man was rolled toward the ambulance. Believe it or not, we were sad and concerned. We actually like people. Probably a part of our undoing.

With one big story occurring right after another, Dee probably wondered what she had gotten herself into by accepting the Clarksville editor's job.

The first time I met our new editor I thought she kind of looked like Dustin Hoffman — you know, where he dressed up to become a woman named "Dorothy Michaels" in the 1982 movie, "Tootsie."

Dee was nice, I guess, but all business, as she started to put her thumb prints on the newspaper and staff. Maybe she was trying too hard to fit in and prove herself. One of the first things she did when she moved into Max's office, was put up a decorative sign on the wall. If I remember correctly, it said something to the effect: "If you need someone to do a man's job, send a woman."

Around the time Dee jumped in the saddle and started giving orders, there was a renewed and concentrated emphasis to find "Good News" to put in the newspaper, which I'm sure had the Chamber of Commerce wetting their pants they were so happy.

Two new features had been introduced to readers: "Neighbors," which was a puff piece about someone's good neighbor doing a good deed; and "Happy First Birthday," a block of photographs of tots celebrating their first year of life.

"Neighbors" ran on Sundays, and actually started before Dee's arrival on the scene. It was Tim and Jerry Manley who came up with the photo illustration, or logo, for this great new addition that was going to enhance the journalism excellence of our paper. (OK. I'm being sarcastic, here. We viewed "Neighbors" as more busy work for the staff, just another obstacle that would take our eyes off the ball—real news.)

So, what was the logo for "Neighbors"? Tim and Jerry had Larry McCormack photograph their hands in a handshake—the "secret" *News Brothers* handshake...Score another one for *The News Brothers*!

Maybe I'm off base here, but I got the distinct impression—after watching Dee interact with the staff—that she didn't like, or respect, men, particularly fat men. We had a couple of overweight guys on the staff, like Ricky G. "Dumbo" Moore and Jim Monday. Both of them always turned around, their big bodies quivering, and headed the other way when they saw Dee coming down the hall. They were scared out of their third helpings of chitterlings and fatback and chess pie by her. Back then, I was lean and mean, and today I'm kind of fat, but by no means Dumbo-sized. Still, the recollection might just be my feeble mind playing tricks on me.

If Dee feared *The News Brothers*, she never showed it. A few weeks after she had arrived in Clarksville, I found a 6-foot-long black, papier mache "land shark"—like the one you used to see on "Saturday Night Live." Someone had left it in the wishing well in the gazebo in front of City Hall. I carried it back to the newsroom,

From left, Rob Dollar, Tim Ghianni and Scott Shelton ride The *Leaf-Chronicle* newsroom shark during a "fishy" encounter at the newspaper in early 1983.

A papier mache shark occupies the desk of City Editor Wendell Wilson, the victim of a *News Brothers* prank in March 1983.

planning to have some fun with it. First, I terrorized Wendell Wilson, by having the shark occupy his desk. Later, I put it on top of the coat rack. The next morning, Dee came in, hung up her coat and then wrapped her scarf around the shark ... while not uttering a word.

While on the subject of the shark, *The News Brothers* found it to be quite a handy prop for their infamous "Jaws" poster, which I believe was the brainchild of "Badger" Shelton.

Anyone who showed up at the newspaper on the day when three grown and shirtless men (Tim, Scott and I) were being photographed as they pretended to ride a papier mache "land shark" no doubt wondered just what the hell was going on...If they missed seeing the poster...now, all these years later, they have an explanation.

Not long after the shark-riding adventure, Scott had Tim and I meet him one day at Camera World, where we had our photo made with Brooks Robinson, the former third baseman of the Baltimore Orioles and member of the Baseball Hall of Fame. Our encounter with baseball greatness turned out to be the damnedest thing I ever saw....There was old "Badger" in his element, lecturing "The Human Vacuum Cleaner" and offering him some fielding tips.

I guess I shouldn't have been too surprised. Earlier that year in mid-January, when all of us shook hands with our childhood hero—The Lone Ranger—Scott "badgered" The Masked Man for one of his silver bullets. *News Brothers* aren't bashful, that's for sure.

Now, getting back to my firing, sometime in late February or early March of 1983 the word came out of City Hall that longtime Police Chief Ira Nunley was reluctantly stepping down, and the city would be looking for his replacement. Mayor Ted Crozier announced a selection process, much of which would take place behind closed doors. People are naturally suspicious whenever you try to do something in secret, so it's no wonder the first thing many people thought was that Crozier—nicknamed "Wild Turkey" apparently from his whiskey-drinking war exploits with the 101st Airborne in what used to be called Saigon—planned to maneuver one of his old Army buddies into the job.

The requirements for applying and interviewing for the police chief's job in the closed sessions included experience or having a degree in law enforcement or related fields from an accredited university. Tim and I kept looking at that requirement.

But it was me who suddenly realized "Hey, I'm qualified!"

You see, *News Brothers* are always thinking, and out of my head popped a most bold idea: *I have a college degree in police administration and three months experience working for a Sheriff's Department, as a student intern. With those solid credentials, what if I submit an application for police chief? I could put myself into the secretive selection process and therefore be in a position to write a story for the newspaper. Chances are, I would not be selected for the job. But, in the event it was offered to me, I would have the option of changing careers and accepting a job that paid at least three times what I was making at the newspaper. And I'd get a badge and a gun and at least one bullet to put in my breast pocket.*

Maybe it was a stupid idea. I don't know. All I know was, I was young, naïve and sometimes foolish 30 years ago.

Of course Tim was all for it, but even the two of us—the most radical of the newsgathering *News Brothers* fraternity—knew that the way to negotiate such intricate plots is to go through channels. You know, let them in on it, get their seal of approval, perhaps even make them think it was their idea.

When I ran with my story proposal to my immediate supervisor, the "newspaperman," City Editor Wendell Wilson, he ate up the idea. He loved it and gave it his blessing. Wendell knew he was either going to get an exclusive inside-look at the selection process ... or perhaps he thought he might get rid of me... and have a "friend" leading "Clarksville's Finest."

Somehow, I was left with the impression that higher-ups at the newspaper, while not encouraging my not-so-undercover mission, had no real objection to it. No one ordered me NOT to apply for the police chief's job or told me it would jeopardize my reporter's job. I thought it was OK with Dee and the newspaper's other top managers. Which, now, with the benefit of hindsight, I'm not so sure was the case.

As I said, Tim liked the idea and approved of it, but he's nuts, you know. I think he just wanted to ride around in the squad car with me, playing with the siren or hollering out messages over the loudspeaker, kind of like Jake and Elwood in The Blues Brothers movie. Joking here. In reality, he saw it as a great newsgathering opportunity, which, when it comes right down to it, was what *The News Brothers* really were all about.

Anyway, with the blessing of authority and blindly believing I was searching for truth, justice and an end to a veil of secrecy pulled over public hiring ... I applied to become Clarksville's new police chief. I submitted my application for the job on Thursday, April 14, 1983, a full day after I had followed the chain-of-command and talked to my boss—"newspaperman" Wendell Wilson, the city editor—about it.

The very next day, Friday, April 15, 1983, Wendell called me over to his desk and announced there had been second thoughts and concerns expressed by the higher-ups, and they wanted me to reconsider my plans to interview for the police chief's job. Regardless of what I decided to do, he said, there would not be any stories, written by me, about the selection process to appear in *The Leaf-Chronicle*. Period. If I insisted on pursuing the police chief's job, then I was told I faced the possibility of being moved from my police and courts beat to another beat in order to remove any appearance of a conflict of interest.

Again, I was young, foolish and after this conversation…pretty damn pissed. This assignment of mine had been approved by my superiors, as far as I was concerned. It was not any sort of underhanded prank. I had the qualifications to apply. And this was a noble journalistic endeavor to raise the curtain on a closed selection process for someone who would have a big impact on the city. I didn't like the idea of the plug being pulled at the last minute. I advised Wendell I had already submitted my application, and I planned to stay in the hunt for the police chief's job. Period.

Wendell reported my decision to Dee Bryant, who called me later the same day into her office, where we discussed my reassignment to another beat. Dee assured me my decision to pursue the police chief's job would not threaten my employment with the newspaper. *The Leaf-Chronicle*, she said, did not want to discourage anyone from seeking a career opportunity. I thought the matter was then closed, but, boy, was I ever wrong.

The deadline for applications came and went and on Saturday, April 16, 1983, there was a front-page story in the newspaper about the 22 applicants for the police chief's job. The story was written by Elise Frederick, the soon-to-be-wife of Scott "Badger" Shelton, and it included my name, biography, and credentials.

That day's paper—which also contained another story about one of those helicopters of the secret 160th falling out of the sky over the Atlantic Ocean near Virginia—apparently was read by someone in *The Leaf-Chronicle* food chain unaware of my plans to either become police chief or get the skinny on Mayor Crozier and City Hall. Maybe the person, in question, simply had not been updated about the situation…I really don't know what happened….But, I can see a familiar figure gagging on his glass of sipping whiskey right now.

Three days later, on Tuesday, April 19, 1983, when I arrived for work, Wendell called me to a back office for another meeting. In his ulcerated-asshole-way, he informed me it had been decided—by someone, he didn't name names—that my last day at *The Leaf-Chronicle* would be 30 days from that particular, rainy day in April. My days at *The Leaf-Chronicle* were over. The time had come to part ways. The "newspaperman" said I could use my available time to look for a new job. Keeping my cool, I thanked him and said I'd give my usual 110 percent over the next month, and when the 30 days were up, the company would have to fire me because I was not a quitter, and I would not quit.

My message of defiance (Remember, *I won't back down!*) was communicated to the top of the chain-of-command. In a later meeting the same day, one that included Max Moss, Dee fired me, effectively immediately. It was nice and polite. Heck, I think we were all close to tears, and could even feel some love. When Tim tells the story, he ends it by saying that he watched through the window to the office while me and Max and Dee, our arms encircled, sang *"Kumbaya."* But, like I said, he's nuts and it never happened.

Rob Dollar, Okey "Skipper" Stepp and Tim Ghianni share a laugh at Dollar's going-away party in late July 1983. Fun was had by all.

Three "Wise Guys" hold plenty of gifts and wear shades in this photograph for a Christmas poster taken in December 1983. From left are Jerry Manley, Tim Ghianni, Okey "Skipper" Stepp, Rob Dollar, Denny Adkins and John Manley.

After I boxed up my personal belongings—with co-workers coming to my desk to express their shock at what had happened—I then handed Max the keycard that allowed me entry into the building. It was called the "Magic Key" by some of us.

"Here you go, Max. There's no more magic left in this key," I said, as I left the newsroom. Going out, I passed Tim, taking off his sunglasses as he walked into the newsroom from the adjacent Composing Room.

"They just got rid of a *News Brother*," I said to him. "They fired me, Flap."

Tim said something witty and clever, identifying those people as ones who apparently he thought loved to copulate with their own posteriors.

"Flash" was gone. "Death" was gone. And Chico The Monkey was still dead.

That night, Tim and Jerry Manley came over to my place at the Malibu Apartments, and we drank beer and watched the movie. I still had a few laughs up my sleeve.

News stories appeared in the local and Nashville media about my firing. It was news, after all. Ace reporter fired for applying for police chief's job. Funny as it seems now, Scott "Badger" Shelton, David "Teach" Ross and Harold "The Stranger" Lynch—all part of the *News Brothers* entourage—wrote some of those stories.

Dee, in explaining my firing, said my actions had "created a conflict of interest" and jeopardized the reputation and credibility of *The Leaf-Chronicle*.

The newspaper, I'm told, received tons of letters to the editor, in support of me, but only ran a few before cutting them off.

A few days after my firing, I ran into my favorite teacher from Fort Campbell High School at Red's Bakery on Riverside Drive. Back in my high school days, Lee Lange, who passed away in 2010, used to call me "Broadway," since I tried to play quarterback and "Broadway" Joe Namath of the New York Jets was my hero.

"Broadway, I read about what happened to you," Mr. Lange said, putting his arm on my shoulder. "Shame on them all. Firing a good man because he applied for another job."

Tim broke the news of my firing to Ralph Nishiyama—Kathy Jane's father—as well as to Rodney Long's mother, Barbara Mack. They were fans of my reporting, and both were quite upset as well.

Not long after I got fired, I had my interview for the police chief's job. I didn't get the job, but I did get to answer questions from a legendary police chief, Joe Casey of Nashville, who was among those on the interview panel.

Many years later, proving again it's a small world, Tim actually got an intimidating letter from the same said police chief after he publicly proclaimed anger at being repeatedly stopped and frisked by "Metro Nashville's Finest" apparently because he had long hair. Or perhaps the word was out that Tim was my pal. At least that's the way I figure it. But I'm nuts, too.

Regardless, now that I was unemployed, I wanted the chief's job. But who do you think got it? George Siegrist, a Montgomery County sheriff's deputy and former Army officer.

Interestingly, just two years later, Siegrist applied for and was chosen to become the police chief in West Palm Beach, Fla. He lost that dream job after only two years. According to published reports, Siegrist resigned in March 1987 while under fire for allegations of racism, intimidation and a criminal cover-up. In the back of my mind, I also seem to remember some lawsuits and something about someone kicking a dog's private parts.

As an aside, my firing from the newspaper robbed me of the opportunity to cover the Kathy Jane Nishiyama murder trial. Instead, Elise Frederick got the assignment and covered it gavel-to-gavel with her future husband and radioman, Scott "Badger" Shelton. The suspect in the case, Charles Eddie Hartman, who had been the trusty behind the wheel of a Dickson County sheriff's vehicle that stopped the teenage girl's car near her home on the night of her 1981 death, was convicted of kidnapping, rape and first-degree murder on May 21, 1983. Two days later, he was sentenced to die in Tennessee's electric chair. On two occasions in the following years, Hartman's death sentence was overturned by the higher courts. Hartman died in prison of natural causes at age 49 on May 24, 2007.

If you'll remember way back to the beginning of this tale, it was someone from the Dickson County Sheriff's Office who tipped Tim that a necklace had been found in the patrol car that Eddie Hartman had kept out too long on that fateful night. And another person, an angry sub-sheriff if I recall, who denied that happened.

I decided, as a matter of principle, to sue *The Leaf-Chronicle* and its parent companies, including some of the editors, for $1.5 million for terminating me without cause.

If I had had my way, I would have hired Court Agate, the imaginary lawyer created in Tim's brain, to litigate my case. Since he wasn't available, one of *The News Brothers* best friends, Clarksville attorney Gary Hodges, stepped up to the plate and took my case.

Many years later, after I had re-established my reputation as a working journalist, I made it possible for both Gary and Tim to become Kentucky Colonels. My old college chums, Don "Gringo" McNay and Bob Babbage, who served terms as Kentucky's auditor and secretary of state, pulled the strings to get those honorary Colonel titles.

Now, Gary Hodges, as fate and irony would have it, also had been the lawyer for Rodney Long's convicted killer, David Frey.

Because Gary had gotten to know Lionel R. Barrett Jr. pretty well during the Rodney Long murder trial, he was able to convince old Lionel to sign on as the co-counsel in my case, as a show of clout and support. Unfortunately, while prestigious, Lionel was best-known for his willingness to take on losing causes and then going on to lose the cases.

But meeting up with the great barrister for the underdog was the reason I was in Nashville the day I reunited with Delmar Harrison.

When my civil case went to court in Clarksville, Tim was there to support me, sitting on my side of the courtroom, infuriating the hell out of *The Leaf-Chronicle* attorneys. His loyalty to me and the brotherhood cost him dearly back at the office.

You see, after he sat on my side, the company attorney glared and glared at him. No one else at the newspaper had any contact with me ... even though the newspaper was 100 feet from the courthouse.

I'll have to say it didn't surprise me to see Tim there. I knew he was putting his job in jeopardy. But to him, like to me, loyalty mattered.

As the hearing concluded, he was grabbed by the corporate attorney just outside the courtroom. "Are you here to support the newspaper?" he was asked, in an angry arrogance.

"Nope, I'm here because Rob's my friend," was his simple response.

He told me that as soon as he got back to the newsroom that day, he again was summoned to take that long walk downstairs to The Big Guy's office.

"Tim, our lawyer said you were openly going against the newspaper in court today," said The Big Guy, apparently thinking that his most-public employee, an award-winning editor and columnist, the conscience of the Queen City—"Tim Ghianni will make you laugh, cry, get angry, become concerned, dream, give up, become involved..." read the ad that ran regularly to promote his Calling Card column—might have to be showed the door if corporate caught wind of his "betrayal."

"This makes us question your loyalty to the newspaper," The Big Guy added, fiddling with a very sharp letter-opener.

"Luther, let me tell you: this isn't about loyalty to the newspaper. You have no right to question my loyalty here. Just look at the hours I put in here over the years.

"This, Luther, is simply about friendship. To me friends come first. Rob is my friend. I was there to support my friend, plain and simple.

"If that's disloyalty to the newspaper, then, well, I'll leave that up to you."

Tim shook Luther's hand and stepped outside to have a smoke, and curiously, found himself laughing.

"Flap" did remain at the paper for a few more years, and continued his fight for the younger people on the staff and for the fat ones as well.

And he never looked back. But he knew his dream of being editor at that paper in the town he had grown to love was over the day he went to court because he was loyal to a friend.

"Management may think that reporters are a dime a dozen. But friends are priceless," he told me. "So it really wasn't even a question as to whether I'd be there in court with you."

Eventually, my lawsuit was dismissed in favor of *The Leaf-Chronicle*. I appealed the Circuit Court decision to the Tennessee Court of Appeals, and the justices reaffirmed the dismissal. In their opinion, the justices noted that Tennessee was an employment at will state, which meant an employer could fire any employee working without a contract, anytime, without having a reason.

Damn law. It even applied to *News Brothers*.

Over the next couple of months, I hung out at my Clarksville apartment, which I shared with my sister, Linda, and one of her twentysomething friends who had just started a career as a barmaid. Tim and I enjoyed the nice young woman's company, especially her intelligent conversation.

Often, while we discussed world peace and problems at the workplace, she'd walk past us in her skimpy bikini, on the way to the pool. "I just love potato chips," she'd chirp, without a care in the world.

Shame on some of you for thinking what you're thinking…I'm really tempted to defend myself here. But, *News Brothers* don't kiss and tell.

I spent most of that spring and summer getting a tan at the pool and watching the Chicago Cubs lose another pennant on television. I also lived it up with the hot redhead I was keeping company with—the same one from my rendezvous back in November after the world premiere of the "Flapjacks" movie.

I was jobless, but not broken. And my gal pal sure kept a smile on my face—like the time she showed up at my apartment, banging on the door, sometime after midnight. She had just left a male strip show and was quite drunk and looking for love in the right place on that particular night.

Oh yeah, I almost forgot…*News Brothers* don't kiss and tell.

Growing restless, with no job prospects on the horizon, I decided to leave town and seek my fortune elsewhere. But, before I was "On The Road Again," *The News Brothers* honored me with a going-away party on Friday night, July 29, 1983. The celebration took place at My Mother's Place...a tavern on Madison Street that had shut down. Tim knew the owner, who allowed us to use the place for our festivities.

Now, *News Brothers* know how to throw a party so you know fun was had by all...Two of the gals at *The Leaf-Chronicle*—Elise Frederick and Laura Warren—baked me a cake. Good thing I didn't have to blow out any candles, which would have been difficult in my inebriated condition.

Another of my *Leaf-Chronicle* colleagues, Sandy Smith, gave me a nice farewell card that brought tears to my eyes. Inside the card, she wrote: "The best of luck to you, 'Death'...You have a lot going for you, and I know you will show us all up one day..."

Three of my old Fort Campbell High School football teammates—Ray Soyk, Mike Perry and Allen "Big Al" Hayes—even showed up at the party to wish me well...Or maybe just to get smashed on the free beer and champagne.

Sadly, my whirlwind romance with the redhead ended this same night, with either a bang or a whimper...It's really too painful for me to remember....Anyway, it was just as well since the relationship had been doomed from the moment of our first kiss...You see, I was a damn nice guy, and her mother actually liked me.

In early August, I moved away to Houston, Texas—where another of my sisters, Adele, and her then-husband, Randy Oatts, lived—to look for work. The very day I got there, Houston got hit for the first time in 20 years by a powerful hurricane. Damn...The Curse of *The News Brothers*, I thought to myself, recognizing the tell-tale signs at once. Hurricane Alecia killed nearly 20 people and injured dozens more. Luckily, I wasn't one of them. My sports car, which was not anchored to a tree like most of the other vehicles in our apartment complex, also survived the hurricane and did not get blown away.

In the meantime, back at *The Leaf-Chronicle*, another *News Brother* had bitten the dust. Jerry Manley resigned to take a job at the daily newspaper in Murfreesboro, Tennessee. Around the same time, Larry McCormack, the chief photographer, turned in his notice to join the staff of the *Nashville Banner*.

By the middle of 1983, there was only one true and original *News Brother*—Tim, old "Flapjacks" himself—left standing at *The Leaf-Chronicle* to battle the forces of evil over the next several years.

The "newspaperman," Wendell Wilson, apparently was another casualty of the police chief affair the following year in 1984. One day, he was reading *Editor & Publisher* magazine and saw his city editor's job being advertised in the classified section. Eventually, he was re-assigned, or exiled, to the copy desk. It wasn't long after that, that he left Clarksville and newspapers, seeking a new career in the world of computers.

I "Googled" Wendell Wilson's name in 2009 and located a photo of him on the Internet. It was taken by a newspaper in Arizona. Wendell, still acting superior and determined as ever, was sitting, toad-like, on a bale of hay outside a prison, protesting the death penalty. The man always did like to argue....All these years later, I'd like to think there was a special understanding between *The News Brothers* and Wendell. We didn't particularly like, nor respect, each other, for whatever the reasons. But, we were always civil to each other. In our movie, we actually "killed off" Wendell, and no one laughed harder in the theater during that scene than the "newspaperman" himself.

Others in *The News Brothers'* entourage like John "Street" Staed and Ricky G. "Dumbo" Moore, soon got the hell out of town, too, heading for parts unknown...maybe Alabama.

Max Moss eventually had enough and got a job as a copy editor at the *Nashville Banner*. Tim stayed on to defend the staff and make his regular visits to Luther's office until 1988, when the *Banner* created a job for him to serve as night city editor.

Tim Ghianni interviews 1960s icon, Tiny Tim, in Clarksville, Tennessee, in the mid-1980s. The entertainer spent the last years of his life as the featured attraction of a traveling circus.

Tim Ghianni (center) interviews Clarksville Mayor Don Trotter, with the help of government reporter Harold Lynch, during a visit to City Hall sometime in the late 1980s.

Tim Ghianni spends some time with a hobo passing through town in the fall of 1982. Ghianni always looked for the unusual for subjects of his award-winning Calling Card column.

He said the guy who hired him, managing editor Tony Kessler, was the fairest and most even-handed direct boss he ever had ... other than, perhaps, "The Silver Hammer." So it shouldn't be surprising to any of you to learn that Kessler suffered his own share of stabs in the back on his way out of journalism.

Dee Bryant remained at *The Leaf-Chronicle* as editor for 11 years and eventually married a local judge—but not the same one that ruled against me in my lawsuit. Now known as Dee Bryant Boaz, she retired from journalism in 1994, but still resides in Clarksville.

In the years that followed came the unexpected deaths of Harold "The Stranger" Lynch and Tony Durr.

Now back to my adventure in Texas. Maybe you're not supposed to mess with Texas, but The Lone Star State was not the place for me—someone who apparently was all hat but no cattle. The cowboy hat just wouldn't fit...

I stayed in Houston for about a month in 1983 before I decided I didn't like anything about the city, other than an occasional foray to Pasadena and that big honky-tonk, Gilley's, where I spent some time pretending to be a cowboy and riding the mechanical bull.

Years later, it probably should be noted here, Tim got lectured by his bosses at his final newspaper destination in Nashville for spending time with and writing a story about Mickey Gilley, the great pianist who is Jerry Lee Lewis's cousin and a Texas legend. "Anyone who cares about Mickey Gilley already knows about him," Tim was told. "No need to waste space on him."

Tim—who knew Gilley did matter in the history of barroom country music, if for nothing else than the fact he had the giant club and provided the backdrop for the genre-bending "Urban Cowboy" movie—ran the story. He was the editor of the section, and he knew he had made the right decision.

Anyway, back to my tale of woe. Returning home, I worked part-time in news at a radio station for a few months and then eventually resumed my journalism career when I went to work in Hopkinsville, Kentucky, for my hometown daily newspaper, the *Kentucky New Era*.

It was now early December 1983. With the approach of Christmas, *The News Brothers*, hurting but not knocked out, pulled a few more punches on "The Man."

Tim, Jerry and I created a Christmas 1983 poster that paid tribute to "The Three Wise Men" who visited with Jesus after his birth...We were "The Three Wise Guys," bearing gifts and wearing shades. The holiday poster also featured Skipper, Denny Adkins, and Jerry's young son, Little John.

At about the same time, we had another year-ending project. After all, *News Brothers* are always thinking. We made a five-minute Christmas video titled, "Miracle on Commerce Street." We rounded up the usual suspects for the short film. One was the son of Raissa Gray, who ran the coffee shop at The Royal York Hotel. Judd Gray was known around town for his thuggish appearance and brushes with the law. But, he was a damn nice guy and should have won an Oscar—or a "Get Out Of Jail Free" pass—for his heart-warming portrayal of a scraggly Santa Claus who saw and knew everything. Our film was no "It's A Wonderful Life," but it was wonderful to us.

Get-togethers after 1983 would be few and far between as *The News Brothers* put their noses to the grindstone, and like cream, rose to the very top of their chosen profession to be recognized as among the best and brightest of practicing journalists in the country.

The road back to the top for me would not be easy. I had to start over and prove myself.

As a new hire at the *Kentucky New Era*—accepting a reporter's job at a substantial cut in pay—I enthusiastically embarked on the long journey to repair my journalism career and reputation.

But, I also refused to give up my *News Brothers* identity. I would not abandon my good sense of humor or willingness to boldly go where no reporter had gone before...

So, just where was one of the first places I went? To a nude dancing bar.

Yep.

Lady Luck winked when the time came for me to get my feet wet as a *New Era* reporter. I got real lucky and got to cover the ruckus down the road in Oak Grove, Kentucky, where The Cat West Showbar opened its doors across from the soldier-rich Fort Campbell Army post in mid-January 1984. Talk about an eye-opening assignment. Hell, I kept both eyes opened, and real wide—for days. There was a lot to see.

Of course, using *News Brothers* logic, I decided to report what was happening at the club by posing as a customer who was having a pretty good time, and a good time is what I had for the better part of a week.

Back then, the club opened just before noon, so I adjusted my work schedule accordingly, splitting my time between the club and the newspaper offices in Hopkinsville. *New Era* Publisher Bob Carter usually was waiting for me, and rather anxiously, when I returned to the newsroom—always happy, but sometimes way *too happy* —each day in the late afternoon to write up my stories.

Mr. Carter sure got a kick out of those daily reports. He wanted to hear all the dirty details, even those that wouldn't be making the next day's paper. But what he really enjoyed was the fact we were selling a lot of newspapers and making a ton of money thanks to the tantalizing story.

At the time The Cat West opened for business, authorities—prompted by complaints from citizens and church groups—had vowed they would find a way to shut it down.

"Those women in there aren't wearing any pastries," declared Christian County Sheriff Bill Dillard, unintentionally providing a bit of comic relief to the controversial story. The High Sheriff, of course, misspoke after an encounter with some of the exotic dancers. "Pasties" was the word he should have used, even if—as he was a lawman—he had doughnuts on his mind.

Twenty-eight years later, The Cat West remains in business as a private club, having prevailed in numerous court battles over the years. As a private club, where customers now bring their own liquor, the dancers no longer have to wear "pastries" or any other covering. They are asked to wear a nice smile, though.

Another of my early *New Era* stories also had some *News Brothers* magic to it.

Not long after the nude dancing saga, I teamed up with a *New Era* colleague, David Riley, then the graphics editor, on a rather shocking story that would have made *The News Brothers* quite proud.

The story was based on a classified ad I had stumbled across while reading the paper. It may be hard to believe, but the ad was seeking applicants for the executioner's job at the nearby Kentucky State Penitentiary in Eddyville, Kentucky.

Shades of Chico The Monkey...I knew exactly what to do with an opportunity like the one that had just been dropped in my lap...What followed was an entertaining story about an electrifying job up for grabs, provided you were someone who had some time to kill...Yeah. I loaded the story with quite a few puns to punch it up, and David Riley assisted with a nice contribution to the story package—an illustration of an employment line, composed of four hooded, ax-carrying executioner wannabes, awaiting their turn to interview for the job underneath a "Help Wanted" sign.

You know, for a minute, I thought about applying for the job....But, I knew there was no future in it for me. After all, I'm against the death penalty. And the hood would have messed up my hair and covered my pretty face.

Anyway, I got off to a running start with my new friends at the *New Era*. But, my heart still belonged to *The News Brothers*.

Proudly continuing my *News Brothers* tradition of being a damn nice guy who looks good in shades, it wasn't long before the *New Era* crew got into the act.

Maybe I started to rub off on them...All I know is, before I knew it, I had an "Injun" name...

Now, hold your horses...Please forgive me my political incorrectness here. Yes we were modern, enlightened men. But we also were newspaper writers, who only worry about being correct when it comes to delivering the news.

Scott Burnside, the newspaper's sports editor for more than 10 years, decided one slow day that everyone in the newsroom should have an Indian name. I guess he probably had been reading too many Western novels. Or maybe he was inspired by the Kevin Costner movie, "Dances With Wolves."

Scott, who had always worn a beard, immediately took the esteemed title of "Scalp on Face" for himself.

Joe Dorris, the *New Era*'s retired editor/publisher and part-time columnist, got the honor of being named next...He was called "Ancient Buffalo."

Now, old Joe—a member of the Kentucky Journalism Hall of Fame who died in November 1999 at the age of 91 after more than six decades of newspapering—was a legendary journalist. He wrote the first news report of the "Little Green Men" encounter in Kelly back in August 1955. And, it was Joe, who, as a cub reporter for a daily Chicago newspaper in the 1930s, had been given the assignment to interview Lou Gehrig of the New York Yankees. Well, Gehrig snubbed poor Joe, not wanting to waste his time on a rookie newspaperman. Turns out some other fellow on the team was more compassionate and offered his time for Joe to get an interview with him....His name? Babe Ruth.

After Joe, the "Injun" naming game focused on me—Rob Dollar (aka "Death" *News Brother*), who forever became known in *New Era* circles as "Bitches Like Thunder."

Joe claimed it was the best title given out and was a perfect fit for me, considering I had mastered The Art of Griping.

OK...I plead guilty...It's true I can get pretty loud on occasion, especially when I get excited....But, I suppose I should count my lucky stars because my "Injun" name could have been a lot worse...Just ask the advertising representative who had to walk around the *New Era* for his entire career known to everyone as "Walks Like Squaw."

There were times, over the years, when life at the *New Era* came close to being like the crazy Clarksville days.

At one point in my *New Era* career, the newspaper fielded a coed basketball team that played a game or two for charity every year. Once, yours truly achieved hoops glory, sharing top scoring honors with a shady teammate who worked as a mid-level manager in the newspaper's Circulation Department. Later, my basketball buddy got convicted of a notorious 1990 murder in

Hopkinsville and spent 13 years on Kentucky's Death Row. His conviction eventually was overturned, and he was given a new trial. In 2009, a Christian County jury sentenced him to life in prison after again convicting him in the murder case.

For many years, I got quite a kick reminding people—particularly those in the Executive Wing at the *New Era*—that one of Kentucky's Death Row inmates had once been a *New Era* manager. Well...I always thought it was pretty funny.

Time marched on, as it does, and I couldn't—actually, I wouldn't—put *The News Brothers* in the rear view mirror. I wondered whether there would be more merrymaking in the future.

But, friends and foes alike knew better...The bond of this brotherhood was too strong to ever break...There would be a lot more laughs on the horizon...It just had to be...Why?

Because....

> All work and no play make *The News Brothers* dull boys...
> All work and no play make *The News Brothers* dull boys...
> All work and no play make *The News Brothers* dull boys...
> All work and no play make *The News Brothers* dull boys...
> All work and no play make *The News Brothers* dull boys...

Rob Dollar chats with Hollywood actress Morgan Fairchild at the 1984 Barbara Mandell Celebrity Softball Tournament in Nashville, Tennessee.

Rob Dollar visits with Peter Fonda in Fulton, Kentucky, in June 1986 during the nationwide "Hands Across America" event.

Rob Dollar interviews Bob Hope during the 1988 Barbara Mandrell Celebrity Softball Tournament in Nashville, Tennessee. At the time, Hope, now dead, was 88 years old. Dollar was working for the *Kentucky New Era*.

Rob Dollar takes photographs at the site of a major train derailment near Crofton, Kentucky, in June 1988. One of the cars on the train contained toxic chemicals, which resulted in an evacuation of thousands of residents in Western Kentucky.

Rob Dollar stands in front of Air Force One while covering the presidential visit of "Bush 41" at Fort Campbell for the *Kentucky New Era* in October 1992.

Tim Ghianni spent 10 years at the *Nashville Banner* as a senior editor and award-winning columnist. The afternoon newspaper ceased publication in February 1998.

Chapter 21
(Rob)

THE YEARS IN THE WILDERNESS

The News Brothers were scattered to the wind now, and there was little, if any, laughing going on in the newsrooms of America.

The boys no longer were together, making merry and making good journalism. The frolicking would stop for more than a quarter of a century—until we were reunited by the evil forces of Korporate Amerika.

Ironically, it was the very same corporate mentality and small-minded people that originally sent us packing that—many, many years later—gave us new life so we could get back to fighting for "Truth, Justice and the American Way."

By the mid-to late 1980s, the original four *News Brothers* still had ink in their veins and were working for newspapers. Tim was at the *Nashville Banner*, Jerry Manley was at *The Tennessean*, Jim Lindgren was at the *Indianapolis (Ind.) News*, and I was at the *Kentucky New Era* in Hopkinsville.

Scott Shelton, who had replaced Jim in the core *News Brothers* foursome when "Flash" went to Indy, was still living in Clarksville. However, he was about to, or already had, abandoned his career as a newsman to take a job as communications director in the Clarksville Mayor's Office.

So, we—Jim, who lived several hundred miles away, being the only exception—were within a short driving distance of each other. But, probably because we didn't work together, there was little to no frolicking for *The News Brothers* for the better part of the next 28 years. Of course, Tim and Jerry worked in the same building—Nashville's legendary 1100 Broadway address was the home for the great *Banner* and remains home for *The Tennessean*—for most of that time and saw each other nearly every day, but it wasn't a *News Brothers* kind of thing. You know, they just did their daily flying chest bump as Tim left work in the mid-afternoon just when Jerry was coming to his night-shift job in the same building. Just kidding…Actually, they just went for walks sometimes and talked about exploding cigarettes and such.

The precious time wasted during these "out-in-the-wilderness" years is my only regret when it comes to my life as a *News Brother*. Hell, there's no telling what we could have done…But, I guess each of us was doing what it took at this time in our lives to make our mark on journalism and contribute to the good in the world.

So, contact was minimal, but it was treasured and memorable whenever it did occur.

On several occasions, when I ventured off to Clarksville for entertainment, I ran into Scott and we talked about those daring days of *The News Brothers*.

Every year, at Christmas time, Tim and I exchanged Christmas cards—and the card we sent each other always was that same "Have a Damn Nice Christmas" card of *News Brothers* lore.

There were telephone calls over those years, too. Both Jerry and Tim called me several times on behalf of their newspapers about big stories I was working on—including the indictment, arrest and federal drug trial of Christian County Sheriff Bill Dillard, who was famous for not only his "pastries" comment but also for being the first-elected black sheriff in Kentucky—seeking my help as a professional courtesy.

Now, the Dillard story—it included links to criminals associated with the "Dixie Mafia," some of whom had been robbing drug dealers around the country while flashing Christian County "special deputy badges"—really "humbled" me….I guess that's the best way to put it after you get a big head and then are reminded of your place in life.

Here's what happened: Hot on the trail of the bad guys during the Dillard investigation, I called the FBI office in Flint, Mich., where a thug with one of the special deputy badges had been arrested and was behind bars.

"This is Rob Dollar, and I'm a reporter for the *Kentucky New Era* newspaper in Hopkinsville, Kentucky," I told the FBI agent who answered the telephone. There was silence. Then, after a long pause, came the response: "WOW!"

In hindsight, I probably should have told the smart aleck I also was almost-CIA agent R. Stanley Dollar.

During the lean years of staying in touch, *The News Brothers*, more often than not, went looking to reach out and touch each other only after hearing about something that reminded them about the old days.

My phone at the office rang on Sept. 18, 1989—the day after Stephen Drake, one of the Rodney Long assailants, was shot and killed by another inmate at the old Tennessee State Penitentiary in Nashville. After I answered the call, unaware of the news, Tim was on the other end: "Good shot!" he said, instead of 'hello."

When the Hollywood movie, "A League of their Own"— featuring Tom Hanks, Madonna and Geena Davis—was released in 1992, Tim called to congratulate me on my second starring role in a major motion picture. (The first was the "Flapjacks" movie.) Actually, Denny Adkins and I were only "extras" in the baseball movie, filmed, in part, during the fall of 1991 in nearby Evansville, Ind. We had "bit parts" in one large crowd scene—along with 5,400 other people.

"Yeah, I was watching the movie and the part with those thousands of fans, cheering and clapping up in the stands, flashed up on the screen... I spotted you and Denny right away. Damn...You guys really stole the scene," Tim joked.

Several years later—on Feb. 20, 1998—the day the *Nashville Banner* shut down and put out its last edition, I called Tim to offer my condolences and support. He landed at *The Tennessean*, which had bought and folded the *Banner*. His maverick ways of doing things right or not at all were pretty much tolerated at the *Banner*, a rebellious little junior partner in a Joint Operating Agreement. His boss there occasionally grunted, but Tim's instincts yielded results. But "upstairs," when he joined *The Tennesssean*, he found out quickly that his way of doing things didn't really endear him. He told me once that what bothered him most was no one really smiled at that paper. And no one sweared, out of fear of offending someone. And in this sterilized new form of korporate journalism, all smokers went outside, so a cigarette load wouldn't do the trick.

Although we hardly saw each other, Tim was always there for me when I needed encouragement—when I needed to laugh.

On one occasion in the early 1990s, I wrote an investigative story about a woman on Hopkinsville City Council, who secretly married a convicted drug dealer still serving time in a state prison. The councilwoman lied to me when I asked her about the marriage. Later, after my front-page story was published in the *Kentucky New Era*, she sued me in federal court. She said I had invaded her privacy, insisting if she had wanted a story about her marriage in the newspaper, she would have invited me to the wedding. The suit also was an attempt to force me to reveal my confidential source for the story.

Articles about the lawsuit—the first ever filed against the *Kentucky New Era*, which was founded in 1869, for a story in the paper—appeared in newspapers around the country. A few of my journalist friends even read about it in *Editor & Publisher* magazine.

After giving a deposition in the case one afternoon, my phone rang and it was Tim. "I'm worried about you. I think you should consider hiring Court Agate to represent you in this case," he quipped, breaking into a sick laugh.

But, as it turned out, I never needed the services of "Court Agate," The suit was dismissed, appealed, and then dismissed again by the 6th Circuit Court of Appeals in Cincinnati—one step away from the U.S. Supreme Court.

The News Brothers reunited for the first time in mid-February 1994, when Scott "Badger" Shelton celebrated his 40th birthday. Now-wife Elise Frederick Shelton arranged a surprise *News Brothers* birthday party at their Clarksville home. Tim, Jerry, and I were in the same room together for the first time in six or seven years. Denny Adkins, still a *News Brothers* hanger-on, also was at the party, because I couldn't get rid of him. One thing I noticed almost immediately….Damn…We were all getting old…

Tim couldn't stay late. He was headed to work at 3:30 in the morning, but he wanted to be there. I think he mostly came because he missed his brothers, particularly his main comrade in arms. Me. Perhaps, he told me later, we can work together again. Slay some dragons, crooks and save a monkey or two.

At the end of July 2003, I became the first of *The News Brothers* to leave my beloved profession of journalism. Although I worked for a family-owned newspaper, the top management had begun using Korporate Amerika principles to run it. At the time of my departure, I was the managing editor, and I was gone, on my own terms, once I determined there was no way I could ever change the direction of a newspaper interested only in making money—and lots of it, at the expense of everything else, including the reader.

One of my last memorable experiences as a newspaperman was a nearly month-long assignment as an "embedded reporter" with the 101st Airborne Division (Air Assault).

In mid-March, just four months before my newspaper career ended, I was with Fort Campbell troops—hunkered down in the Kuwaiti desert, just miles from the Iraq border—when the bombs and missiles started exploding with the launch of the Iraq War. By placing myself in a war zone, my duty as a war correspondent, albeit short, was undertaken at great personal and financial risk—with questionable life insurance protection, no medical insurance, and absolutely no coverage from the newspaper's workers' compensation policy. Everything I did in the theater of operations—whether looking down at hostile Iraq while flying in a helicopter or riding in a convoy to God only knows where—had to be weighed carefully…

There's an old adage I've always considered good advice: "Lead, follow, or get out of the way." As a newsroom manager, I always made it a point to lead by example.

No one else at the *Kentucky New Era* had stepped forward to go off to war, so the fortysomething editor—me—was the one who went…Someone had to be there with the troops to witness and report this huge story for our loyal readers.

Rob Dollar poses outside a small village in Kosovo in August 2001 while reporting for the *Kentucky New Era* on a peacekeeping mission undertaken by Fort Campbell's 101st Airborne Division (Air Assault).

Rob Dollar is shown aboard an Army Chinook helicopter, en route to Camp Bondsteel in Kosovo, where he and some local government officials spent a few days visiting troops as part of a goodwill mission.

Rob Dollar rappels down the wall at the Air Assault School at Fort Campbell in October 2000. His opportunity to tackle the wall was part of the day's activities for the 2000-2001 Class of Leadership Hopkinsville-Christian County.

So, off I went into Harm's Way, carrying my helmet, gas mask and body armor—as well as the nagging thought in the back of my mind that it was quite possible I might never come home.

If there's one thing a newspaperman learns early in his career, it's that life can play some awfully cruel tricks. I made it back from Kuwait—without a scratch—but two of my colleagues left behind to do the newspaper's work in Hopkinsville weren't as lucky.

On my first day back at the office, my immediate boss, David Riley, told me he had been diagnosed with Non-Hodgkin's lymphoma—a cancer that would take his life two years later. On Saturday, April 19, 2003, only a few weeks after my return from Kuwait, David called my house to inform me that our top reporter, E. L. "Lynn" Gold, had dropped dead of a heart attack while mowing his yard.

At the time of his death, Lynn was 49. It's no joke he was considered the Mike Wallace (Think "60 Minutes") of the Hopkinsville news media. Public officials and businessmen got real nervous whenever this guy E.L. Gold was on the other end of their telephone call. A bulldog of a reporter and early pioneer of computer-assisted reporting, Lynn had been a coal miner who, in mid-life, got his college degree and became a journalist.

Nothing, and I mean nothing, ever got Lynn down about the profession of journalism...Not the low pay, long hours or even lack of appreciation from the big bosses and public. This bearded, mountain-of-a-man was damn happy to be a reporter. "This is the best job I've ever had," he'd tell me, slurping a milkshake at his desk as he worked on some story that was sure to give the paper's new young publisher an ulcer.

Now, *New Era* Publisher Taylor Hayes, who certainly was no Bob Carter, really admired me for having the balls to run with the dogs of war. Visiting with me in my office, before I left the country, I remember him telling me he had actually considered going with me on this great adventure—as my photographer. But, he confessed, he realized after considerable thought that he was just too important to the newspaper to put his life at risk. Pretty funny, huh? The man with the money was too important to die, but good, old Rob was expendable because he was no VIP...Our little pep talk really made me feel good about my decision.

During my newspaper career, I was never a stranger when it came to volunteering for something no one else wanted to do. Back in August 2001, I reported on Fort Campbell troops on a peacekeeping mission—from war-torn Kosovo, traveling with several area mayors and VIPs who were part of a goodwill trip organized by Army officials. I had pitched a fit to go, and *New Era* President Chuck Henderson, a soon-to-be Civilian Aide to the Secretary of the Army, had the clout to make it happen for me.

And, in January 1991, I had volunteered and was chosen to be part of a 10-person media pool from the Fort Campbell area that was supposed to deploy to Saudi Arabia to cover the 101st during the first Gulf War. However, the pool—which also included legendary Nashville television newsman Chris Clark—never made it out of the United States. The Army canceled our trip about one week before the air war got under way, with little explanation for the decision.

News Brothers, as everyone finds out, are always the first to volunteer for dangerous assignments, even if it means having to walk through the fires of Hell to get the story.

I'm certain one of my Army friends, David H. Petraeus, appreciated my can-do spirit. The retired four-star general now is the Director of the CIA, something that makes me smile. Remember, I was an almost-CIA agent, and if things had turned out differently, I might be working for him today, fighting the War on Terror.

About two months after I returned to the States from my overseas assignment as an embedded reporter, I got an e-mail from Petraeus, then a major general still in Iraq commanding the 101st Airborne Division (Air Assault) at locations around Mosul.

Petraeus' daughter, Anne, a college student, was interning for the summer at the *Kentucky New Era*, and she was under my supervision since I was the newsroom manager.

"*…Also glad to hear our daughter will be gainfully employed this summer. I hope that you'll find that she's a pretty good writer,*" Petraeus wrote. "*I know that she's excited about the opportunity to learn about the newspaper business. Don't hesitate to work her hard! Best/ Air Assault— DHP*"

In the spring of 2011, Petraeus, finishing up his final command as an Army general, was in charge of the war in Afghanistan. He sent me and a few other Hopkinsville friends his "challenge coin" as the commander of NATO and International Security Assistance Force (ISAF) troops in Afghanistan. It was quite an honor.

My exit from the newspaper world came about four years after the *New Era* shamelessly fired my longtime friend and the paper's former top editor, Mike Herndon.

Mike, as a top manager at the newspaper, once refused a hefty raise in pay, telling the big boss he could not in good conscience accept the money when many of those who worked for him had been denied salary increases for two or more years due to a slumping economy.

A great newspaperman, Mike put 30 of the best years of his life into practicing journalism in his hometown of Hopkinsville and succeeded his father, Cecil Herndon, as *New Era* editor in the fall of 1990.

It was Cecil Herndon who had hired me at the *New Era*, and I used to joke with him that he was the one responsible for all the havoc I had created in Hopkinsville over the years. An insurance salesman before he became a newspaperman, Cecil died at the age of 82 in mid-April 2010—nearly 20 years after his retirement from the *New Era*.

Now, Mike Herndon, too, had gone toe-to-toe with the new publisher in the post-Bob Carter days at the *New Era*, doing everything in his power to protect his people from the evils of Korporate Amerika.

He was not happy with the new way of doing business at the family-owned newspaper: Like treating your employees like cattle...Hiring consultants to tell the big boss what he wanted to hear...Allowing non-editorial executives to undermine the authority of top editors by blatantly interfering in newsroom matters...Putting pressure on reporters to steer clear of controversy and focus on puff pieces...And finally, what may have been the final straw, or damn close to it, the introduction of a company "mascot" to lead the corporate cheer for bigger and bigger profits.

Unbelievably, the *New Era* spent thousands of dollars to buy an air-conditioned costume for "Read The Rooster," and then management actually had the gall to look for volunteers in the Editorial Department to wear the costume at public events.

Mike Herndon was a popular public figure in the community, and the news of his firing in March 1999 was buried in the newspaper. It was announced to the public in a "news brief" that noted—in "Korporate speak"—he had "vacated" his job. The entire affair was shabby treatment for a decent man, loyal employee and great boss. He deserved much better.

Mike's successor—a highly-regarded and experienced newspaper manager recruited from a Virginia paper—lasted less than three months on the job before the powers-that-be at the *New Era* called the county sheriff and had him escorted from the building. You'd think a newspaper, in the business of providing information to the public, would feel compelled to offer up an explanation. But there was none—not even to the people who worked at the newspaper. The guy who had been editor just kind of "vacated" the face of the earth...well, Hopkinsville, anyway.

Funny thing, many years later, sometime around November 2008, I saw him on national television ...At the age of 73, he had gone back to college somewhere in Tennessee and joined the basketball team, soon apparently becoming the oldest player ever to score in a college basketball game.

When the new editor met his demise in Hopkinsville, I wasn't around to watch the soap opera. Disappointed and angry over the Mike Herndon firing—particularly the fact the publisher had initially "massaged" the truth and told me to my face that Mike had decided to leave the editor's job on his own—I had left the *New Era* and Hopkinsville to go to work for a newspaper in Fayetteville, N.C.

I returned to Hopkinsville to become the *New Era*'s managing editor the following year, in the spring of 2000, at the urging of David Riley, who by then was the newspaper's editor.

Kentucky New Error.

HOPKINSVILLE, KY., MONDAY, MARCH 22, 1999

Rooster is vacated; move stuns everyone

**By GRACE LEWIS
And CYNTHIA HOSKINS**
Mike Herndon Hinee

SHORTTIME NEW ERA mascot Read the Rooster has stunned the community by announcing he will vacate his high-profile position with Hopkinsville's daily newspaper.

Rooster said NEW ERA management "helped him make up his mind" to leave the job he had held since last June upon his return to work from a two-week vacation.

"I believe it's for the best," Rooster said. "I'm overworked, frustrated and I'm sick and tired of fighting management officials over this silly dress code."

Rooster said "philosophical differences" with NEW ERA management also played a part in his decision to fly the coop.

"I can't communicate with those bird brains any more. The NEW ERA has become a real CLUSTER-CLUCK lately," he explained.

NEW ERA Publisher Taylor Hayes said there are no immediate plans to fill the position vacated by Rooster, who was known for wearing sunglasses and loud Hawaiian shirts.

"Just like any other business, our newspaper must deal with change in a variety of areas," Hayes said.

"Until the mascot's position is filled on a permanent basis, I guess we just won't have one. But I have the

utmost confidence that Jeff Jobe or Buff and Lott will help us out of this mess after we pay him another small retainer."

Sources close to Bibb and Lott indicate Rooster's successor already is on the drawing board.

The new mascot — Wiggle the Weasel — apparently will reflect the newspaper's philosophy of anything goes as long as it makes a buck.

A news conference at the Chamber of Commerce is expected sometime next week to introduce Wiggle the Weasel.

Rooster becomes the second top NEW ERA official to vacate his job this month.

Longtime Managing Editor Mike Herndon vacated

his job on March 2.

Herndon — who, like Rooster, looked way cool in sunglasses — was just a little chick still in school when he started writing sports stories for the NEW ERA.

After graduating from Hopkinsville High School in 1965, Herndon enrolled at Hopkinsville Community College, and then the University of Kentucky.

Herndon was editor of the UK student newspaper, the Kentucky Kernel. When he wasn't busy organizing beer blasts at the Sigma Nu Fraternity House, Herndon stayed busy at the student newspaper, routinely angering university officials with his hard-hitting style of journalism.

"Where did this little troublemaker come from," the university president cried. "Maybe we can get the folks at that chicken-shit newspaper in Hopkinsville to take him off our hands."

Sure enough, Herndon was lured back to the NEW ERA when then-publisher Bob Carter said the paper would fold if he didn't come home quick.

NEW ERA, Herndon covered everything from the Women of the Moose to school board meetings.

Herndon earned a reputation for getting stories no other reporter could — like the time he drove miles to the scene of an airplane crash in a cornfield. Yep, he got the story, even if he did forget to put film in his camera. But who needed a picture when Herndon could make it much more interesting with his words?

As a city editor and managing editor, Herndon had a sterling record for hiring only the best writers and photographers. Who could forget the reporter who spent his

weekends writing sobering stories from a bureau inside the County Jail? Or the "Graceful" reporter who didn't mind wearing a little black dress and flirting with the commanding general at Fort Campbell to get her stories.

Maybe the smartest one of them all was the young man from Oak Ridge, Tenn., who came to work one day, took a good look around him and then never came back.

SOMETIMES YOU EAT THE ROOSTER AND SOMETIMES THE ROOSTER EATS YOU: Managing Editor Mike Herndon chows down on a fine feathered friend.

R. ROOSTER

City editor, yes. Managing editor, yes. Food editor, now wait just a minute...

By BENITA CORLEY
Mike Herndon Hinee

MIKE HERNDON'S award-winning journalism career may have included various roles and spanned three decades, but it's what he didn't accomplish that delights Ray Duckworth.

Duckworth said he is so happy Herndon didn't serve as a food editor or a travel editor.

Herndon might have been tempted to write about one of his more memorable trips with Duckworth.

It went like this:

Driving home from St. Louis, Herndon suggested that after getting to the east side of the city and interesting with Interstate 57 that the pair stop and eat lunch. Duckworth, having made the trip to St. Louis before, suggested Herndon travel north on I-57 because he didn't remember there being any eating places south of the I-57 junction.

Herndon obliged and shortly after taking the north-bound lane pointed out to Duckworth that the first sign for an exit would be at Dix — 7 miles away. As they travelled north, seeing nothing but flat land and cornfields, Herndon let loose.

"Boy, Duckworth, I can't wait to get to Dix," he quipped. "Is it Big Dix or Little Dix?"

Herndon soon found out. They exited the off ramp to find only a small, round convenience store. The pair went in and made their pur-

chases — a soda and a pack of crackers — and returned to the car.

"Boy, Duckworth, I sure am glad we came all the way to Dix just for a pack of nabs and a pop!" Herndon insisted. "You noticed how big that store was didn't you? When the two of us went in, the clerk had to step outside because the store was too small for all three of us to fit in!"

Herndon insisted that Duckworth drive for a while. And as their 14-mile side trip neared its end at the I-57/I-70 junction, Herndon spoke up again.

"This is why I wanted you to drive south," Herndon said. "I want to see this desolated exit down here. Why, Duckworth, there's a Cracker Barrel!

There's a Stuckey's! But no, that's got to be my imagination because there's not supposed to be anything here! Say, I sure am glad we went 14 miles out of our way to go to the big city of Dix! This sure is a nutritious lunch."

Needless to say, the experience was buried a time or two more as the pair concluded the four-hour drive from St. Louis back to Hopkinsville. And naturally, Herndon repeated the story to all whom would listen in the coming days ... months ... years.

"Yes," Duckworth says now 10 years later. "I sure am glad Herndon wasn't the newspaper's travel editor or food editor. Otherwise, all 16,000 subscribers of the New Era would have learned, too."

A promising future
Hope, idealism and optimism beam from the face of this young person as she prepares to embark on the career of their choosing. The big one on the right is unidentified.

NEW ERA/John Summers

Looking for a home
This mild-mannered journalist is among the many individuals vacated each month at the county Animal Shelter. The adoption fee is waived for the pictured animal. Animals can be adopted at the shelter on Russellville Road from 10:50 a.m. to 4:30 p.m. Thursday through Friday. They are kept for one week and then destroyed.

NEW ERA/Grayson Hood

The newsroom staff of the *Kentucky New Era* produced this fake newspaper front as a farewell gift to Mike Herndon when he was fired from his editor's job at the Hopkinsville newspaper in March 1999.

It was quite clear by this stage of the game that newspapers had become nothing but a business, and there was little anyone could do to fight the quality-killing changes and other Korporate influences on the journalism profession.

The late Pete Wright, a former photographer for *The Associated Press* and *New Era* colleague, put it best one day while we pondered the future, moaning about the latest Korporate hatchet job. "It's The Golden Rule," Pete reminded us. "He who has the gold, makes the rules."

Pete's nickname was "Little Buck." He had left big-time journalism and relocated to nearby Trenton, Kentucky, in order to take care of his seventysomething father, "Buck" Wright, who had health problems. Pete was 49 when he started working at the *New Era* in December 1995—already a living legend from his AP days of photographing the biggest news and sports events in the world.

It was a widely-circulated Pete Wright photograph that, in part, led to Woody Hayes' firing as head football coach at Ohio State the morning after the Dec. 29, 1978, Gator Bowl in Jacksonville, Fla. Pete and his camera were right there when the 65-year-old coach slugged a Clemson player who had been knocked out of bounds on the Buckeyes' sidelines following an interception.

Old Pete—ironically, he died of cancer in May 2000 at age 53, several years before his sick father passed away—used to share another tidbit of wisdom with us: "Sometimes, you get The Bear, and sometimes The Bear gets YOU!"

Eventually, I went to work for the City of Hopkinsville, as a mayoral aide, helping out my longtime friend, Rich Liebe, who was in his second term as the mayor of Kentucky's fifth-largest city. "Da Mayor" and I did some, as he would say, "extra good" things at City Hall. There were initiatives to address flooding, economic development, retail trade, downtown revitalization, and deteriorating inner-city neighborhoods. We also opened an aquatic center for the community's children and refurbished Fort Campbell Memorial Park—the city's tribute to the 248 soldiers killed in the December 1985 Gander air tragedy. Our work at the park included convincing the Army to donate the shell of a UH-1 "Huey" helicopter for an eye-catching static display.

Politics and a new mayor ended my city government job on Dec. 31, 2006. Interestingly, Dan Kemp had become Hopkinsville's new mayor after my boss decided not to seek re-election. Kemp was the former attorney for the *Kentucky New Era* and the guy who had drawn up my will and the paperwork protecting the newspaper from civil liability when I went overseas as a war correspondent. While at war, I received hundreds of e-mails, thanking me for the great job I was doing, including one from the future mayor. Oh, well. In the end, hero worship, I suppose, is greatly overrated.

Later, after leaving City Hall, I worked a federal appointment for the U.S. Department of Commerce/Bureau of the Census as a public affairs official responsible for promoting awareness of the 2010 Census in 21 Western Kentucky counties. Tim told me I was the hardest working U.S. government official he'd ever met in his life, and someone who actually got results—participation rates increased for all my counties, from 4 to 21 percent, compared to the 2000 Census rates.

It was during my hectic years at City Hall (2004-2006) that a rebirth of *The News Brothers* took place. By this time, I was pretty gray and long in the tooth. So was Tim.

I convinced Tim to come up to Hopkinsville a few times to do stories for *The Tennessean* on the "Little Green Men" incident at Kelly—having helped organize a festival to mark the 50th anniversary in 2005—and the special friendship between local Green Berets and Robin Moore, a new resident of our city and author of such best-selling books as "The Green Berets" and "The French Connection."

The City of Hopkinsville proudly declared a "Tim Ghianni Day" and even made old "Flapjacks" an honorary mayor to show our appreciation for his positive stories about Hoptown, "The Pearl of the Pennyrile." As for that parade Tim wanted—with floats and marching bands—well....it just never worked out...

Tim enjoyed these trips and our friendship that had survived the long and winding roads, so he began scheduling feature stories that would push him up in my part of the world. He called me when he was working a story in Guthrie, Kentucky, where we both had friends and where he had earned the admiration of Robert Penn Warren. I also met up with him in Fairview, Kentucky, when he did a travel piece on the Jefferson Davis Monument, a presidential-style obelisk in the middle of the cornfields of Kentucky's Mennonite country.

While on business in Nashville, I ventured over to *The Tennessean*, where both Tim and Jerry worked, and presented them with Keys to the City for their support of "Da Mayor" and the City of Hopkinsville.

My Nashville visits also gave me an opportunity to visit with another former *New Era* colleague, Ray Duckworth, who was my roommate when we worked together at *The Fayetteville Observer* in Fayetteville, N.C. For about a year (1999-2000), "The Kentucky Boys" put out some award-winning newspapers in The Tar Heel State while fighting killer hurricanes and record-setting ice and snow storms. Ray eventually spent nearly a decade at *The Tennessean* before he saw the handwriting on the wall and left newspaper work for a relatively safe government job in his native North Carolina.

People who met Ray and became close friends with him knew he was capable of letting out the funniest laugh ever heard if he really got tickled about something. The laugh—some thought it sounded like a wounded loon, or maybe a flock of mad geese—caught quite a few strangers off-guard over the years...OK. It actually scared the hell out of them. And that could be pretty funny, too.

Nowadays, Ray often writes happy notes and Facebook updates about his good life. You know, he even gets excited about drinking a Cheerwine on his deck, while watching the planes fly over his neighborhood. Ray, it would seem, has managed to put those days as a hard-charging newsman behind him.

In August 2007, the gutless, hypocritical slimes of Korporate Amerika finally picked off Tim, but only after the fight of their good-for-nothing lives. He wouldn't back down, either and as the pressure on him mounted for him to leave, he became more determined to stay long enough for them to make him leave. And pay him something for the effort.

Jim's newspaper career had ended in 2005, thanks to the same corporate suits and their short-sighted logic. It took them longer to get Jerry. He was officially retired as a newspaperman on June 30, 2011. He told Tim he was surprised when they handed him the paperwork and told him he had just retired. Tim asked him where he'd been parking his head the last few years. How could he not see it coming?

During these years of gloom and doom, *The News Brothers* rose from the ashes and began to meet more frequently to make some noise about the fall of American journalism.

The original four *News Brothers*—Tim, Jerry, Jim and I—had a reunion in October 2009 in Nashville. One year later to the month, we reunited again in Clarksville. Jim couldn't make that reunion, but Tim, Jerry, and I were there along with Scott "Badger" Shelton, David "Teach" Ross, Billy "StrawBilly" Fields and Frank Wm. "Wuhm" White.

Between jobs, during these "out-in-the-wilderness" years, I made it my personal mission in life to use the new technology to spread the story of *The News Brothers*. Keeping that goal in mind, we started making movies again—and lots of them,

Thirty years later, they call these movies, "YouTube" videos.

Yes…*The News Brothers* are back, but it's like we never left.

And, in most cases, we're larger than ever.

The News Brothers reunite in October 2009 at Centennial Park in Nashville, Tennessee. From left are: Jim Lindgren, Jerry Manley, Rob Dollar and Tim Ghianni.

An October 2010 reunion took place in Clarksville, Tennessee. The above photograph was shot in front of the Montgomery County Courthouse, just across the street from *The Leaf-Chronicle* building, in downtown Clarksville, Tennessee. From left are: Jerry Manley, Tim Ghianni, Scott Shelton, Rob Dollar and David Ross.

Rob Dollar is shown at Camp Thunder, on the Kuwait-Iraq border, in Mid-March 2003, just days before the start of Operation Iraqi Freedom.

Among hundreds of embedded reporters, Dollar was issued the identification badge at left to cover the combat operations of one of the two Screaming Eagle aviation brigades.

Chapter 22
(Rob)

LIFE'S DEFINING MOMENTS

Every person on this earth has experiences that shape the course of their life, for better or for worse. They're called defining moments...They help make you who you are...Sometimes the experiences are obvious when they happen, and other times it may take years and years to acknowledge their effect on your life.

On March 20, 2003, I found myself taking cover in a trench—wearing a gas mask and a nuclear, biological chemical warfare suit—out in the remote Kuwaiti Desert, only miles from the Iraq border. Operation Iraqi Freedom was under way, and Saddam Hussein had just launched his first missile attack of the war on Camp Thunder, where about 4,000 soldiers and most of the helicopter assets of the 101st Airborne Division (Air Assault) were based. Several embedded reporters—including me, then an editor for the *Kentucky New Era*—were with the men and women of the 159th Aviation Brigade when the fighting broke out.

Huddled in that trench, with 20 to 25 Fort Campbell soldiers, I vividly remember a battalion chaplain leading everyone in prayer as we waited for the incoming missiles. At that moment, no one knew if we were going to live or die. Fortunately, the one enemy missile headed directly for us was shot down by a Patriot Missile Battery, only minutes before hitting its target.

Later, I found out just how lucky we had been...When Saddam launched his missiles into Kuwait and at our camp, two of our Patriot Missile Batteries were down for maintenance. The third, the one that engaged the enemy, fired three missiles—one misfired, one missed the target, and the third destroyed the incoming Iraqi Ababil-100 missile

My old pal, at the time the commander of the 101st Airborne Division (Air Assault)—Maj. Gen. David H. Petraeus—had fought for authorization to put Patriot Missile Batteries at Camp Thunder, which had been a former Iraqi Army camp during the first Gulf War in 1990 and 1991.

His foresight probably saved thousands of American lives that day—including mine. Had the missile not been shot down, the Iraq War would have gotten off to a catastrophic start. "If it had hit right here, it would have taken out lots of people," one of the soldiers at Camp Thunder told a newspaper reporter.

After the initial attack, there were more than a dozen other alerts that first long day of the war—warning of incoming missiles, possibly carrying biological or chemical agents—that had us running back and forth, from our tents to the trenches.

During a breather, between the mad dashes, I picked up my satellite telephone and called my newspaper back in Hopkinsville, Kentucky. We were isolated out in the desert, and I wanted to try and get some information on what was happening…I also wanted to hear a comforting and reassuring voice from home.

The voice that answered my phone call belonged to a relatively new copy editor I had only recently hired. "Hello, Rob," he said. "Hey, we're on deadline right now and real busy. Can you call back? We'll talk to you later."

CLICK.

The memory is funny all these years later. But, I wasn't laughing when I thought my life was hanging by a thread.

The terrifying experience of trying to stay alive during war, for me, was a defining moment in life. Scared shitless, I remember praying and promising God if he got me out of this mess, I'd never sweat about any of the little stuff in life again and appreciate everyone around me.

This defining moment, in later years, was reinforced while I was working in the Mayor's Office. I represented the City of Hopkinsville at dozens and dozens of memorial services and funerals for Fort Campbell soldiers killed in Iraq and Afghanistan.

At these solemn occasions, I often interacted with the grieving families. As it turned out, a few of the soldiers who had shared the same trench with me at Camp Thunder may have later made the supreme sacrifice for their country.

While at City Hall, sometime in the late spring of 2004, Hopkinsville Mayor Rich Liebe and I went to Fort Campbell to visit with Gen. Petraeus, who had returned home from Iraq and was preparing to leave the post for his next command. During that meeting, we thanked him for his friendship and service. We also presented him and another good friend, then-Division Command Sgt. Maj. Marvin L Hill, with certificates that made them Kentucky Colonels.

I'm sure I've had other life-changing experiences that probably qualify as "defining moments" in my life.

Like the time Potsie's (Actor Anson Williams of "Happy Days") future sister-in-law broke my heart in high school. Or when I experienced my very first, end-of-the-world "haboob" in the Kuwaiti desert...Maybe the tragic deaths—at 53, 49, and 52— of three cherished friends and colleagues, within a relatively short, five-year time span.

But, until only recently, it was difficult to pinpoint any significant experiences that stood out for me as defining moments during my Clarksville days.

Then, out of the blue one day, some ghosts from my past knocked on the door. Through connections on Facebook, I was reminded about the long-ago slayings of Rodney Long and Kathy Jane Nishiyama, which occurred in the earliest days of my journalism career.

The triggerman in the Long slaying, David Frey, came up for parole in 2010, and Debbie Dover Azar, of Atlanta., Ga., used social media to coordinate a letter-writing campaign to keep him in prison. She contacted me and asked for my help.

Debbie is the mother of three grown children. She said she'd been Rodney's girlfriend at Austin Peay State University at the time of his disappearance and slaying in February 1982. And proving it's a small world, she also was an Army Brat who had known me during my teenage years at Fort Campbell.

In the meantime, I also discovered that a Hopkinsville acquaintance, Polly Forns, was Kathy Jane Nishiyama's first cousin. For years, Polly, who works at a Hopkinsville funeral home, was unaware of my role as a reporter in the murder case, and I did not know of her connection to the Nishiyama family.

Anyway, with these contacts, I began to relive that early part of my life when I was a brash, young reporter who thought, like most young people, I was going to live forever.

It was no picnic taking that walk down Memory Lane.

Thinking back to the days of the Long and Nishiyama murder cases turned out to be painful therapy for me, Back when the murders occurred, things were happening so fast that everything was like a blur, and I never really gave much thought to what, if anything, I was feeling at the time.

Maybe becoming a *News Brother* and blocking out the horrors was my way—the only way—to cope over the years with that awful chapter of my life...I don't know...

I never forgot the grisly details of what happened...But now, in this mental playback mode, I was finally being bombarded with the suppressed, or pent-up, emotions from that time so long ago.

What made the two teenager murders even more terrifying to me was the fact they were so random. You or I could have easily been the victims—driving along a city or county road on the way home, or going for a hamburger at Wendy's. I can remember being out and about in Clarksville on both of the murderous nights.

Actual court testimony revealed that Eddie Hartman, convicted in the Nishiyama case, had pulled over at least three other people while driving a Dickson County patrol car the night Kathy Jane disappeared. One of those other victims, Betty Diane Smith, of Palmyra, testified Hartman was impersonating a law enforcement officer and "terrified" her and her daughter, following them for more than nine miles before stopping their car on Tennessee Highway 149, near Palmyra, around 7 p.m.

There but for the grace of God go I....

Not being able to get rid of that thought is something that really messes with your mind.

It's a fact, in the most trying of times, the bond with your "battle buddies" is strongest, and you cope by looking out for each other and uniting as one...

And, I guess that's kind of what happened 30 years ago when two teenagers died senseless deaths, bringing about a defining moment for me and some other newspapermen who would go forward in life to try and always do the right thing as *The News Brothers*.

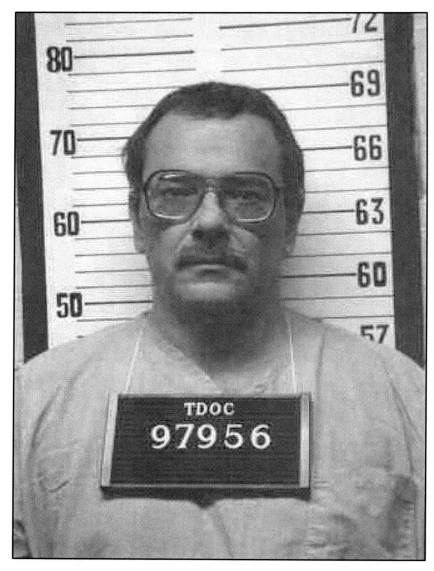

Here is a prison photograph of David Frey, who was the convicted triggerman in the Rodney Wayne Long slaying. He remains behind bars for the 1982 crime.

Chapter 23
(Tim)

A LETTER TO THE PAROLE BOARD

I usually do not get involved in news stories. Yet the stories that propelled *The News Brothers* affect my life to this day.

At least once a week for the last three decades, something reminds me of those hard and horrid days, when death roamed Clarksville and fear reigned.

Sure, my friends and I had fun. But we also suffered. I still do. The cold sweats greet me at night. My stomach tightens. When my own daughter or son are out of my sight, I grow terrified ... even if I know where they are supposed to be. I can't help it.

Of course, Rodney Wayne Long and Kathy Jane Nishiyama had places they were supposed to be, too. They just never made it home.

My kids probably think I'm too strict. I am an old dad, now 60. And my family is the most important thing in my life. And, unfortunately, I know what can happen.

I tremble when the wind shakes the storm door at night, when a car I've never seen passes slowly by the house, when coyotes howl and the moon is full. When doves cry....

Occasionally, I still hear from Barbara Mack, Rodney's mom, and Ralph Nishiyama, Kathy Jane's father. In this new world of instant communication, we're actually Facebook friends. When we visit, they always ask about Rob, how he's doing. How I'm doing.

We all share a bond. Of course, the loss suffered by the two families is much more significant than mine. They lost their children.

All I lost was a piece of my soul. A big piece.

In the spring of 2010, Barbara called me to ask for help when one of her son's killers, David Frey, came up for parole.

Anyway, I wrote this letter to the state parole board on April 19, 2010:

In regard to parole hearing for David Frey, TOMIS Number 0097956

My name is Tim Ghianni.

I am a freelance journalist in Nashville, Tennessee.

I am writing today to loudly oppose any potential parole for David Frey, the convicted murderer of a young man named Rodney Long.

I spent 34 years as a daily newspaper journalist before being "bought out" (better than being laid off) three years ago.

In my time as a newspaper journalist, I came to know the details of way too many stories of the darkest underside of the human spirit.

I found no darker tale than that of the cold-blooded murder of Rodney Wayne Long. Rodney was a good kid, a football player at Austin Peay State University.

Prior to my time as the primary news editor at the local newspaper in Clarksville, I spent time as sports editor and came to know the football players and coaches at Austin Peay State University.

I did not know Rodney when he was alive.

But I feel like he is with me every day due to the vile and cowardly act of David Frey and Stephen Drake. Thankfully, Drake has died in jail.

And if all is right with the world, then Frey too will die in jail. I hope not violently, as Drake did, but of old age, a beaten old man who killed for the sake of killing.

There is no acceptable defense for this kind of slug-like behavior. Frey and Drake duped Rodney into giving them a ride to the edge of Clarksville where they killed him for his car so they could escape the cops who were looking for them in a string of burglaries.

I never understood why they didn't just drop him off on a deserted highway and then keep going.

They didn't need to murder him. They just wanted to.... for the cold and cruel thrill.

As the (associate) editor and human interest columnist at The Leaf-Chronicle in Clarksville, as well as the one who oversaw the Sunday newspaper, I came to be in charge of the coverage of this case as well as another case, the murder of a teenager named Kathy Jane Nishiyama, at about the same time. That killer, Eddie Hartman, already died in jail as well. He died on Death Row.

Anyway, it was a time of deep trauma to the town.

And as I became more and more knowledgeable of the case, following its twists and turns as they searched for Rodney's body and then the killers, it made me increasingly sick to my stomach.

I came to know and love Rodney because I came to know and love his mother, Barbara Mack. I spent a lot of time with her during the search, time with her when his body was found and I attended the funeral that traumatized Rodney's hometown of Rainbow City, Ala., and nearby Gadsden, Ala.

Rodney's murder, and that of the young Nishiyama girl, changed my life. I still have nightmares recalling those days. Both young people are frozen in time by the images of handsome youth that we ran, almost daily, with the stories of their disappearances and murders.

It is said that newspeople are supposed to be cold and distanced. But as I assigned my top reporter, Rob Dollar, to cover the bulk of the breaking news stories (I did some of those as well), I also, as the local columnist, had to help the people of Clarksville come to terms with what had happened.

That meant funerals and trials.

Mostly it meant murders and grieving families.

I am not a death-penalty advocate. But what I am is a believer in justice. No, Frey shouldn't be dragged off and dumped at roadside while people shoot him and laugh.

That's what he did with Rodney, though.

He should spend his life in prison, perhaps regretting what he did. Or maybe answering to a higher power.

Please do not allow anyone to convince you that this truly bad man should walk free... unless he can somehow figure how to bring Rodney back and erase the scars that are still felt by me, by my friends in journalism from that era and most of all, by Rodney's mom and family.

Feel free to contact me if you need me to say this for the record.

Tim Ghianni

Barbara, who truly is dear to me, had asked me if I could attend the hearing in early May 2010 and perhaps testify if she needed another voice.

I planned on being there so I could stare into those evil eyes of David Frey one more time. Those plans were dashed when The Great Flood of 2010 washed away half my Nashville home and closed the highways on the night before the hearing.

Still, she called me when it was over. And I love her. What a strong and wonderful woman.

There was no parole for David Frey. May there never be any parole for Frey. I am a forgiving man, for the most part.

But I hope he rots in hell.

Chapter 24
(Rob)

IT WAS THE CHEMISTRY, STUPID

At this point, nearing the end of this book, I think our readers have a pretty good idea about the birth and roots of *The News Brothers*.

For those who missed the moment of realization: We found each other and came together as a Band of Brothers—holding on for dear life—to save our sanity after the tragic murders of two teenagers traumatized a city and robbed us of all hope and innocence.

Years from now, when this book is out of print, and those of us now alive are taking well-deserved dirt naps, people looking for the answers in life will surely stumble across a photograph of this bunch of damn nice guys, wearing shades and with wistful, world-weary grins on their faces.

And, when they do, they'll want to know more than just the reason for our existence on this earth. They'll wonder: Who were *The News Brothers*? What was it that made these guys so special? What was behind those mysterious shades?

Some will search the pages of history and compare us to "The Fugitives"—Robert Penn Warren and his fellow writers and poets who put the literature spotlight of the world on Vanderbilt University back in the 1920s and 1930s. That's fair enough, as old RPW was among Tim's fans, after old "Flapjacks" spent a good bit of time in Guthrie, Kentucky, the town near Clarksville where folks still speak with Mayberry-like familiarity about "Robert Penn." In fact, Thomas Warren, the poet's brother, befriended

Tim and sent copies of his Guthrie writings to "Robert Penn." Others of the Warren clan also sent the nation's first poet laureate the musings of *The News Brothers* co-founder with the melancholy and poetic soul.

Others may think back to "The Rat Pack"— those fun-loving and hip cats (Frank Sinatra, Dean Martin, Sammy Davis Jr., Peter Lawford and Joey Bishop) who invented the concept of "cool" out there on the Las Vegas Strip during the late 1950s and early 1960s. With "Flap" and me both being of Italian descent, well, I guess you could draw that Frank and Dino parallel.

There might even be a very few, if we're really lucky, who are reminded of the talent and love for humanity that comes across in the great music of The Beatles—the original Fab Four (John Lennon, Paul McCartney, George Harrison and Ringo Starr). Again, with old "Flap" requesting that the four-letter-word-rich "Working Class Hero" be played at his "Farewell to this Earth Party"—when the time comes—that's not a bad assessment. And, yours truly, often sings "Band on the Run" while raking leaves in the front yard.

Of course, we're not them, but there are some similarities. Like all of the great men in these other well-known Bands of Brothers, *The News Brothers* simply clicked… They were perfect fits for one another, just right for the time and place in everyone's lives… "It's the Chemistry, Stupid!"

The truth be known, I always saw a little bit of "The Fugitives," "The Rat Pack," and even The Beatles in the life's work of *The News Brothers*. We were serious. We loved to drink and have fun. And, in the end, all we needed—and wanted—was love. Plenty of it.

This is all well and good, but, there was another group of infamous merrymakers who were more in line with our way of thinking and of handling problems in the workplace. They were some of "The Boys of Summer" and could have given *The News Brothers* a run for their money.

Now, this might sound strange, but I always thought *The News Brothers* were very much like the notorious, and legendary, free spirits on the great New York Yankees baseball teams of the 1950s.

I like baseball, and I always pictured Tim and myself—the heart and soul of *The News Brothers*—as the Mickey Mantle and Billy Martin of the newspaper world.

In the early 1980s, Tim was the rising star at *The Leaf-Chronicle*, our Mickey Mantle, the guy we were pinning our chances of future success on...this at a newspaper already long-recognized as one of the very best in the state of Tennessee.

The Yankees, of course, with "The Mick" in center field, appeared in 12 World Series, winning seven, most of them during the 1950s when they were the powerhouse team in Major League Baseball.

Off the field, Mantle hung out with his teammate and best friend, Billy Martin, an All-Star second baseman with a quick temper, and several other Yankee players who liked to have a good time away from the ballpark—Whitey Ford, Yogi Berra, Hank Bauer and Bill "Moose" Skowron.

Like *The News Brothers*, the Yankee merrymakers were true and dedicated professionals who worked hard at their game to be winners, while fighting back against the stress, fatigue and back-stabbing that comes with being the best of the best.

So, when the time came to play, they played just as hard as they worked. And then the next day, sometimes after staying out all night, they showed up at Yankee Stadium and beat the pants off their opponent. *The News Brothers*, in their days of glory, pulled the same kind of all-nighters before showing up at work and producing an award-winning newspaper.

"Flapjacks" was like "The Mick" in many ways. Mantle could run like the wind and swing the bat and hit homers by the bushels, while old "Flap" was one dude who could write and move people to tears with his wonderful words....Just like "No. 7," old ladies and little kids loved Tim and asked for his autograph. Younger women offered inviting glances. Colleagues saw in him the promise and potential for greatness...He might even become a future editor of *The Leaf-Chronicle*. Everyone, it seemed, was a

"Flap" fan except maybe for "The Big Guy," who always liked Joe DiMaggio better than Mickey Mantle.

Me? I was the spitting image of "Billy The Kid," right in the middle of everything and always mad about something. I was damn good, and I didn't mind making sure everyone knew it...Like Billy, I didn't have to look for trouble. It usually found me. Most often, I was the instigator....I couldn't help it...Billy Martin took his teammates to The Copacabana Nightclub in New York City to celebrate his 29th birthday with a good, old-fashioned brawl, and I persuaded *The News Brothers* to become experts in "The Art of Exaggerating Our Adventures," and getting police officers drunk for entertainment purposes at The Camelot. And, of course, "Billy The Kid" and I shared another trait—we always had one eye on the ladies, the other on our cocktail.

The other *News Brothers* also had their counterparts on the Yankees, when it came to The Art of Merrymaking. Jim "Flash" Lindgren, with those boyish good looks, was *The News Brothers'* Whitey Ford, and Jerry "Chuckles" Manley, with his quiet demeanor and way of saying dumb things that needed to be said every now and then, was our Yogi Berra. The only thing is we just couldn't get old "Chuckles" to wear a catcher's mask instead of that silly, yellow aviator's hat.

As for Scott "Badger" Shelton, he was our "Moose" Skowron....Both steady and reliable, with animal nicknames. And David "Teach" Ross, a future teacher and molder of young minds, was the *News Brother* who had a head on his shoulders—just like Hank Bauer, a smart man who would become a successful manager for three Major League Baseball teams, including the 1966 World Champion Baltimore Orioles..

When the Yankee merrymakers were out on the town, just like us in our heyday, nothing was sacred and no one was safe from the pranks and tomfoolery. Least of all themselves—and ourselves.

But, all good things must come to an end. The management of the Yankees finally concluded Billy Martin's nightlife was a bad influence, especially on Mickey Mantle and Whitey Ford. I guess Yogi Berra already was a lost cause. Maybe Moose and Hank, too.

Anyway, they broke up the merrymakers by trading "Billy The Kid" to Kansas City the month after the May 1957 Copacabana brawl.

The Leaf-Chronicle broke up its merrymakers, *The News Brothers*, for good—at least for a few decades—when they fired me in mid-April 1983. Much later in life, after they were older and wiser, "The Mick" and "Flap" gave up alcohol, but not the beautiful friendships with their highly-combustible, best pals for life.

No more "Flap" and "Death" together at *The Leaf-Chronicle* had the same effect as no more "Mick" and "Billy The Kid" together in the Yankees clubhouse—the party was over. There would be no more fun, for anyone.

In the past 30 or so years, if you've paid attention, you had front-row seats to witness The Dumbing Down of America. And, of course, it was greed—one of the seven deadly sins—that destroyed everything in this country that once was good and important. Like baseball, our national pastime, and newspapers. Today, in Major League Baseball, we have mediocre players, with little talent and multimillion-dollar contracts, earning 10, 20 or more times annually what "The Mick" and other baseball greats got paid in their primes. As for newspapers, well, they no longer are relevant to the everyday life of most Americans, with the exception of some good, local news-oriented weeklies—like *The Todd County (Kentucky) Standard*, published by one of my former *New Era* staffers, Ryan Craig, and the *Nashville Ledger*, put out by Tim's old *Banner* pal, Lyle Graves.

Nothing personal. It's just business. Maybe nowadays, that's the way it is and has to be…But nothing can ever make us forget….When "Mick" swung for the fences, when his best friend stood there to (sometimes literally) prop him up, when there was greatness on the baseball diamond. When newspapers mattered…

Tim Ghianni, with more than 30 years as a professional journalist, earned national recognition for his column-writing at three Tennessee daily newspapers.

Chapter 25
(Tim)

THE WORLD ACCORDING TO TIM "FLAPJACKS" GHIANNI

During my four decades in journalism, I have been blessed with the opportunity to showcase my writing in columns that appeared in three different Tennessee daily newspapers.

Over the years, I probably wrote thousands and thousands of slice-of-life columns—one or more each week—that put the spotlight on ordinary people in the community going about their daily lives.

My column-writing earned me many prestigious journalism awards, but more importantly it brought me much joy and satisfaction. Because when everything is said and done in this world, it's all about the people.

Many of my columns brought to life unusual characters most people would never meet on their own.

Like Okey "Skipper" Stepp. I spent many summer afternoons sitting with Skipper on a bench in downtown Clarksville. He was either the true-life inspiration for the movie character "Forrest Gump," or a Teller of Tall Tales....extremely tall tales. To those of you in the Boomer generation, he also reminded me of the elderly Jack Crabbe, the dream-weaver and narrator of the book and movie (starring Dustin Hoffman) "Little Big Man."

Then, there was W. Robert Cameron, a hobo who saw himself as the "Savior of the Cosmos." He was on a secret mission to save the world.

The late and lazy but lovable Tony Durr, our editor at *The Leaf-Chronicle*, stumbled across W. Robert, near a railroad trestle, while out jogging one morning and instantly recognized him as a perfect subject for one of my columns.

The guy, after all, was on his way to Austria to see the chancellor.

After I interviewed W. Robert, I gave him a half-pack of smokes and a $5 bill for food. His story made for a damn good column. I liked talking with him because he took great interest in my own tales of movies and bands, of charity, Skipper, Santa Claus and *The News Brothers*.

Before he left town, I found out that W. Robert was in danger of being arrested for vagrancy, so I appealed to the police officer who had been dispatched to check out the "drifter" near Shoney's restaurant.

"W. Robert doesn't belong in jail," I told the officer. "He needs to get to Austria to see the chancellor."

What could the officer do? He laughed and promised to get him to the edge of town.

Here are 17 of some of my best columns—focusing on interesting characters, *The News Brothers* story, the Long-Nishiyama murder cases, and legendary journalists—published over the years in *The Leaf-Chronicle*, *Nashville Banner* and my blog, "They Call Me Flapjacks."

THE CLARKSVILLE *LEAF-CHRONICLE*, CALLING CARD

(Feb. 12, 1982): Savior of the Cosmos

The savior of the cosmos and I spent a pleasant 90 minutes or so sitting on the gravel embankment of the L&N railroad trestle by Shoney's parking lot Thursday afternoon.

No one's going to believe this column, anyway.

The man with all the answers to the world's problems sat at the edge of the railroad tracks, sucking at bottles of Falls City beer he pulled meticulously from the pocket of his worn Army field jacket.

It was shortly after noon and he couldn't waste a lot of time. He has to get to Austria ... without a passport ...hitchhiking ... as soon as possible.

W. Robert Cameron—"that name will do ... use that ... it will be official soon..."—is going to Vienna, Austria, to see his old friend, the chancellor.

"Austria's as good a place as any and better than most," he said. "They have more exports than imports. They have a good balance of trade.

"You've got a lot of gray hair," he said. "You know, it's really nice to sit here in the sun. You must know a lot, you've got all of that gray, curly hair. How old are you?"

Robert put his forehead down into his small, weatherbeaten hands, his long, gray-streaked hair falling around his wrists.

"Let's relax for a minute. All of this laughing is robbing my head of oxygen."

With that he exploded in laughter, the aroma of Falls City buffeting my face. He punched me and laughed again. "You know what beer does for you cerebrally?"

Anticipating that this conversation about beer was going to finally get us back on track toward the purpose for his Austrian pilgrimage, I said "Yeah, the guys who made beer first sure were smart ... must have been Austrians...."

Robert laughed at my naiveté, and brushed some spittle off his full beard and mustache. "The Pharaohs first made beer back in Egypt."

I asked the explorer his age.

"What's age?" he elbowed me conspiratorially. "I'll tell you my age if you hold your hand up and promise on the sun, the only star that's out now, that you will not tell anyone."

Then, not waiting for me to swear by the sun, he whispered: "I'm three eight and a half. But I tell everyone I'm three one. How old are you?"

"I'm three oh," I answered.

"Man, you've got a lot of gray hair."

Robert then cried a bit. "I want to go to Austria. I want to go home. But I have no one to go with me. But if they shoot me, that's okay. I have my cosmic self." He shot his arm straight to the heavens.

I then asked him if Austria was his home. "I'm from Idaho, Montana, Wyoming," he said. "Of course, it doesn't matter where you are from."

It's where you are going that's important, according to Robert. And where he is going is Austria, where if the border guards try to stop him from entering without a passport, he will get them drunk. And if that doesn't work, he will tell them to let him have one phone call. "I'll call the chancellor," he said. "I read all about him in the *Cleveland Plain Dealer* and I wrote a whole page to him. And I called him and he remembered me."

What's he going to tell the chancellor? That is the mysterious part of his mission. "Sadat knew," he said, quietly.

Robert, who carries a small suitcase as well as his backpack, has been on the road a long time, "but what's seven years in the whole of time?" he asked.

He signs his name as a star, with the lower left corner open—to allow the cosmic rays to penetrate.

His cosmic powers have enabled him to communicate with the president of a shoe company. "I had a pair of shoes stolen and he's going to replace them with three pair," said Robert.

"Cosmic beams can destroy everything," he said, motioning at the hamburger joint and motel-cluttered skyline from our perch on the embankment. "I don't want that power.

"I can see as much difference between the buttons on your coat and the thread as I can see between your blue eyes and the color of your hair. My eyes are blue, too, but they are more of a gray-blue. The sun really shines in your eyes.

"I had a girlfriend when I was your age. She's probably your age and married now. Her name was Tammy... Tammy of the river. We used to fish a lot together. I can find her anytime I want to.

"You know it's almost over for this continent, don't you?" he asked.

"Nobody's ever going to make as much money as we need unless we change things. We need to get drunk as we can and confront the police. They have good ideas, if you understand me.

Some of them are scared because some of their daughters have had bad encounters with juvenile men, but not all of them have."

He stumbled as we descended the steps and landed, headfirst, in the weeds at the side of the embankment. I freed him from his topsy-turvy position and helped him don his backpack.

And I wished him luck on his trek to Austria.

The Clarksville *Leaf-Chronicle*, Calling Card

(March 5, 1982): Rodney's Funeral

RAINBOW CITY, Ala.—The little boy tightrope-walked along the concrete retaining wall. He was a cute little towhead wearing tennis shoes and dirty jeans. He couldn't have been more than 7 or 8.

He was scampering around the front of the Tabernacle in Gadsden, Ala., Wednesday afternoon. Things were happening that he didn't quite understand, and he wanted to talk to somebody.

The adults wearing fancy suits and somber faces didn't want to talk to him.

"I'm one of Rodney's best friends," he said, smiling, interrupting a sober discussion I was having with Austin Peay State University flanker Ondra Woods.

We had been discussing Rodney Long's funeral, the event, which had drawn 1,600 people to the Tabernacle, a large percentage of whom would later attend the graveside ceremony in Rainbow Memorial Gardens.

It was the final chapter in a gut-gnawing 2½ weeks for the people of Rainbow City.

Rodney was their pride and joy, a sensitive, religious fellow, a gifted athlete. Three weeks ago, Rodney, a freshman football star at Austin Peay, left the APSU dormitory to get a late-night hamburger.

He never returned.

Police officers, public officials, friends, relatives and teammates from Rodney's Southside High School days flocked to Clarksville. They wanted to find Rodney, to bring him home.

As the developments in the case unraveled, it seemed likely Rodney had been killed. The people at Rainbow City retained their hope.

That hope collapsed Sunday, when Rodney's body was found in the northern part of Montgomery County. Investigators believe he was approached by two fugitives, desperate to flee Clarksville, who tricked him into giving them a ride and then shot him twice with a .38-caliber revolver.

The violence has touched us all, but it has cut at the souls of the citizens of Rainbow City.

"He was the best high school receiver I've ever seen. I loved him to death," said Billy Ray Williams, vice president of Coosa Valley Bank and a long-time friend of Rodney's family. Billy Ray is starting a Rodney Long scholarship fund for Southside High students.

"Some of the people, I don't know if you'd say they were bitter, they were shocked. We had a lot of faith that he'd be alive," he said. "It's just hard to realize why. He was the type of boy who would have let them have the car if they wanted it...Our people here don't hold anything against Clarksville. I think Rodney really enjoyed it there. It's just one of those things."

Brian Mintz was Rodney's lifelong friend and the quarterback who threw passes to Southside High star Rodney Long. Brian, who plays at Jacksonville State University, wrote a poem tribute to his friend which was included in the funeral bulletin and which he read during the service.

"I wrote it last Wednesday when I was beginning to think that Rodney might not be coming back," he said as he rubbed his eyes before the service. "Being as close to him and to God, I wanted to represent him in a way I could remember for the rest of my life."

Brian said his friend was typified by "his love for all people. He befriended everyone. It's so ironic that he has to die while trying to help somebody."

"If I had one last day to spend with Rodney, we'd go fishing, we'd lay out on the riverbank and laugh…"

Lloyd Matthews coached Rodney's midget football team. The burly worker at the Goodyear factory in Gadsden remembers those days well. "Rodney was the kind of kid who could have been a pro football player," he said. "You know, I was laying on the couch before I came over here and I said to my wife how sad it was, that it was 19 years wasted. And then, I said 'No. It was 19 years of memories.' He touched an awful lot of people."

While the spiritually oriented people of Rainbow City continually turn to scripture for explanations of this tragedy, the hurt shows on their faces.

Even though he had viewed the body, the little towhead was unable to comprehend fully the sadness, the anger, the hurt on his elders' faces.

"He was better than you," he told Woods. "But you were good. You know why Rodney was good? He had the moves. He practiced every day."

The little towhead pantomimed catching the football, in imitation and tribute to his dead hero.

"I have his last football towel. It's real special."

The Clarksville *Leaf-Chronicle*, Calling Card

(March 10, 1982): Peace for Kathy

It was silent in the cemetery, save for the crisp winter wind and the chirping of mockingbirds as they soared through the silver-blue sunlit sky.

Kathy Jane Nishiyama is at peace in the Garden of Crucifixion.

The remains of the 16-year-old Northwest High School student were lowered into the ground on a grassy knoll overlooking Resthaven Memorial Gardens Tuesday afternoon.

As the gravediggers cranked the silver-colored coffin into the rich earth, the approximately 200 cars which had wound their way through the cemetery in Sango began their mournful creeping back into Clarksville.

The long, sad day was over; the final chapter was written in the young life of the girl with the haunting smile.

Of course, the Nishiyama story itself will continue, as investigators move on to make an arrest or arrests in the case and as the subsequent trial unfolds. We still don't know how or why someone apparently abducted and killed Kathy last Nov. 16.

Those answers will be forthcoming.

But as far as the attractive young girl is concerned, the story is over. Her remains were found a bit over a week ago in a remote section of Houston County, the examination bearing stark witness to her brutal death.

The hell of her last hours on earth will be told often while the investigation unfolds.

But she is finally at peace.

Her friends, family and Clarksvillians whose heartstrings the story tugged saw her to that peace Tuesday.

The nearly two hours of funeral ceremony began at 1 p.m. at the First Baptist Church on Madison Street.

That smiling photograph of Kathy that we have become all too familiar with in the last 3½ months looked on from the altar at the silver casket decked in rainbows of flowers.

As preachers read scripture and spoke words of condolence and salvation, a steady undercurrent of weeping and sobbing filled the church.

A curious mixture attended the ceremony. Kathy's parents, her mother scarcely able to control her emotion, and their friends wore the somber clothes befitting this most somber occasion.

Law officers, who have lived with the Nishiyama case day and night for months, also congregated at the church.

The most personally involved of these officers, Montgomery County Sheriff's Investigator Bill Wheeler, stayed with the family through the afternoon. His wife, Wanda, remained at his side, clutching dearly a yellow ribbon. Mrs. Wheeler had spearheaded a campaign to encourage Clarksvillians to hang yellow ribbons until Kathy came home. Now, she is at home.

The members of the Montgomery County Rescue Squad, who spent so many hours searching for Kathy, joined their colleagues from Houston County, who had helped in the discovery and recovery of the girl's remains, as honorary pallbearers. They lined the walkway to provide a cordon of salute and honor at the church entrance.

The stars and stripes flew at half-staff at the Montgomery County Rescue Squad's garage on U.S. 41A.

Other authorities, including Assistant District Attorney General Dan Cook, sat at the back of the sanctuary and stood a few paces from the family at the cemetery. These men, in their conservative suits, were attending the ceremonies out of respect for the family, but also in their official capacities. Cook and his colleagues huddled off to one side of the grave, taking notes and discussing the case as the cars bearing mourners wound from the cemetery.

There were also many of Kathy's school friends, many in Levis and work shirts, others in their Sunday best, in the crowd of mourners.

Kathy's boyfriend, David Lin, watched the proceedings in eye-glazed silence.

Most of the mourners at First Baptist followed the white McReynolds-Nave hearse to the cemetery for what Resthaven owner Milton N. Marshall called the biggest turnout for a graveside service in the cemetery's existence.

The prayers complete, the sobbing continuing, the mourners filed beneath the blue canopy over the silver casket. Kathy's mother, Gabrielene, leaned heavily on her stoic husband, Ralph, as she struggled to make it through the sad day and to a waiting car.

According to Marshall, the Nishiyamas bought four cemetery plots 10 years ago.

Those plots remained vacant until Tuesday, when the remains of the girl with the haunting smile were buried.

The mockingbirds' chorus broke the windy silence and a palomino munched on the grass in a field nearby.

Kathy is at peace.

The Clarksville *Leaf-Chronicle*, Calling Card

(July 4, 1982): Me and Skipper

Me 'n' old Skipper sat on a bench.

It was hot in Clarksville. Boy was it hot.

But it bothered me a lot more than it did Skipper. A guy who has spent his life wandering the high seas and the carnivals of the world is accustomed to discomfort.

The noxious breath of the late-afternoon traffic was trapped in the brick-lined gulley of Third Street.

Skipper reached his arthritis-gnarled hand to the pocket of his T-shirt and fished out a Salem.

"I'll sit out here until late in the evening in the summertime," he said. Then, as he lit his cigarette, Skipper glanced down Third Street toward downtown. "After six o'clock you can look all the way clear to town and never see a soul. When I first came to Clarksville, there were all kinds of things to see here. Man, it's dead now. I've never seen such a town. Next week they're going to start rolling the sidewalk up at 9 o'clock and I'll have to run because I'll be sitting on the bench."

The bench is a deep blue wooden bus stop bench, a recent addition to the sidewalk in front of The Royal York Hotel.

Skipper is likely to spend much of the rest of his life on that bench. "This is as good a place as any."

And he's seen them all.

Skipper was born 70 years ago in a small West Virginia mining town.

His wandering began at age 11 when his dad moved the family to Hawaii. That was the first of the many sea voyages which eventually gave Skipper his nickname.

Skipper was christened Okey Stepp at birth. "I don't know why in the hell they named me that," he said. Now, he goes by several names, including Skipper and Red.

"I answer to anything, just so they don't call me late to payday or late to eat," he said, breaking into his high-pitched laugher.

Skipper, who describes himself as happy-go-lucky, looks and sounds so much like the cartoon character Popeye that you almost expect him to sing "I'm strong to the finish 'cause I eat my spinach."

"I have been around the world three times," he said. "I've been in every state in the union. I worked in carnivals for 25 or 30 years. I was in the merchant marine from 1938-45. I've lived out of a suitcase damn near all of my life.

"I've worked everything from rides to concessions in the carnivals. I've been a barker. I've worked in oil fields, as a truck driver, as a cook...you name it.

"I liked carnival life the best...always on the move. The merchant marine was all right except for all of that water. I guess that's part of the job. Five ships were shot out from beneath me during the war. And, I was shot in the stomach and leg when a Japanese plane shot at our ship."

Both of his stick-like arms are covered with tattoos: a couple of flowers, one of the ships he was on is memorialized in a tattoo he received in China and way up on his right shoulder is the face of a Hawaiian woman.

"That's one of my wahinis," he said, with a laugh. "That's what they call women in Hawaii."

Speaking of women, Skipper laughed when asked if he had a woman in every port in the old days. "I would have been a damn poor merchant marine if I didn't...same thing with the carnival."

Finally, at 54, he did something he had been "dodgin' all my life"—he got married. Eight years later, his first wife died in Florida.

A buddy up here in Clarksville then asked him to come visit. "I figured I might as well. I didn't have anybody."

He met his wife, Mary, here eight years ago and that was enough to get him to stay. Health problems have cut into their time together. Mary lives in Summit Heights, Skipper in the Royal York.

"I go see her three times a week and she calls me three times a day. But she is not able to take care of me and I'm not able to take care of her. So, we decided it would be best if I lived here."

That decision was made a bit over a year ago after Skipper was released from the Palmyra Intermediate Care Center, where his rheumatoid arthritis and faulty heart had kept him for the previous two years.

Living downtown, in a hotel full of self-reliant souls, has been good for Skipper.

"When I came here, I was using a walker. I got rid of the walker and used a cane. Then, I threw the cane out and I ain't used nothin' since.

"A lot of it is the environment. I'm relaxed here. I don't have to worry about nothing. My Social Security is taking care of me...so far."

Skipper dug a bottle of heart pills out of his trousers pocket. "Damn pill is as big as a horse pill," he said, as he washed it down with a healthy gulp of heavily-sugared coffee. "When I can throw away these pills, I'll be happy."

Cold weather and arthritis don't mix, so in the winter "I just stay in my warm room and read. I read historical books about how they settled the west and how they settled Kentucky and Tennessee. For Westerns, I like to read Louis L'Amour. But, other than that, I like historical books."

Which is a big reason for Skipper's vocabulary. "Too many people think I've got a better education than I have. Most of my education came through traveling.

"I've been through college: I've been through the back door and out the front!"

Skipper likes the States the best of any country in which he has traveled. But he would like to go back to Australia.

"That's the place," he said, a glimmer in his worldly eyes as he formed the contours of a woman's body with his hands. Then, he laughed. "I can dream, can't I?"

The rambling is over. 'I guess I'll end up here," he said. "It's as good as anyplace. It's home after I have spent my life rambling over hell and creation."

The Clarksville *Leaf-Chronicle*, Calling Card

(Oct. 27, 1982): Skipper's birthday

It was hot…boy was it hot.

The flames shot toward the ceiling of the room. The four men—two in their mid-20s, one almost 31 and one 71—did their best to keep the fire alive as they sat around the round, brown Formica table at 1:30 a.m.

The air was heavily laden with the mingling scents of pancakes on the griddle, sausage grease, coffee and burning wax.

The flickering light of the flames eerily illuminated the bottom halves of the faces of the four men as they sat in the once darkened room, laughing uproariously and singing.

Tears welled up in the old man's eyes and, rising slowly to his feet, he summoned all of the breath in his 100-pound body and blew out the flames.

There was a round of applause from the other three and the old man sat down, gingerly, in his chair.

This was not some strange wee-hours pagan ceremony.

It was Skipper's birthday.

Several months ago, I wrote about Skipper, whose real name is Okey Stepp.

Skipper, who lives in The Royal York Hotel, is familiar to Clarksvillians who work downtown. During moderate weather, the former merchant marine and carny can be found sitting on the bench in front of the old hotel.

Not the shy, retiring type, the old man, who resembles the cartoon character Popeye in appearance as well as mannerisms, engages even the casual passerby in pleasant conversation.

Well, since that time, the frail-looking, white-haired "saltiest old dog in Clarksville" has become one of my favorite people.

Sunday was Skipper's 71st birthday, a landmark for the old fellow, whose body is ravaged by arthritis.

But Skipper doesn't complain about his shuffling, arthritic stride, nor does he complain that the malady of age has locked up his fingers so that he can barely hold the menthol cigarettes he enjoys so thoroughly.

"I just take each day as it comes," is Skipper's philosophy. "I don't worry about what's happened and I don't worry about tomorrow either.

"The first thing I do in the morning is read the obituary columns. If my name isn't there, I enjoy the rest of the day."

To honor our friend, reporter Rob Dollar, Dennis Adkins and I took Skipper out for a birthday breakfast as soon as the presses rolled Saturday night.

The old fellow was looking forward to it, which was obvious by the fact he dressed up in his best-looking sweater and wore shoes shined to Army gloss.

The old man wanted flapjacks, one of his favorite foods ever since his days as a short-order cook. So, we took him to G's Pancake House on Riverside Drive.

It was probably a strange sight to see the old fellow and his considerably younger friends as we walked into the restaurant, with a birthday cake, a wrapped gift and a card.

"Can you open up the back room for us?" I asked the befuddled waitress. "We are having a birthday party for our buddy and we're going to sing and everything. We don't want to disturb the customers."

The folks at G's cooperated with the strange 1 a.m. request. And, after flapjacks and what Skipper called eggs "staring me in the face," it was time for the party.

The room was aglow with the celebration as well as with the heated feeling cast by the flames of 71 candles.

The waitresses even got into the spirit of the occasion by teasing our old friend about his age and inviting him to "go party."

At 2 a.m., Rob and I walked Skipper back into the lobby of the hotel and helped him get his booty—one box still half-filled with cake and another containing the billfold we had given him—into the elevator.

"Thanks, fellows," said the old salt, his watery eyes showing his appreciation. "You know, there's not many people who give the time of day to old people."

We're just glad to call him our friend.

THE CLARKSVILLE *LEAF-CHRONICLE*, CALLING CARD

(Nov. 14, 1982): Party at The Roxy

Franklin Street was ghostly quiet Saturday night...as it is on most nights.

Clarksville's downtown streets were being traveled by few cars and I was the only pedestrian trodding the cool stillness of Franklin. I definitely was the only person wearing sunglasses while walking the quiet, blackness of downtown.

It was a different scene 24 hours earlier, when madness, pandemonium reigned supreme on Franklin.

A score or more of people—including Mayor Ted Crozier—were wearing sunglasses on that incredibly different street scene.

The focus of Friday night's activity was The Roxy Theater, that stately old movie house, a reminder of the matinee days of our youths, days when theaters were cavernous, ornate structures, walls covered with neon and bright colors and the foyer floors composed of rich marble.

Like most old theaters, The Roxy has long been abandoned as the place where movies are shown. The more comfortable, economical, neighborhood quadruple theaters are now the rage.

That's progress, I guess.

But the old Roxy, which dominates Franklin, which once lit up downtown with gaiety and light, is normally a sad sight to those of us who remember those days.

The flowing, orange neon which climbs the side of the theater spelling "R-O-X-Y" over and over again, flashing signals of merriment into the night, has been stilled except for the random occasions when theater owners George Terrell and Jimmy Maynard have staged a community play or pageant.

The two have big plans for the future of the old theater. And I hope they achieve them...contrary to the hopes of some that the theater will be demolished in favor of a parking lot. "Pave paradise, put up a parking lot..." is how the old Joni Mitchell song describes that dilemma.

But Franklin and The Roxy came alive Friday, a night which Crozier officially proclaimed *"News Brothers* Night" in the Queen

City. It was the night in which we staged the world premiere of a project which obsessed us for the last 2½ months: "Flapjacks: The Motion Picture."

It was a project which was designed to blow off steam and satisfy some creative urges for *The News Brothers*, members of the newsroom staff here at *The Leaf-Chronicle*.

The project, well, some say it snowballed out of control, but I prefer to say it blossomed, from a home movie into something we staged as a premiere, complete with gala arrival, visiting dignitaries, interviews with the media, musical and choreographed entertainment, lovely and talented young ladies and champagne.

All of this was designed to raise money for three worthy local charities: Cops for Christ, The Mustard Seed and the Firemen's Toy Drive. We raised a few hundred dollars—every penny to go to the charities.

Terrell, who was of so much help throughout the project, literally turning us loose to use the theater and providing us with suitable attire for the main event, guessed there were 150 people at the theater for the 8 p.m. show.

It was an all-night happening, beginning with the hour-long performance by the Sommer Saults, members of the 101st Airborne Band, who perform as a combo on nights and weekends.

The Clarksville High School cheerleaders also donated their time to perform some rigorous routines.

The Fire Department helped us out by hauling *The News Brothers*, E.T. (Christopher Turner) and Santa Claus to the theater, where Crozier awaited to present us with the official proclamation.

It was a night which only ended when the sun shined, a night I'll never forget. The neon lit the street. The Roxy was alive with music, laughter and good cheer…all in a good cause.

Saturday night, I wandered through the silent theater, remembering the laughter and the joy of the night before.

The deathly stillness inside the wonderful old shrine raised goose bumps on my forearms.

I switched off the lights and then locked up The Roxy. The party was over...

The Clarksville *Leaf-Chronicle*, Calling Card

(Dec. 10, 1982): The death of Chico

Chico's dead.

His mangled body was found in a remote area off Rossview Road.

He just wanted to be free of the bars of confinement. He wanted to roam. He wanted to pick caterpillars off trees and eat them.

Sitting in front of the television in his warm house on Dunbar Cave Road just wasn't enough for the adventurous scamp.

But, he was a little too brave for his own good...and he paid the price when his young life was snuffed by a marauding dog or dogs.

I am writing the final chapter in the life of Chico, the squirrel monkey who belonged to Sgt. 1st Class Carl Hirlston and his wife, Janice.

Chico was special to the Hirlstons, who purchased him while honeymooning in Hubbard, Ohio, last January.

"He was six months old when we got him," said Mrs. Hirlston.

Chico's intelligence enabled him to break free from the back yard cage he stayed in when not rambling around the house.

"He was smart," said Mrs. Hirlston. "I guess that he'd watched my husband open the cage often enough that he figured it out."

Chico became too smart for his own good. After making good his escape in July, he romped in the nearby woods, staying near home but always eluding capture.

You may remember the Sunday morning in mid-August when you picked up *The Leaf-Chronicle* and read the screaming headline: "Deputies Go Bananas: Monkey At Large!"

The Hirlstons weren't in town on that Sunday. The monkey already had been free for two or three weeks, and they had given up hope that Chico would be found.

"We figured something had happened to him," said Mrs. Hirlston.

When they returned from Ohio in mid-August, they found out—from the newspaper story—that Chico had been seen a few days before and he was very much alive.

That August story basically centered on the fact that a man phoned the Sheriff's Department to report he had seen a monkey near Rossview Road.

At first, deputies figured it was just so much monkey business on a hot August night. They found out differently when they arrived at the scene.

Deputy Freddie Maxwell described the activity that night: "He was up there, just jumping from tree to tree," he said, guessing that the fugitive was between 3 and 6 months old.

The monkey, scared into the trees by dogs, could not be lured down.

The Humane Society then came in to see what could be done.

A couple of days later, the search was abandoned, most people figuring the weather or some beasts had killed the monkey.

That changed in late-November, when another Rossview Road resident reported seeing a monkey. This time, the report was taken seriously. The Hirlstons' hope was renewed.

The Humane Society put a live animal trap out. This contraption allows an animal to enter a cage through a door at one end of it. When the animal touches the bait at the other end, the door drops closed.

Society volunteers checked the trap daily, placing fresh fruit inside and near the trap, in hopes of luring the wily beast. Each day, the volunteers reported seeing the monkey looking from a distance while the fruit was being put in place.

On Nov. 26, when the volunteer took fruit to the cage, the body was found.

"What can I say?" said Mrs. Hirlston. "We were hoping we could get him back."

Chico's close friendship with the Hirlstons' dogs may have been a factor in his demise, according to Mrs. Hirlston. Evidently, he trusted dogs just a bit too much and that trust may have caught up with him.

Why was it that the story of the elusive monkey captured the imagination of our city?

I think it was mainly because we live in such depressing times, with headlines grabbed by terrorists, murderers and bleak economic forecasts. There's not much any of us can do about any of that. But, this little squirrel monkey, Chico, gave us something to cheer for, a furry little hero, an underdog.

Now, he's dead.

THE CLARKSVILLE *LEAF-CHRONICLE*, CALLING CARD

(Jan. 16, 1983): The Lone Ranger

My heart was thumping mightily as I sat in the darkened auditorium, the strains of that oh, so familiar tune quickening my pulse.

Moments before, I had been cheering, stamping, applauding as the greatest of the good guys eliminated another evil threat in the old West.

The hero on the screen raced off on his white horse, his faithful Indian sidekick riding beside him on a pinto. The crescendoing trumpets blared as "The End" flashed on the screen.

The houselights came up in the auditorium of the Convention Center at Hopkinsville's Western Kentucky Fairgrounds. Within minutes, the crowd was on its feet, as a familiar figure in white hat, blue cowboy suit, red bandana and sunglasses edged his way through the throng.

I looked at my friend, Rob Dollar, a staff writer for *The Leaf-Chronicle*, and asked:

"Who is that sunglassed man?"

"Why, don't you know?" he said, a gleam in his eyes. "That's The Lone Ranger."

Clayton Moore, 68, wears sunglasses now instead of a mask. That's because of legal hassles that came up when a movie, "The Legend of The Lone Ranger" was made a couple of years ago.

"They said I was too fat and too old to be The Lone Ranger," said Moore. "I'll get my mask back."

Others have played the part, but to those of us who grew up in the early days of television, Clayton Moore is The Lone Ranger.

Rob and I weren't the only adults at Saturday's grand opening extravaganza sponsored by Chaney & Chaney Insurance Corp.

There were plenty of youngsters, who have witnessed the exploits of the masked man in reruns.

But there also were plenty of what Moore called "big guys" in the crowd, those of us in our late-20s and early-30s who grew up with The Lone Ranger. That group included me, Rob, my brother, Eric, and WJZM Radio News Director Scott Shelton.

We all had cheered as the masked man defeated Western villains on the old flickering RCA, back when the dog was still listening to the master's voice on the RCA trademark.

And we all cheered anew as Moore carried us back to those thrilling days of yesteryear.

We were easily primed for our excitement. Prior to Moore's appearance, we watched "The Lone Ranger," the first of two feature films Moore and Jay Silverheels (Tonto) made. That film was made in 1955. They made 169 television episodes.

Moore opened a question-and-answer session by yelling "Hi-yo Silver, away!" in the authoritative tones which filled our living rooms 2½ decades ago.

The session was laced with The Lone Ranger's straight-shooting philosophy. Some might say the mom and apple pie voicings are corny.

I disagree. As Moore said, "The Lone Ranger always speaks the truth!"

His voice cracked when he spoke of Silverheels' death three years ago. "He'll live throughout eternity. Scout, Tonto, Silver and I will keep riding forever."

In a brief photo and interview session afterward, Moore broke more sad news to us: the white horse he posed with at the fairgrounds was a "loaner." The real Silver died in 1972 at the age of 33.

Feeling uncomfortable calling him "Mr. Moore," we addressed him as "Lone Ranger." He didn't mind. That's who he is, after all.

Before he left, Moore autographed a black costume mask I pulled from my pocket. He may not be able to wear a mask, but to me he will always be the masked man. That mask will hang on my wall forever.

The sunglassed man climbed into a black luxury car and sped away.

"Hi-yo, Silver, away!" I yelled after him. He smiled and waved back.

As the snowflakes pelted us in the empty parking lot, Dollar turned to me and asked:

"Who was that masked man?"

"Why don't you know," I said. "That's The Lone Ranger."

There were no silver bullets. Tonto and Silver are dead.

But, The Lone Ranger rides again.

THE CLARKSVILLE *LEAF-CHRONICLE*, CALLING CARD

(Feb. 4, 1983): Fighting the law

The story you are about to read is true. The names have not been changed because no one—except maybe me—is innocent.

I was surrounded by dozens of dirty, unshaven men, many in manacles and accused of crimes varying from assault to drug possession.

And soon it would be my turn to tell my case to the judge, to throw myself on the mercy of the court. How did I find myself in this spot?

I guess you could blame The Lone Ranger.

My Don Quixote-like battle with the criminal justice system began Jan. 15, as I was driving back from Hopkinsville, Kentucky, with my brother, Eric, and WJZM News Director Scott Shelton. We were overjoyed because we'd just met Clayton Moore, The

Lone Ranger, the man who preserved justice in the old West. Another lawman cut that joy short.

Glancing in my mirror, I saw a state police car a quarter-mile to my rear. I lifted my foot from the gas pedal, dropping down to 45 mph in the 55 mph zone. The blue light began flashing.

"Oh, no (or something to that effect)," I said.

"Let's make a break for the state line," said Scott, obviously hungry for a radio exclusive about desperadoes eluding police.

I pulled over, walked toward the trooper and explained I was a friend of The Lone Ranger's and obviously no criminal...

Stone-faced Trooper Rudy Adams, complaining about working on a brutal winter's day, just wanted the facts. He handed me a citation for going 70 in a 55 mph zone. It said I had to pay $62.50 or go to court at 9 a.m. Feb. 2.

I wore my brown Tweed coat—the closest thing I have to a lawyer's suit—when I arrived in court.

"You're not on the docket. This is Criminal Court," said one nervous clerk. "You have to arrange a hearing later."

I showed him my ticket. "This is when it says I should be here."

"You know, you can just pay and not bother with court," he said, a note of hope in his voice.

"I'm innocent!" I said, in stern F. Lee Bailey tones. I learned later that the trooper had made a mistake in assigning my court time.

Karen Williams, an attractive young woman from the county clerk's office, tried to pacify me. "Rudy's off today," she said. "I'll call and see if he'll come in."

I said she shouldn't bother. He wasn't here, I was. The charge should be dismissed....

She wasn't listening. She was chatting with "Rudy" and telling him they would hold off my hearing until he could get there. The fact everyone called the trooper "Rudy" and yet couldn't come close to pronouncing my name worried me a bit.

I stood in the back of the courtroom as the parade of "bad guys" passed before the judge. I was startled when I looked over to the holding tank and saw one guy squashing his nose against the window, watching my every action. I affected a Bogart sneer and stared him down.

Shortly after Rudy entered the courtroom, the judge asked, "You ready, Rudy?" I relinquished hope.

The judge called something which could have passed for my name.

"That's *Ghianni,* your honor," I said in somber Perry Mason tones as I strutted to the bench.

I looked at Rudy and tried to break the ice. "Sorry I got you up this morning, Rudy." He nodded.

Rudy testified he had me on radar and as far as he could tell, I was speeding.

I surprised him by asking if his radar unit had been calibrated recently. I knew I would lose, but I wasn't going down easily.

I proclaimed my innocence and talked a bit about The Lone Ranger.

The judge paused, the wheels of justice probably turning in his head. "I'm going to find you guilty of going 65 and fine you $20 plus court costs of $37.50."

I took the defeat with dignity. Rudy met me outside. "Tim, I hope there are no hard feelings."

"No, Rudy. I don't think I was speeding, so I don't like paying $57.50. But, you and the judge thought I was. That's that."

"I try to be right all the time," Rudy said. "But I'm human and I can make a mistake....I just have to weigh the amount of good I do against any mistakes." He seemed like a pretty good cop.

As I drove—slowly—back to Clarksville, I began humming, then singing the old tune: "I fought the law, and the law won."

THE CLARKSVILLE *LEAF-CHRONICLE*, CALLING CARD

(Feb. 13, 1983): Two senseless deaths

I stood at the edge of Oakland Road, appreciating the silence, the solitude.

Needing a little time to sort things out Friday, I climbed behind the wheel of my Duster and drove.

I came back more confused than ever, still wondering about life's cruelties, ironies, inevitabilities.

I was struck with déjà vu as I stood on the road, peering into the distance. I'd never been here before. Rodney Long had.

I never knew Rodney. I do not know, nor do I care to meet, David Frey or Stephen Drake. But Rodney's life intertwined with the lives of Frey and Drake a year ago Friday.

This quiet road in the rural northern part of the county, near the Kentucky state line, was not so quiet on the night of Feb. 11, 1982, when two blasts from a stolen pistol shattered the silence of this pastoral area, terminating Long's life.

"Rodney Long's Life Short," was the screaming headline across the top of our front page a couple of weeks later, the day after the body of Long, 19, was found a few short yards from where I stood Friday.

He was wearing the referee's shirt he wore when he officiated some church basketball games, the same shirt he wore when he dropped into his dormitory room later on and told his roommate he was going for a late-night snack. It was the same shirt he died in a few hours later.

Friday, while I drove a nowhere sort of drive, I found myself following the fatal trail of a year before.

Norwood Trail is lined with fine homes, owned by fine people...the types of homes burglars find attractive. In one of these homes, burglars David Frey and Stephen Drake found the gun which Frey used to kill Rodney. Not long after robbing that house, Frey and Drake learned they were "hot." After being questioned by police, the two began looking for a way out of town.

They had been waiting behind Wendy's on Riverside Drive for a while when the young Austin Peay State University football player pulled up to order some burgers "to go." The men approached Rodney's car and told him their car was broken down and they needed a ride.

"Sure, as long as you don't have a gun," Rodney joked, a joke which proved sadly ironic later.

Later that night, Rodney's life-blood was spilling, quite possibly in the same spot I stood Friday.

Clarksville, reeling from the unexplained disappearance of another youngster, Kathy Jane Nishiyama, was in shock when Rodney's disappearance was reported.

"He's just a boy out sowing some wild oats," said many people, possibly out of hope rather than conviction. Everyone feared Kathy was dead. We didn't need to lose another bright, young person. His mother, Barbara Mack, said her son wasn't that type. Sadly, she was right.

The clues came in a torrent, our headlines chronicling the trail to the grisly discovery: "Long's Car Found"..."Wallet Found: It's Rodney's"...and finally "Rodney Long's Life Short."

The trauma was hardly over for this city. Within hours of each discovery in the Long case followed the discovery of clues leading to the remains of Miss Nishiyama.

The back-to-back funerals of both young people further traumatized us. We shared the agony of the grieving parents and asked "Why?...Why?"

The Long murder trail ended a few weeks ago and Frey and Drake are serving long prison terms. The Nishiyama case is as yet unresolved.

The trauma of a year ago lingers. Has our world turned so sour that our young, our beautiful, our best and brightest, are not safe?

I'll never forget the shudder I felt when City Editor Wendell Wilson called to tell me Rodney's body had been found. ... I had just returned from a matinee of "On Golden Pond," a film celebrating the wonders of life and aging gracefully.

"They found Rodney," said Wendell, softly. The movie-enhanced glow was replaced by a bilious burning in my stomach's pit.

None of us should forget what happened a year ago, when we were shocked into recognition of the dark underside of the human spirit.

When I began driving Friday, I was hoping to make some sense out of life.

Instead, I stood on the side of Oakland Road and asked "Why?"

THE CLARKSVILLE *LEAF-CHRONICLE*, CALLING CARD

(Feb. 23, 1983): Bowling for charity

I felt like Rodney Dangerfield in the beer commercials.

Rodney, bowling with Mickey Spillane and some of his buddies, rolls the ball down the lane, giving his portly frame some jiggly body English. As one would expect from the man who gets "no respect," the ball bounces off the pins.

The thunderous rumbling of balls and crashing of pins enveloped me Sunday afternoon as I stood at the head of the lane.

"There they are, those wonderful guys, *The News Brothers* on lane 7…That's Tim Ghianni who's getting ready to bowl now…He's such a nice-looking guy. He's Italian, you know…"

I looked over at Al Williams—the boisterous, to put it mildly, master of ceremonies—and I forced my trembling lips into a nervous grin.

When I agreed to bowl for Big Brothers/Big Sisters, I figured no one would be around to watch anyway, so why not? There were 300 participants and at least as many onlookers in Sunday's charity event.

Prior to Sunday, I had bowled three times in my life. I gave up the sport 19 years ago. When I don't do something well, I generally don't do it…at least not in public. I have this peculiar quirk: I hate holding myself up for public humiliation and scorn.

I would have declined Sunday's opportunity for humiliation except that it was for Big Brothers/Big Sisters and was called "Bowl For Kids' Sake."

It is a worthy organization which helps provide adult companionship to children from single-parent homes, giving children a more positive outlook on life.

My friend, WJZM News Director Scott Shelton, received an invitation at the same time I did. Scott's the newest member of

The News Brothers, a group staff writer Rob Dollar and I formed with the purpose of raising money for charities and having fun along the way.

The three of us decided to enter the event as a *"News Brothers"* team, complete with our uniforms of yellow T-shirts and sunglasses.

"The sunglasses cut down on the glare from the bowling lanes" I explained to one person who stared at our unorthodox outfits.

"I think we're supposed to get one with the finger holes just tight enough so you can hold the ball and not so tight that your fingers get stuck," I muttered to Rob as we selected our bowling balls. I think he admired my knowledge of the sport.

We strutted to the scorer's table to sign in. "You get one practice roll," said the scorer. I know that doesn't sound like much, since I hadn't bowled in 19 years...but as it turned out, my bowling skills had not tarnished a bit.

After figuring out which fingers went into which holes, I calmly strutted forward, aimed carefully and sent the ball rumbling toward destiny. One pin fell.

"I've still got it!" I exclaimed in mock delight, disguising my nausea. My game improved after that. In the first frame, I dropped five pins. "That's 2.5 pins per ball," said Scott, obviously proud to be playing in such sterling company. Rob didn't fare much better.

Scott, who warmed up with a strike, had strikes on his first two frames. Rob and I decided we should use Scott's bowling ball. "It's magical," said Rob.

Suddenly, we caught fire, literally humiliating everyone else in the jam-packed bowling lanes. "*News Brothers! News Brothers!*" the crowd chanted. "Go, Timmy. Go!" roared another faction. Hold it...Hold it....What am I telling you here?

Scott finished with a game of something like 130. Rob finished at 115 and I had 96. I did finish with a flourish, however, with two strikes in the final frame.

I turned to accept the wild cheers of the throng, proudly puffing my chest, hoping to hear my laurels broadcast by emcee Al Williams.

Al didn't even notice. "That's Mayor Ted Crozier on lane 13," he said. "He can really do it, can't he?"

I sat down in lonely agony and unlaced by shoes. "Aw, cheer up, Tim," said Rob, patting me on the shoulder and offering me a Life Saver. "The main thing is that we helped raise money for charity."

"Yeah, but I just don't get no respect," I muttered.

THE CLARKSVILLE *LEAF-CHRONICLE*, CALLING CARD

(March 11, 1983): City Hall shark

Just when you thought it was safe to walk the street of the Queen City...

The tipster sounded nervous. And scared. It was no apparition that he saw...rather it looked like a refugee from a Steven Spielberg film.

Or perhaps someone was making a sequel called "Jaws III: Attack on City Hall."

"I know you're going to think I'm drunk or something," said the breathless tipster, by way of introduction over the telephone.

"But, I just thought you ought to know that there is a huge fish...the biggest fish I ever saw...down by City Hall," the informant said, giving Staff Writer Rob Dollar time to absorb that bizarre mental image.

"I was downtown to pay my electric bill," the anonymous man continued. "On my way back home, I drove through Public Square. And there in the wishing well or whatever that is across the way from the mayor's office is this huge fish."

Rob at first ignored the "hot story" as a crank call. It was 11 p.m., an hour when some of our more bizarre citizenry crawls out of the woodwork. (I know, because I am often out at that hour.) But there was something about the caller that bothered Rob. He didn't sound drunk. He sounded genuinely nervous about the huge fish.

So Rob finished his reporting duties for the night and went out into the chilly, misty blackness of downtown Clarksville, wheeling his black MG down to Public Square He didn't really expect to see the huge fish.

"When I drove up and saw it, it shocked me," said Rob. The newspaper's crime reporter is accustomed to grisly sights. It is the unexpected that sends chills up his spine. The monstrous fish was unexpected.

"There was this GI and his girlfriend or wife standing near it, looking at it. It was by far the biggest fish I have ever seen. I got out and asked them about it. They said they were scared to get too close to it...I was pretty darned scared, too."

Rob paused, gulped then extended his hand to quickly touch the 6-foot-long black monster.

The shivering touch enabled him to determine it was not a real fish, but rather a papier mache shark.

Upon close examination, it resembled the "land shark" of the circa-John Belushi episodes of "Saturday Night Live."

When Rob discovered the shark was not hazardous to his health, he picked it up, with the idea of bringing it back to the newsroom and finding it a home. He obviously was fishing for a laugh.

But, he ran into difficulties. I don't know how long it has been since you tried to get a 6-foot shark into an MG. It doesn't work.

Which explains the other strange sight some of you may have witnessed Tuesday night: a man walking the streets of downtown with a shark slung over his shoulder.

The shark's next victim was City Editor Wendell Wilson, who arrived at 6 a.m. to realize there had been some fishy going on in the office overnight. The shark was sitting in his chair, sprawled across his desk.

Now, as I sit here in the newsroom, several issues are troubling me.

First of all, I wonder where the fish came from. Investigation has revealed that it previously dwelled on the roof of a house on Seventh Street.

Does the appearance of the fish hold "Godfather" symbolism, i.e. "Joey's sleeping with the fishes?"

I actually doubt the fish had such dark implications. But there may have been political overtones in the placement of the shark by the merry prankster/pranksters.

After all, it was placed on the wishing well in Public Square. Could it have been an editorial prank aimed at Mayor Ted Crozier, whose office is just a few scant yard from the well?

Crozier—who I happen to like—is nothing if not the "Jaws" of City Hall. For example, witness his honor's response when informed of the fishy incident. "Whoever put the shark there made a mistake because we emptied the water out of the gazebo long ago to save the taxpayers money."

The other thing that bothers me is what to call the shark, now that it has found a home here at *The Leaf-Chronicle*. Some folks want to call it "Jaws." I've heard "Mack The Knife" mentioned as a possibility.

I am pulling for "Hizzoner."

NASHVILLE *BANNER*, OPINION PAGE

(July 30, 1990): Fond farewell to the old cowboy

The old cowboy looked across the Formica table. A pink/white smile—punctuated by down-tilted stress lines—lighted his pasty face

He forked a bit of lemon pie, washed it down with coffee.

"I've got no regrets," he allowed. "Lived life the way I wanted to.

"I mean there are some things I wish I'd done differently. But, you know, I've had a helluva good life."

Harold Lynch's laughter turned to breath-labored gagging.

"So, how've you been?" he asked.

It was typical of the old cowboy to wonder about me when his own life was drawing to an end.

Harold was no saint. You can ask his grieving wife and the two kids.

He was a kind human being. That's plenty.

Harold didn't look much like the cowboy of our respective youths the last time we "rode the range" together over pie and coffee at Shoney's in Green Hills.

He was pale, weary. A cowboy riding a hospital bed doesn't get much sun.

"You're looking good," he said.

I couldn't return the compliment. I wouldn't lie to him. Never have. I should say never did.

He died the other day. He was only 43.

The long battle with lung cancer ended the way he said it would.

"I don't know much about this stuff," he said, as we galloped the range of memories. "Sometimes it's not worth fighting.

"But the doctor told me that the only good thing about it is that when I want to call it quits, I can."

Monday night, Harold told the doctors to turn off the life-support machinery.

I can imagine that in his heart he was smiling. He had control over one final act. He died Tuesday night.

Harold was one of the stalwarts of my former place of employment, *The Leaf-Chronicle* in Clarksville.

Actually, he was in his second tenure there. He left Clarksville 20 years ago to work at the *Nashville Banner*. After stints on the state and outdoors beats here, he moved back to the Clarksville paper.

All *"News Brothers"* drank too much when we were younger. Harold drank more than any reporter I ever knew. He kept it up when we moved on.

A beer in one hand, Marlboro bobbing beneath the mustache, the old cowboy drawled us through rodeo adventures into endless neon nights.

A Stetson and boots covered both ends of his lanky, arthritis-gnarled frame. All were souvenirs of his bareback-riding days.

He changed out of the cowboy duds for good the last time he overcame a deadly obstacle, when he returned the last case of "dead soldier" Sterlings for deposit, when he rediscovered joys of loving family and sobriety.

Yet, he remained the old cowboy in my heart.

With the beer well in his past, a more upbeat Harold greeted the world.

He'd talk with relish about the war he'd won, enemy hops undone.

A year or so ago, doctors told the old cowboy he had cancer in one lung. "Well, take it out," he commanded.

They did. He thought he had it beat, that the remaining lung would be healthy. One more enemy vanquished.

He talked about vacations with his kids, wife and old friends.

"I want to take you to my favorite fishing spot," he allowed to a riding buddy.

A few months ago, the cancer returned for a final shootout.

The old cowboy didn't give up.

And, to the credit of the newspaper in Clarksville, they didn't give up on him either. He returned to work whenever he could.

Scarcely audible, he still commanded authority, respect, love.

He was planning on returning to work right up until he had them pull the plug.

The last time the old cowboy and I rode the range, we watched the afternoon sun's angle splash color across the Formica table.

We laughed a bit. I cried inside, until he saw the tears behind my eyes. "Take it easy," he smiled.

Then I understood. He had called to suggest we "have coffee" that day because he wanted to say goodbye.

When the waitress brought the check, the old cowboy tried to rope it in with his thin, near-bloodless hands.

"I'll get it this time," I said, rustling the check away. "You get it next time."

He didn't protest. He simply nodded.

We both knew there wouldn't be a next time, that the old cowboy would ride into the sunset owing me a pie wedge, a cup of coffee.

We walked slowly to the parking lot and I grabbed his arm and hand.

"Don't worry about me," Harold said. "It's good to see you again."

A few years ago, he would have tipped his Stetson.

Nashville *Banner*, Real Life

(Oct. 3, 1991): Toasting Tony Durr

The little guy with the Hemingway beard smiles from the 5-by-7 photograph as he embraces the tall guy in the dirty fedora. Laughter, life, triumph spark from their eyes.

They didn't know it, but that 9-year-old picture marked the last time the two would ride the range together full-tilt.

Well, there was one clear night, just before the Persian Gulf crisis, when the phone rang at 2 a.m. "Take a glass of cognac outside and toast the Big Dipper," said the cheerful voice from God knows where. "I'll be doing it here."

Where was he? Can't remember. I do remember pouring a snifter and holding it to the sky. "Here's to you, Tony. I love you."

A few days ago, Tony Durr's ashes were dumped from a Coast Guard cutter off Kodiak, Alaska.

They found his body on the floor of his Coast Guard barracks apartment in Alaska. An apparent heart attack victim, he collapsed reaching for the phone.

Tony was born under a wandering star. He was a man of dreams and schemes. And little to show for it in his 44 years.

He'd been a newspaper editor in his Cajun home of Louisiana. And in Clarksville. And San Antonio, Chicago, Anchorage and Kodiak.

How could Tony be dead I ask, as I look at the photo, mental soundtrack playing The Pilgrim (Chapter 33), an old Kris Kristofferson song. "He's a walking contradiction, partly truth and partly fiction. Takin' every wrong direction on his lonely way back home." I laugh at the memory of the slice of life frozen on the 5-by-7.

Tony had returned to Clarksville—where I was associate editor of the newspaper—to attend the "world premiere" of "Flapjacks: The Motion Picture."

I was Flapjacks. Still am to the endangered species of compatriots in that poor-man's "A Hard Day's Night." Our film—the "premiere" raised several hundred dollars for charities—chronicled *The News Brothers* and their search for a "missing person" named Tony Durr.

Tony wasn't really missing. He'd just lost his job in Clarksville. But he rebounded into greener Rupert Murdoch-funded pastures in San Antonio. The movie made fun of us and of him. He/we loved it.

Jobs came as quickly as failure for Tony. Finally, two years ago, he escaped to the merchant marine and then the Coast Guard, wandering the globe, romancing the soul. "I was in a bar brawl in Seoul," he'd write. Or "Cleaning Up the Exxon Valdez mess." Or "I'm in the Suez. War's starting. It's exciting." "Miss you," he'd sign off. "Love, Tony."

The dispatches carried baggage of sadness. He'd left another job or another wife (he had three, four or five, depending on what version of his life he was recounting).

"Tim, the thing I wish I could learn from you is how to work hard at things," he said in one melancholy-fueled phone call. Memories of failures succumb to thoughts of books we'd planned, laughter we'd shared.

"Here's another fine mess you've gotten me into, Durr," I said on more than one occasion as our dreams snagged on reality. We'd laugh. Vibrating, belly-tightening laughs, unlike most I can recall in my almost 40 years.

Those laughs were shared on foggy Cumberland banks, sweaty San Antonio cantinas, always in our hearts. "You know I'm full of it. And you still like me," he'd say, selling himself short. "In your whole life, if you have four friends who you know you can count on to always be on your side, you are lucky."

The other night, I donned the soiled fedora and stood in the yard, looking for the Big Dipper.

Nashville *Banner*, Real Life

(Dec. 17, 1992): Saluting Skipper's voyages

Me and ol' Skipper sat on a bench. It was hot. Boy was it hot.

In another life, a guy with long, brown hair sat frequently with an arthritis-gnarled gentleman on a bench outside The Royal York Hotel in downtown Clarksville.

Now renovated into apartments, the run-down grand hotel was home to hard-knocks survivors, including a merchant of coarse wisdom named Okey "Skipper" Stepp.

He looked like Popeye, this one-time adventurer who would nurse his coffee loaded with sugar, suck mightily on menthol 100s and describe the world according to Skipper.

The guy with long brown hair listened and laughed, writing a column or two about the old guy for the local newspaper.

The first one began with the ungrammatical first paragraph of today's column.

But it *was* hot. And we were on the *bench. Often.* At least during the summers.

Because of his arthritis, Skipper could scarcely move during the cold weather. In his concrete cubicle above the chipped "Fireproof" neon sign of the old hotel, the radiator would belch at super-high during a winter hibernation that included as companions dog-eared Zane Greys and a sports-blaring old radio.

During the summers, Skipper would shuffle around downtown, visit his friends, curse injustice. And smile that toothless grin.

"Don't like to use those choppers," he'd say, gumming his customary breakfast/lunch of scrambled eggs and milk-gravy-soaked biscuits in the hotel diner. Flapjacks on the side. Wash it down with plenty of sugary "joe."

"Hey, boy, ain't you got nothin' better to do than waste your time talking with some old bum."

Lots of times there were "better" things—life's calamities—going unattended. But Skipper's friendship helped the brown-haired guy weather the worst of times, usually with laugher.

"I was living in Hi-why-ee when the Japanese bombed Pearl Harbor," he'd say, eyes watering. "I had an outdoor terrace, and I heard this noise. I went outside and looked up and these Zeros were coming right over my head. Horrible."

Or there was the Merchant Marine ship shot from beneath him by a U-boat, forcing him to splash around, awaiting rescue.

"Didn't worry about the sharks," he'd recall. "Just wanted to get out of there alive."

Or panhandling in Chicago when the Italian guy slipped him a fin and told him to go buy a plate of spaghetti. "It was Al Capone!" Skipper would howl. "He coulda killed me. He was a nice guy."

And the tales of his carny barker years, flavored with a con man's guile. His X-rated romances in exotic ports. His early years as an orphaned Depression world rover so tough his spit would bounce.

Skipper often took the brown-haired guy on verbal replays of those voyages—real or imagined—as they whiled sultry summer's nights on the hotel bench.

The brown-haired guy helped Skipper move from the hotel, as he entered years of illness, nursing homes and hospitals.

Then, as brown hair began to gray, Skipper's friend eventually moved to Nashville and this newspaper.

The Royal York's gone upscale.

When Skipper died recently at 81, there was no funeral.

His remains went to medical research, as he always promised. "Just a damn shell," he'd shrug.

When he heard the news, the guy with the now very gray hair hoisted a cup of sugary joe to the ceiling.

A tiny tear. Followed by a smile and a not-so-distant memory.

Of me and old Skipper sitting on a bench. It was hot. Boy was it hot.

"THEY CALL ME FLAPJACKS," BLOG POST

(April 7, 2009): The workingman's journalist

Eddie Jones wasn't the kind of journalist who made headlines or who was heralded by all of the media pundits.

Eddie was a workingman's journalist, the kind who rolled up his always neatly starched white sleeves and jumped into the fray.

Eddie was 85 when his heart finally gave out on him Sunday, April 5, 2009, in Nashville.

In a lot of ways, he was an anachronism. He began his newspaper writing career as the *Nashville Banner's* television reporter, when he didn't own a set, in the years after World War II.

It should be mentioned that he was a WWII fighter pilot, seeing much action, particularly in the skies over Italy. It was just a few years ago that he made a trip back to the land that he had helped liberate from the fascists. I'm sure he enjoyed a touch of the grape while there.

Early on in his newspaper career, he covered the rise and fall, in quick order, of Hank Williams. He rode the jam-packed special train from Nashville to Montgomery to cover the funeral proceedings.

He left journalism for awhile to head the Chamber of Commerce and then to run for mayor of Nashville, a race he lost.

Then he went back to his true love in 1987 when he became editor of the *Nashville Banner*.

I went to work for Eddie a year later and stayed on his staff until the *Banner* folded ... or was folded ... by *The Tennessean*, senior partner in the JOA.

Eddie quickly rebounded, going to work as the "go-to-guy" for a large P.R. firm in Nashville.

I went on to work for *The Tennessean*, where I stayed until I applied for and was accepted for a buyout in the summer of 2007.

But my heart always belonged to the *Banner*, which was a local newspaper in the truest sense. It was not a *USA Today* wannabe, where six-inch stories and graphics and pie charts took the place of words with soul.

Instead, it was a paper that tried its best to actually cover the cares of the community it served.

Oh, we weren't always right. It was a newspaper we were putting out, not The Great American novel. But we scrapped and fought and were by far the better NASHVILLE newspaper.

Eddie was the kind of editor who stood behind his staff rather than stabbed his staff in the back.

When I was in charge of political coverage, sometimes we pissed off the politicians. They would come to Eddie. Instead of caving in, Eddie would call me into his office. Often with the "offended" ... and by the time the meeting was over, there were handshakes all around.

He also encouraged me to write a slice-of-life column, detailing the concerns of the common man in Nashville. Yes, it was gritty and yes the people I wrote about weren't in the demographic charts of those who figure into the newspaper coverage formula these days.

But he knew these people mattered. I didn't have to explain to him that the purpose behind my column was to show that we are more alike than different, that we share the same hopes, dreams, fears and ambitions, whether we are living in a tent city, a tenement or a luxury condo.

Probably my favorite night as a journalist came in the winter of 1993, when he and I flew up to Washington to visit with the delegation and to sign up the services of a Capitol Hill-oriented news service.

That night we left the hotel, a block from the White House and went to a nearby lush haunt. I don't know the name, but it was filled with the politically wealthy and healthy.

We began the night with a Heineken. Then a scotch. Then wine with our steak dinners and brandy afterward. The beverages were enjoyed thoroughly. But while we took our time over the food and drinks, I listened to Eddie tell me story after story about Hank Williams, Gov. Frank Clement, the struggles of the World War II Flying Ace and more.

And he was just as enthusiastic about my own stories, of my time spent in the business, of my own adventures with guys like

Muhammad Ali, O.J. Simpson, Magic Johnson, Johnny Cash, Gov. Lamar Alexander and a group of guys that are known still as *The News Brothers*.

If Eddie had wanted to, he could have been a part of that fraternity of my friends who reported and drank our way to prize-winning journalism with a fight-for-the-little-guy attitude back in the early 1980s.

He was a boss. But he was a great man, too.

In the years since the *Banner* folded, I have often called him to seek his counsel and just to smile.

Yes, journalism didn't always fit into a bland mold of regurgitated pablum that is slanted to protect the image and feelings of Korporate Amerika.

Eddie, who fought the war to make sure every little guy retained his rights, never lost touch with his East Nashville roots

I loved the guy. May he rest in peace.

Thanks Eddie.

"They Call Me Flapjacks," Blog Post

(Jan. 23, 2010): 'Maverick' Battle had a soul

Another old-time journalist died Friday, Jan. 22, 2010. Bob Battle was a good guy. He loved the *Nashville Banner*. He went on to write a column for Williamson A.M., the Gannett suburban product, after circumstances killed the city's very good afternoon newspaper.

Anybody who knew and loved Bob remembers the *Banner*'s last day. While others drank and partied about a job lost, Bob wailed and wept, for the *Banner* was a living, breathing entity, squashed by korporate journalism and greed. I helped him to the door. I didn't think he'd make it. A part of Bob Battle died out there where the Gannett reception desk now stands sentry.

Those who still walk the earth who are considered unfit for korporate journalism lost a treasured alum today. Some of those who used to love newspapers and considered PR a necessary evil rather than a corporate-sanctioned co-collaborator were there on the final day of publication of the *Nashville Banner* almost 12 years ago.

That newspaper—a truly local newspaper in a world where news increasingly was and is being determined by demographic studies and corporate trend-spotters—was sold out from under 100 people, most of whom still loved newspapering better than the promised land of public relations. Many of them have bounced well into that sector. Good for them.

But then there are the "mavericks" ... people who cannot by nature succeed in the world of news-gathering as determined by the gods of Rochester or the Space Coast or wherever they may entrench themselves.

Bob Battle was one of those. Yes, he wrote his final column for the Gannett suburban product targeted for the richest county in the state. And I'm sure those columns were as hard to edit at the end as they were if anyone had to edit them back in the old days.

But Bob had soul. And he had institutional knowledge. He knew everyone in Nashville and knew where they drank. He was to the drinking journalist what Eddie Jones was to the smoking journalist: the real deal. The "Hello, Sweetheart, get me rewrite" kinda guy.

If there was a greatest generation for journalists, it would be guys like Bob, Eddie, Jerry Thompson, Fred Russell, John Bibb, Gene Wyatt, Edgar Allen, Jimmy Carnahan, all dead.

I'm fortunate to have spent time with each of those men and to have considered them friends.

To these guys the story was the thing, not the spin. Little thought was given to how it would play in Green Hills or Belle Meade or if it would impact sales at mall boutiques negatively.

Yes, Bob had his faults. He sometimes even bragged about them. Yes, he liked his white wine in the bottomless glass after he gave up the harder stuff. But he also knew when to seek out the opinion of journalists, perhaps a generation or at least a half-generation younger, and ask for advice or even proof-reading of a column or a business story.

When Garth Brooks first began to make a little noise, Bob told everyone that Garth would be as big as Elvis one day soon. And he was right. No surprise. Bob knew his shit.

This rambling comes as I'm sitting in my basement, my own fortress of sorts, which, among other wall-decorations, has the final edition of the *Nashville Banner*. My farewell column to that newspaper is right above Bob's.

Good company to the end, I figure.

He was a good guy to start the day with during my 10 years at the *Banner*. He usually was there at 4:30 or 5 when I arrived at work, generally beating not only me but even Tony Kessler, Jane Srygley, Mike McGehee, Left-Hander and C.B. Fletcher.

Sometimes, perhaps, Bob hadn't had a lot of sleep. And perhaps there was that more than faint hint of the night before on his breath. But he kept on going. He was working for a newspaper he loved, a living and breathing dinosaur.

Well, those dinosaurs are extinct now.

In an era when backing down and back-stabbing are the keys to success, not just in journalism but in Amerika, some still are able to keep their dignity even in a world where perhaps they are out of step. I treasure the fact that I could call Bob Battle a friend.

I don't drink much or any at all now. But maybe I can figure out how Bob kept that one glass of wine from ever getting anywhere near empty.

I'll never be able to really figure out why the world decided it didn't need journalists like Bob Battle, dedicated to a newspaper and its audience and not bottom line figures. People who didn't back down when they knew they were right.

R.I.P.

Rob Dollar, Tony Durr, Tim Ghianni and Jerry Manley savor the moment outside The Roxy in downtown Clarksville, Tennessee, following the world premiere of *The News Brothers* movie in mid-November 1982.

Chapter 26
(Tim)

"THIS IS THE END"

It may be my favorite picture of my newspaper career. It's not one of the shots I got of O.J., Ali, Waylon and Willie. John R., Magic, Henry Aaron. It's not even the one that Johnny Cash Kristofferson, Kris' son, took of me and his pop singing one day at the corner where the Tally-Ho Tavern—which we both frequented lives ago—once existed.

Nope, it's a photo of a quartet of journalists—three guys I loved and me—sitting on a curb on a deserted downtown street. A bottle of cheap champagne by our feet. Likely a trail of empties followed us to that spot, like so many broken hearts.

We'd just finished screening a movie called "Flapjacks: The Motion Picture," a crude-by-today's-techno-standards Super 8mm film that chronicled the birth of *The News Brothers*. I don't need to go into it here. Buy the book if one ever becomes available. (Yeah, Mr. Dylan, I am workin' on it, so quit riding me about it. Damn, Zimmy....)

I write pieces of *The News Brothers* book now and then. Sometimes I laugh. But at times like this it hurts. The movie featuring those four men—including that dashing young man in the yellow fedora—is a skewering of pop culture, society, ruthless authority and the korporate mentality. But for all of its rudeness and satire, it also is a love letter to newspapering.

Working as a newspaperman was my life's goal. It was ripped from me a few years ago, although I still have the pleasure of writing for a living and for life.

Some of the fellows in the picture didn't become journalists on purpose. The guy in the white top hat, my pal and still-colleague in *The News Brothers* business, is Rob "Death" Dollar. He'd been destined for a job in the CIA when a newspaper job and family ties came calling. He had career setbacks, thanks to corporate politics and big money small-town bullying, but he went on to a distinguished career as a journalist. You'd probably not have expected that if you looked into the bleary eyes of the guy in this Saturday morning, 2 a.m. photograph. Of course, you'd have to remove the shades to see those eyes.

News Brothers always wear shades because our futures are always so damn bright, as life has proven.

Rob was on my staff and he was the best police reporter I have ever known and, though I never worked for him, I've been told he was a good and fair boss, willing to go to the mattresses for his troops after he moved to his hometown to take over the daily.

Jerry "Chuckles" (damn he hates that nickname) Manley is the guy in the green tuxedo. I know you can't tell colors in this black and white picture, but he's the guy on the far right, his arm on my shoulder. And that tux is green.

He looked like a drunken and somewhat overweight leprechaun that night. Hell, many nights for that matter. I remember one night he and I went to see the Little Ole Opry—Jack Greene, George Morgan, Jeannie Seeley, Little Jimmy Dickens—in a not-very-secret after-hours club behind Pal's Package Store in Clarksville. It was a joint that perked up at about 10:30 on Friday and Saturday nights and featured the Grand Ole Opry stars who came up to Clarksville after finishing their weekly shows. If I remember correctly, it was corporate Opry clout that caused this Little Ole Opry to close. Not surprising.

After the Little Opry show ended and Jerry dropped me off at my house, he drove back to his. When a dog came running out in front of his blue Prelude, well, he chose wisely. He left the road and rolled the car. "I didn't want to kill the dog," he explained to me the next day. *News Brothers* are, as we like to say, damn nice guys. I think he only took one sick day, but he looked like something the ... well. .. dog dragged in...

Jerry was, like me, never planning to be anything but a newspaperman. It was his calling. As a writer perhaps his words didn't sing. But as an editor who finds holes in stories, who asks the right questions, who writes headlines, who exercises humanity with staffers, he was among the best in the business. I love the guy like a brother.

Then there's the dark-bearded Cajun in the purple fedora, Thomas Anthony "Tony" Durr. He kinda stumbled into journalism by accident. His life, it turned out, was one big accident after another, leading to ultimate tragedy.

He had been a computer guru with a company out of Florida. When he sold his company's products to the newspaper in Clarksville, he pretty much came along as part of the deal. I mean, early newspaper computers had a lot of problems.

What could be better than hiring an editor who helped hone the system and plopping him in the newsroom to try to keep things straight?

Of course, Tony's greatest contribution as an editor is that he also liked to play golf, so he pretty much relinquished the control of the newspaper to me, coming in for conversations or calling in, but I was the associate editor and, well, he figured I could take care of things. (Actually I shared the authority with another sub-editor, a guy who had a face like a death mask and a personality to match.)

Tony was what they call an "idea" man. With the help of Rob and Jerry and a few other brave souls who lived hard but worked harder for the sake of good newspapering, we executed some of his ideas.

We also had plenty of our own, and Tony, to his credit, knew enough to step out of the way if *The News Brothers* were chasing a story, covering a tragedy or consoling a grieving mother whose murdered daughter's skull had been mistaken for a milk jug when the dogs dragged it out of the woods.

Tony really wasn't a *News Brother*, but he enjoyed the fruits of our hard work in his role as editor of the newspaper.

Jim "Flash" Lindgren isn't in this picture, because he was young and went home by 1:30. He was like our little *News Brother*, among the original foursome. We loved him and took him on our outings and figured he'd carry on the tradition, which he did in Indianapolis, where he now sells bogus penny stocks to unsuspecting retirees. Nah, that's not true. He's distinguished himself in journalism and in academia at Butler University. (That's the school that keeps on almost winning the NCAA title, choking in the big games. Talk about "The Curse of *The News Brothers*....")

But this is about the picture and I'm kind of getting off the track here. But that's my right, as I am the writer of this piece and I no longer report to soul-snuffing corporate bean-counters and butchers of hope and dreams.

What this photograph represents to me is love of friends, for sure, but love of friends who also were in love with the act of committing good journalism.

Proud, hard-smoking, far from pure or Puritanical, these good and decent men prided themselves on being solid newspapermen.

At the time this picture was taken, that's the way we all figured it would be. Newspapers would be around forever and we'd be able to enjoy the ride and the responsibility and, especially, serve our duties as members of The Fourth Estate.

This picture was taken in Clarksville, Tennessee, where all of us worked together and where I spent the first 14 or so years of my newspaper career.

Tony had already gone on to his next job, weekend editor of the *San Antonio Express-News*, by the time we coaxed him to fly up to spend the weekend in my apartment and go to the movie. I remember him as a perfect house guest, a good gumbo cook and a guy who loved my old cat, Sly ("C'mon, get up and dance to the music.")

Sometimes now Rob and I joke that this early morning after the movie premiere was at the peak of our careers and we should have driven off into the Cumberland River or disappeared like Jim Morrison after the police arrested us while the credits rolled. That statement may raise questions, but I'll answer them another time, perhaps in the book.

This is about newspapers.

It turned out it wasn't our careers' peak. For another decade or even two, there still was newspapering being committed around Tennessee and even in some of the other colonies and commonwealths.

Not too long after this photo, Jerry went on to a short stint at the *Daily News Journal* in Murfreesboro (Yes, that used to be a helluva paper and not a shopper at all) before landing his dream job as a copy editor at *The Tennessean*.

He'd wanted to work there because John Seigenthaler was his hero and because he loved that newspaper, the one that was delivered to his home down in Petersburg, Tennessee, when he was a kid and playing Tiddlywinks and Mumbly Peg, while getting sugar drunk on Nehi on the town square ...

Of course he may not have done that at all, but I never can figure out what he might have done in Petersburg. I think he kept his pants on most of the time.

He rose fairly quickly at *The Tennessean* because he is, was, remains, a great newspaperman. He not only was content, he was jubilant that he was going to spend the rest of his working days at the paper he had loved all his life.

I was still in Clarksville, sucking on smokes, listening to the scanner and minding the night shift when he'd call me and say "I just wrote a good headline and thought, man, a million people will look at this headline tomorrow." Of course, there weren't a million Tennesseans sold then. But there were probably four or five times more than the measly 55 copies they sell daily now. OK. OK. I'm kidding. I don't know what the circulation is or how the "Internet" clicks factor into the equation. Mind you, there's still good work being done there, but you can only stretch a staff of five so far.... Well, that's an exaggeration, but bean-counting is the name of the game and they have continued to lop off staffers.

But Jerry was in his glory back in his early *Tennessean* days. Sometimes, as he still lived in Clarksville part time, he'd spin by my house at the conclusion of both our shifts and we'd chase the dawn. "C'mon, man, let's go for a ride in this Pink Cadillac..." and Bruce Springsteen would scream from the speakers as we played chicken with deer and ran full-tilt on reckless adventure, sometimes to Nashville or Guthrie, Kentucky, once to laugh at death on an interstate overpass. But we don't need to share that story here. Glory Days, indeed.

Rob's newspaper career also was glorious for nearly 24 years as he became the backbone of the *Kentucky New Era* in his hometown of Hopkinsville, Kentucky He helped turn that small-town, daily rag into a respected, hard-news paper. He made enemies. But he earned a lot of respect from his staff and even from his bosses. That's back when bosses in upper management showed respect to their staffs. And sometimes the bosses even deserved it.

Me, well, I was the last *News Brother* to leave Clarksville, taking a sip of brandy and turning out the lights on my last night in that newsroom. I had been hired by Editor Eddie Jones and Managing Editor Tony Kessler at the *Nashville Banner* and served a variety of jobs for the 10 years I was there. In whatever role, I was also the designated No. 2 man, the bullpen, if a decision needed to be made. I loved the *Banner*, which eventually was killed by greed, both corporate and personal. I went down with the ship.

Because I was in the middle of an adoption, I accepted the offer of a job that wouldn't force me to move. I went to work for *The Tennessean* and served as a copy desk staffer, entertainment editor (about six years), senior entertainment writer, senior features writer and then, as they apparently—at least I interpreted it that way— were trying to make things uncomfortable enough for me to leave, I was moved to night cops. Almost a full-circle career.

I figured that buyouts were going to come, so I held on for the better part of a year, working the night shift, never seeing my kids. One of the few pluses of that job was that my boss was Jerry, who had been on my staff in Clarksville, but had been more of a comrade than an employee.

When my buyout did come through, Jerry could hardly stand it, keeping his head down and hugging me quickly before he went out the door. He was going to be night editor for another four years, but I was the last full-time staffer he'd ever have, at least as far as I know.

Of course, I survived and continue to squeak out an income but hold my head high as a freelance journalist, writer and even part-time news-writing instructor and journalist-in-residence at a local university. My family and my forays with Rob and the occasional other *News Brother* or Americana star help keep me sane (so to speak).

Rob finally left his newspaper job on his own terms, resigning as managing editor, after disagreement with the way his paper was going, his staff was being treated and his powerlessness to change it. He wouldn't backstab his people. Money talks. Good men (and women) walk.

After reluctantly leaving journalism, he went on to serve as deputy mayor in Hopkinsville, and later had a pretty good temporary job with the federal government, responsible for overseeing public relations and community outreach activities in 21 Western Kentucky counties during the 2010 Census.

When he accomplished that task with great success, the Census Bureau gave him a lapel pin and said, "Attaboy." Now, in polite terms, he's in "transition" or "between opportunities." But, he keeps pounding the pavement to get a job, and he'd make anyone proud. Hell, I'm proud of him.

Tony left San Antonio for newspaper jobs in Chicago, back to San Antonio, Anchorage and Kodiak, Alaska. He tried to recruit me for each one, but I knew he was never going to be at one place long enough to pin my hopes to his career. I did get trips to San Antonio and Chicago out of the deal, though.

It would have been my luck to have moved to Anchorage just in time for his firing there. Even if he'd taken me to Kodiak from there, he also got fired there.

I occasionally would talk with him after he left newspapers and joined the Coast Guard. He seemed happy, had survived his seventh or eighth divorce. With me in Nashville and him in Alaska, we'd find the same star in the sky late at night, look at it, and talk to each other on the phone while sipping brandy.

But there always was the hope he'd go back into newspapers. He didn't know where or when, but he figured he would. I'm sure he would have wanted to come wherever I was so I could cover for him. But I loved him.

Tony's Coast Guard career ended one apparently lonely night. An empty bottle of prescription medicine—perhaps what he took for his crippling migraines—was found by his body after he didn't show up for duty the next day. It was called a heart attack, but even his family isn't sure of the circumstances. Nothing about Tony was uncomplicated.

It should be noted that the other original *News Brother* not in this picture, "Flash" Lindgren rose to great heights as a senior copy editor in Indianapolis, before his paper was consumed by korporate cannibalism and he exited rather than compromise his principles. Apparently his *News Brothers* training "took."

There were others who joined, proudly. Scott "Badger" Shelton was a correspondent for *The Tennessean* (by the way, Rob was for a time, too in his Hoptown days.) Scott also was a radio newsman, who became infected by *The News Brothers* and their enthusiasm while covering us as a news story. (Our movie was designed as a fund-raiser for a variety of worthy causes.) I don't know if Badger left journalism to go into a media relations job or if journalism left him. Regardless, there was ink in his veins.

John "Street" Staed left Clarksville to pursue the heights of management superstardom in the news business. He reached them all right and even admitted once, in a note he wrote in jest, that he was a "management puke" and no longer worthy of the *News Brothers* affiliation. Perhaps not ... until he was lopped from his lofty position and turned back into a reporter. Last I heard he was working part-time at a newspaper in Anderson, S.C., while training to be a respiratory therapist or Popsicle salesman.

I think Ricky G. "Dumbo" Moore has so far survived as a newspaperman. The sports editor in Clarksville back when the Brothers raged, he's some sort of high-falutin' copy editor or something in Chattanooga. I'm sure he worries, though, as he's not getting any younger, is overweight and has a variety of health woes.

There are others ... Harold "The Stranger" Lynch died long ago of lung cancer. Billy "StrawBilly" Fields left newspapering early enough to survive and he now is a high-ranking government official in Nashville (as if that's a good thing). David "Teach" Ross, who reported the news for radio, television and newspapers, got out when he could and now is a schoolteacher in Dover, Tennessee. He also plays guitar in roadhouses at night.

I could go on, but I want you to envision this picture of four guys who just wanted to be newspapermen, who loved each other and loved exercising the First Amendment as well as helping the underdog and uncovering corruption and, always, sticking to their principles.

On the far left is Rob. As I said, he's "between opportunities." Then comes Tony. His life ended in despair, a pill bottle and a heart attack apparently to blame.

The happy fellow with the yellow fedora is me. I left newspapering on my own terms, but I both regret and resent what has happened to newspapers since. My heart aches for my profession and its people as well as for the readers who no longer are fully served, for the underdogs who are ignored and for the fact big business and government go unchecked while a country is in despair.

You see, I got a buyout four years ago. In the months and years after that came a wave of buyouts and layoffs, shrinking a once proud staff to just a few. It's not just a Nashville malady. It has happened everywhere there is or has been a newspaper. The bottom-line is key. Sacrifice enough people so the CEO can get a $1 million bonus or whatever.

My old friend Jerry toiled in the trenches of middle management, a night editor without a staff, for almost four years after I left.

Then on Thursday, June 30, 2011, while he was on vacation and bound for the annual Manley family pig roast and clambake in the countryside near Petersburg, Tennessee, he was notified his job was being vacated. Time to pack up your stuff old man.

I'm sure he was told "Thanks for all you've done."

Several other good people—including an exceptional young journalist and rock drummer named Nicole Keiper (I put her name in here because she's still young enough to hire, folks)—got axed. As did Ellen Margulies, who spent 25 years at the morning newspaper.

There were many more corporate-wide. Some didn't expect it. For that, I am most sorry. I'd been telling them it was coming. But nobody really accepts that the worst will happen. Until it does.

By the way Larry McCormack—the official *News Brothers* photographer (I'm not sure if he took this shot as it was 29 years ago and very late on a night when $2 champagne was involved)—did make the cut and remains employed. At least last time I checked.

I could go on and protest what happened to the guys in the picture, but I'm particularly angry with the way Jerry was treated. He had his dream job, and the corporate guys, who come and go, took it away from him.

I'm sure he'll bounce back. Or at least roll back.... Maybe he can return to Petersburg to play spin-the-bottle with the local school marm. I don't know.

All I really know is that when I look at this picture, it used to make me happy. Still does, until I realize that the four men there just wanted to spend the rest of their lives as newspapermen. And, for whatever reason, those dreams were crushed.

They say daily newspapers are dying. The reason is simple. People, not necessarily me, but I am a good example, are being dumped on the curb as the korporate juggernaut kills a most wonderful profession.

It's not over yet, of course. So beware if you remain in a newsroom. George W. Bush never had an exit strategy, but you sure should. Does anyone want to be the last one standing in America's newsrooms? I don't know and I assume it would be some korporate type with a parachute, anyway. I do know that's one story no *News Brother* would want to report ... turning out the lights on what once was a noble profession.

There are a few things that come with a life spent in newspapers, triumphs and friendships as well as nightmares from tragedies covered, human beings in suffering.

One thing you never forget is the stench of death.

Tim "Flapjacks" Ghianni (left) and Jim "Flash" Lindgren sing "The Ballad of *The News Brothers*" with street musician Mike Slusser on Lower Broadway in Nashville, Tennessee, in October 2009.

Tim "Flapjacks" Ghianni and his political ally Abraham Lincoln discuss *The News Brothers* Address" during an encounter at Fort Negley in Nashville, Tennessee, in the spring of 2011. Of course, Honest Abe is dead. This is acclaimed Nashville-based impersonator Dennis Boggs.

Jerry "Chuckles" Manley smiles for the camera after a nice breakfast with fellow *News Brothers* Rob "Death" Dollar (left) and Tim "Flapjacks" Ghianni (right) in Nashville, Tennessee, in August 2011.

David Riley (right) visits with then-Hopkinsville Mayor Rich Liebe (center) and Scott Burnside, the former sports editor at the *Kentucky New Era*, in early November 2004 at the annual Veterans Day Parade.

Rob Dollar (right) and David Riley discuss the news budget for the next day's newspaper at the *Kentucky New Era* sometime during the Spring of 2000.

Chapter 27
(Rob)

THE BUSINESS OF BEING HEARTLESS

Every day, when I wake up, I thank God for allowing me to practice journalism for 24 years and work as a newspaperman in the days when newspapers mattered to so many people in this country.

They don't anymore. I know because there was a time when I used to read a newspaper—maybe even two or three—every day of the year. That's something I no longer do.

You see, I'm not able, in good conscience, to give my loyalty to a newspaper—any newspaper.

It probably has a lot to do with a late friend and great newspaperman, David Riley. I can't—and I won't—forget what was done to this good man on his deathbed.

David was a true Renaissance man, someone who had many skills and could have worked anywhere, doing just about anything he wanted to do.

A retired U.S. Naval Reserve officer, he was nominated for a Pulitzer Prize in photography for a picture he snapped in July 1979 while on active duty aboard the USS White Plains. The image dramatically captured on film shows a Vietnamese refugee scaling a cargo net on the side of the ship after his rescue at sea.

David also was the author of a book on military medals and a whiz with computers, so much so that the Kentucky Bureau of *The Associated Press* routinely called upon him for help with graphics and other projects.

I worked alongside David Riley—we called him "Commander Layout"—for 20 years at the *Kentucky New Era* in Hopkinsville, Kentucky

In 1999, he realized his lifelong ambition, which was to become the editor of his hometown newspaper—the *New Era.*

A few years later, David got sick and was diagnosed with Non-Hodgkin's lymphoma.

Just three months before he died of the cancer in mid-April 2005, David was relieved of his duties as the *New Era* editor and reassigned to the newly created job of Opinion Page editor.

With the hiring of a new editor, the change-in-command was splashed across the front page of the newspaper with great fanfare, amounting to what some readers and friends saw as a public humiliation for a man who had loyally served the *New Era* for 24 years.

At the time of this event, I was working at City Hall. I remember I was so angry, not only about what had happened to David, but also because of the reaction—or really the lack of a reaction—of those still working at the newspaper. There was no uproar or revolt. Most, if not all, of the people out there quietly shook their heads in disbelief. Far too many, I suspect, just turned their heads the other way, not wanting to stand up or speak up for a decent man.

Now, maybe the person who made the decision—"The Decider"—believed in his heart he was doing David a favor by lessening his work responsibilities while he fought for his life. That's what we'd all like to believe....But, I don't know.

What I do know is losing his cherished title of editor broke David's heart. It crushed his spirit. So, I can't help but believe the situation could have been handled differently—and with some compassion.

David and I were as close as brothers. This was a man whose entire life was about doing for others. I had returned to the *New Era* from North Carolina in April 2000 and accepted the managing editor's job only because I wanted to work with him again and help him succeed as editor of the paper.

Our friendship had no bounds. David always made me look better than I was, and when he got himself into one helluva mess by breaking a cardinal rule of journalism in September 2001, I rode to his rescue and put a remedy in place that allowed him to keep his job as *New Era* editor.

What he did—or failed—to do is not important nor worthy of discussion as I've always believed it was unintentional and the result of unrealistic demands placed on him by the top management of the newspaper.

In the months leading up to his death, David showed up for work almost every day. But, he also spent a lot of time in the hospital, and I was a frequent visitor. Sometimes, I would bring him a bag of White Castle hamburgers. We talked about a lot of things, but because we both had ink in our veins, nothing was talked about more than our love of newspapering.

Just weeks before he died, the job reassignment was still on his mind when I visited him during one of his many stays at Vanderbilt University Medical Center in Nashville, Tennessee.

"Rob, why don't they want me?" he asked me, tears welling up in his eyes. "I've always been loyal and worked hard. But they've never wanted me for their editor...I'll never understand it."

I had no answer for my friend, no answer that would comfort him, anyway.

Eventually, David left the hospital to go home to die. On a Wednesday morning—April 13, 2005—after his two teenage daughters had left for school, he passed peacefully, with his wife, Toni, there with him. Only three days earlier, some of his closest friends—Ray Duckworth, LaMar Bryan, Jennifer P. Brown and me—went to see him in the beautiful log cabin house he had built with his own hands. We laughed, reminisced and said goodbye to a dear friend during that final visit on a warm, sunny spring day. There were few words when it was time to go. "Dave, I'll see you later," I said, trying to maintain my composure. With a grin and nod, he responded, "See you, Rob."

After David's belongings were packed up and removed from his office, a colleague gave me something she said David surely would have wanted me to have—a hand grenade desk display, with the words "Complaint Dept. Take A Number" printed on it.

I had given the decoration to David as a gift on what turned out to be his last Christmas. David and I, always standing shoulder-to-shoulder, had fought the newspaper wars for two decades, and he so appreciated the irony of life.

He placed the grenade display in a prominent spot on his desk, where it could be seen easily whenever someone entered his office those last few months of his life.

David chuckled when he told me there was one person in particular who often glanced at the grenade, with a puzzled look on his face, not really knowing what to make of it.

He didn't have to tell me who the fellow was…..It was an easy guess…David would wink at me, then whisper softly, "Rosebud."

At David's funeral, I was given one of the biggest honors of my life when I served as the only non-family pallbearer. I helped carry my friend to his final resting place knowing, beyond a doubt, that the Hopkinsville community and the journalism profession were damn lucky to have had him.

In the years since David's death at the age of 52, I've come to realize the world has changed—and not for the better. In this day and age, loyalty to anyone or anything is asking too much, particularly when you know for certain that the loyalty won't be returned because it costs too much.

Stories like what happened to David Riley used to be a rarity. Now, they're so common that people don't even get upset.

Of course, it's not just what's happened to newspapers, but the sickening decline in quality, relevance and readership is most certainly a reflection of the sad state of today's society.

It's always been a cold, cruel world. But, until the last 10 or 15 years, never that cold or cruel for the decent souls who go through life trying to do "The Right Thing."

In today's turbulent economic times, where "The Bottom Line" is king, not only do the good die young, but they're also spit on and humiliated long before there's an opportunity to retire and enjoy the golden years with dignity.

Nowadays, life has become all about business, and that means NOTHING apparently is personal anymore. It's acceptable to be greedy. It's acceptable to be heartless. It's acceptable to create chaos and misery for others in this world as long as you get YOURS—and plenty of it.

If the world ever should have slowed down the money-making machine, it probably was on Sept. 11, 2001, when terrorists attacked America, killing nearly 3,000 people in New York City, Washington, D.C., and Pennsylvania.

On 9/11, as I walked into the *New Era* newsroom that beautiful Tuesday morning, I was greeted with the breaking news that a plane had just hit the World Trade Center in New York City. Of course, at the time, no one believed it could be anything but an accident. That all changed seventeen minutes later when the second plane crashed into the South Tower.

Immediately, as the managing editor of my newspaper, I scrambled my staff to cover the local angles of what would become the story of a lifetime. Once assignments had been made, I made a mad dash to the newspaper's boardroom, where the weekly management meeting was in session.

As I burst through the doors, the powers-that-be glanced up from their financial papers with a perturbed look on their faces...You know, the kind of look that screams out something like: "WHY ARE YOU INTERUPTING MY IMPORTANT MEETING? THIS BETTER BE GOOD!"

"A second plane just hit the World Trade Center...America's at war," I blurted out to the bosses of money.

My declaration of war was greeted with blank stares and an uncomfortable silence...No one let out a cry of horror. No one suggested that we pray. No one asked for more details. No one jumped up to go and check on their families.

Finally, after what seemed like an eternity, the big boss meekly responded: "OK...Thanks for letting us know."

And, with those words, it was back to the meeting and the business of making money...Of course, it was the same story elsewhere, I'm quite sure.

There was money to be made…Gasoline prices at service stations around Hopkinsville mysteriously skyrocketed in the hours after the attacks as unnerved motorists formed long lines to fill their tanks. Sad, but true.

Korporate Amerika, in these new times, isn't satisfied with just making a profit. The profit margin has to grow by leaps and bounds every year, and it doesn't matter who or what is destroyed in the process.

Take a look at The Gannett Co. newspaper chain. Just over the past few years, hatchet men and women eliminated the jobs of thousands of journalists at Gannett newspapers around the country.

Dear old "Flapjacks" (as you'll read very soon) was among the targets. He never backed down, But, he was shown the door, a buyout not a layoff. His position was never filled, figuratively or literally.

As recently as last summer, 700 reporters and editors got the ax—even while the corporation had no trouble whatsoever paying out multimillion-dollar bonuses to executives and bean-counters for massaging the profit margin for greedy stockholders.

It's perhaps too easy to point to Gannett, because the corporation is such a mammoth target.

The bottom-line principle guiding that chain's "reductions" is no different than that found at newspapers and media corporations nationwide. Journalists from Chicago to Los Angeles to Denver to Seattle to Knoxville and points in between have fallen, fled or faked it just to keep their jobs.

Yep. Nothing personal…It's just business.

The out-of-work journalists, I'm quite sure—as many are my friends and all are my comrades—feel otherwise. No one should forget those let go were real people…They were someone's husband, wife, daughter or son.

Among the latest casualties, as previously mentioned, was my friend and fellow *News Brother*—Jerry "Chuckles" Manley. At the time he was sent packing in 2011, Jerry was a 59-year-old newsroom manager at *The Tennessean* in Nashville, Tennessee, with many years of good journalism left in him.

But, it didn't matter. He had to go, with a lot of others, to pay for those outrageous bonuses, golden parachutes and to keep the corporation's profit margin healthy.

There was a time in this country when successful companies valued good and loyal employees. CEOs recognized that a competent workforce was the key to success. And, they understood that appreciated employees made all the difference between a good product and a bad product.

"Flap" carried almost 3½ decades of nationally honored and honorable newsroom experience out the door and into the night at *The Tennessean*. It was the same story for "Chuckles."

Worse still...and something I can't get out of my mind...How much did David Riley's lack of being appreciated add to his pain in his final, brave days?

But quality and compassion apparently don't matter much in the new business world models, where people are disposable. You don't take care of them. You use them up, and then look for new ones to throw under the bus. To hell with loyalty. Ditto for morality and ethics.

Take a look around now, folks. I don't care if you are working in retail, in an office or in a factory: Bad behavior, when unchallenged, doesn't just go away. It digs in and puts down roots, growing like a cancer. It's nourished by the scared, self-serving enablers, who fail to stand up for what's right, choosing instead to look the other way whenever a wrong is committed in the workplace.

It is what it is, unfortunately...

The News Brothers never were strangers to the heartless side of the human spirit. I saw it at its ugliest many years ago shortly after leaving Clarksville, when, as a still wet-behind-the-ears reporter, I was called out to the scene of a fatal shooting.

A distraught man had been inside the Shoney's restaurant in Hopkinsville on a busy Saturday morning, arguing with his girlfriend. Upset, he abruptly left the breakfast table and went outside to the parking lot, where he retrieved a rifle from his truck and shot himself in the head.

When I arrived at the restaurant, the man's body was lying on the pavement, beside his truck. Police already had roped off the crime scene and placed a coat over the man's head. Still, there was no way to shield the people at the restaurant from the horror of the public suicide. There it was for all to see: A dead man...A huge pool of blood...Blood and brain matter dripping from one of the windows of the truck.

As I waited for the coroner to arrive so that I could ask him some questions for my story, I couldn't help but notice that the tragedy seemingly was having little effect on the restaurant's business.

People were casually going in and out of the eatery like any other normal Saturday morning. Many had small children in tow. Some of the hungry customers glanced over at the police officers standing over the dead man's body, but no one seemed bothered or upset by the grisly sight.

The steady stream of unnerved customers struck me as being odd and inappropriate.

"What in the world is wrong with these people?" I asked myself. "How can anyone in their right mind still have an appetite after seeing something like this?"

As I stood there, an apparent curious customer, well-dressed and looking satisfied with his breakfast, walked out of the restaurant and up to me, a toothpick still in his mouth.

"What happened here?" the man asked me.

"A suicide," I responded.

With my answer, the man paused, looked at me and said: "You know...that old boy must have really been upset about something."

The stranger then strolled over to his expensive car, climbed in, and drove off on his merry way to chase The Almighty Dollar.

Heartless? I thought so. But, probably not to someone who worships at the throne of the moguls on Wall Street. Hell, Mr. Compassion probably would be a great CEO...You know, one of those "job creators"...The great Americans who are CONSUMED with the idea of making more and more money ...

even though they already have more money than they'll ever be able to spend in a lifetime.

The News Brothers saw what was coming way back in the early days of Korporate Amerika, when all of a sudden one day, being heartless became a virtue.

Believe me. Not everyone was fooled when the Captains of Industry replaced company pensions with those volatile 401K plans that were going to make us all millionaires.

My friend "Flap," it should be noted, did not actively participate in the 401K at his last and depressing stop. He spent the money on toilet paper, so he claims, only half-joking. At first I thought he was foolish, but now as I sit here, I believe it was a wise investment.

I have a prediction, or maybe it's a wish or even a promise: When the clock on this earth finally runs out (you pick a date when, as all the wackos and soothsayers do… one of them will be right), ALL of the heartless, money-chasers in this world better be ready to pay a huge price for their deadly sins of greed.

After all, The Man Upstairs is the ultimate Chairman of the Board. And, like *The News Brothers*, there's no fooling him…

With apologies to The Beatles, "In The End, the money *you take* is never equal to the money *you make*." That's not a problem for the good and decent who don't want anything to do with blood money.

The News Brothers pose for a group photo during their 2011 reunion in Clarksville, Tennessee. Clockwise, from front left, are Rob Dollar, David Ross, Jerry Manley, Tim Ghianni, Jim Lindgren, Rick Moore, and Scott Shelton.

Chapter 28
(Tim)

11-11-11

"This could be the last time, maybe the last time, I don't know," I said, smiling at my own spoken-word version of an old Rolling Stones tune as I stepped toward the front door of G's Pancake House on Riverside Drive in Clarksville.

It was a Friday night in the Queen City—Nov. 11, 2011. Now, if you happened to be someone who likes number games or looks to the stars for answers, then this was no ordinary day.

It was 11-11-11, with flapjacks on the menu for *The News Brothers*. The boys were back in town for some merrymaking at a big reunion—maybe their last.

G's Pancake House, not surprisingly, was one of the stops on this rendezvous with the ghosts of the past.

Back when *The News Brothers* roamed and reported in Clarksville, G's had been the scene of many late-night meals. It was where we shared the tears and the cheers of Clarksville with our readers.

Nearly three decades later, not much had changed at the place. It even smelled the same, stepping in from the moist, cool of November by the Cumberland and quickly being enveloped in the aroma of griddle cakes, pancakes… Hell, let's not be formal. We call them flapjacks.

It was at G's—this family-friendly eatery—where my nickname was born, I recalled as I glanced at a table and saw a bacon-spattered copy of the local newspaper. I hardly recognized it as the same paper where I once gave 80 hours a week, my sanity, my life.

But, if I had it to live over again, I'd do it pretty much the same way, because what we did back then mattered...It made a difference...Whether it was Skipper or Chico The Monkey or the blood-drenched hillbilly homicides, a plane-load of "Fallen Eagles" or those teenagers who visit me in my sleep.

"Man, I'm 60 next week," I said to my old friend, Jerry "Chuckles" Manley, who on this night had forgotten his yellow aviator's cap, his on-screen trademark for all the *News Brothers* adventures.

"I got it out, but left it on the table," he said, slapping himself in the face and damn near falling over.

Like a true brother—as are all the men I would see on this night—Jerry had listened to me as he drove U.S. 41A up from Nashville for this gathering, celebrating 29 years, almost to the day, since our film, "Flapjacks: The Motion Picture," a kind of a warped story of my life—I am "Flapjacks," after all—and the lives of Rob and the rest of *The News Brothers* played at The Roxy on Franklin Street.

"Life's not easy, man," Jerry said. "But I turned 60 two days ago. And I'm not dead yet."

"Chuckles" laughed and spit a sunflower shell on the floor by the doorway into the pancake joint. Most of the old nasty habits, and *The News Brothers* had plenty, have been supplanted by more life-friendly things. Where Jerry and I used to chase the nights with smokes and jokes and perhaps mixtures of beer and coffee and pickled pigs' feet, he's now chugging bottled water and chewing sunflower seeds.

Me, well, I'm talking a lot, sharing the deepest of secrets, which is what *News Brothers* do, whether we've seen each other two weeks ago or 20 years ago. We all need someone we can lean on. And in my case, other than my wife, *The News Brothers* have always been the ones who offered their shoulders. And the gallant camaraderie, the undying bond with the now old men in shades remains untrampled by time.

"You know man, this is 29 years since the premiere, but 30 years, almost to the day, from our 30th birthday party," I reminded my old friend.

Remember, Jerry and I threw ourselves our own birthday party on Friday, Nov. 13, 1981, with the good-time fumes of that night and a football game two days later turning out to be the end of innocence for a group of young newspapermen.

Three days after that party, Kathy Jane Nishiyama went missing. And all hell broke loose, eventually triggering a self-protective madness—the birth and growth of *The News Brothers*—that carried us through to the end.

Jerry laughed. "I know I still owe you half for that keg," he confessed. "I tell you what, I'll buy the one for our 90th."

More likely a keg of Mylanta at that point, if ever reached. But I laughed. Jerry had taught me one thing all those years ago when he said he'd pay me back for the other half of the keg: Never trust a *News Brother*.

During our drive up from Nashville, I told Jerry about this book, about how Rob and I were still chasing those spirits, those ghouls, the pain in our souls by writing the story that changed our lives forever.

"Maybe you can edit it, or at least read through it," I said. "You're still the best line editor who ever was cut off at the knees by the heartless bastards who run what they call 'journalism' nowadays."

Recently laid off by the company to which he'd given most of the last three decades, Jerry laughed and shrugged. And popped a sunflower seed in his mouth.

By the time we got to G's, we already had spent a couple of hours in Clarksville.

First, we met Rob—my partner in coordinating this and other gatherings by the *Brothers*—at our old friend Frank Wm. White's printing shop, about a block from the church basketball courts in downtown Clarksville where Rodney Long had refereed youth games the mid-February 1982 night he was abducted and executed by vile slugs. Yep, I'm seeing slugs again, just thinking about them.

Frank, a damn fine reporter back in the day and an even better human being, had printed up a poster for this special gathering—again, the last, perhaps?—of the band of merrymakers who made the city smile even while we cried inside.

The poster is our own take on the old "Sgt. Pepper's" album cover, but we can't show it in this book because we don't want to be sued by those other carefree merrymakers, or at least the two that are left. Yeah. Yeah. Yeah.

Rob and I told Jerry and Frank more about our book and how it had helped us again, rescued us from the darkness of life in the 21st Century, where the Global War on Terror continues even while America, the beautiful, collapses beneath the corruption of economic policies.

One nation, under God, with liberty and justice for all.... Yeah. Yeah. Yeah.

While this book is the *News Brothers* story as told by me and Rob, it also has plenty of starring roles from Jerry, you'll remember. The sweet-souled fellow with the yellow aviator's cap always was a scene-stealer and I've cherished his friendship for going on 40 years now. Others, of course, include Frank, Ricky G. "Dumbo" Moore, Jim "Flash" Lindgren and Scott "Badger" Shelton. There also are special appearances by others in the Brotherhood, like David "Teach" Ross and "Da Mayor," aka Rich Liebe.

As I've mentioned, the boys, those who could or who cared, were back in the Queen City of the Cumberland for the annual *News Brothers* reunion, a chance to remember when we were young and the hero was never hung, to paraphrase my old pal, John Lennon, who, of course, was gunned down outside his home in New York City in December 1980. Still miss my old friend.

When Frank showed us his handiwork with the poster, we knew right away it was guaranteed to raise a smile with the lucky recipients at the 11-11-11 reunion. Rob and I dreamed up the photo idea and the words, but it took the amazing graphic-art skills of former *Kentucky New Era* employee Tracey Lewis and a man with a great eye and heart—Frank Wm. White—to perfectly execute it

The poster is of "Flapjacks' Lonely Hearts Club Band." Hope John and George don't sue us. Yeah. Yeah. Yeah.

Anyway, it's a tribute to the faces of our careers, including Skipper, Harold Lynch, John Glenn, Chico The Monkey, The Lone Ranger, Kris Kristofferson, Tiny Tim and an assortment of *News Brothers*, Beatles and dead prizefighters.

Flapjacks were on the menu at this *News Brothers* reunion at G's Pancake House in Clarksville, Tennessee, on Nov. 11, 2011. Scott "Badger" Shelton (left) and Mrs. Badger (Elise Frederick Shelton) smile for the camera. Looking on are David "Teach" Ross and Jerry "Chuckles" Manley.

Tim Ghianni (right) and Rick Moore talk about the old days at *The Leaf-Chronicle* while waiting for their flapjacks.

Rick Moore (foreground) signs his name to the newest *News Brothers* poster, while his old newspaper friends admire his writing ability.

Scott Shelton waits for his fellow *News Brothers* to autograph his poster at the 11-11-11 reunion.

After visiting with Frank and thanking him for his work and his generosity, we ventured over to *"News Brothers* Headquarters" for the night—the Riverview Inn—the hotel where the out-of-towners were going to stay if they didn't decide—as Jerry and I had—to take one more long ride into the darkness when the evening ended. Of course, when we were younger, that ride often ended after dawn. On this night we hoped to be home and in our beds by 1 or 1:30.

Before we got started with the festivities, a few incidentals—like making sure The Roxy lights were turned on and getting the word out to any stragglers that we were starting the night with flapjacks at G's—had to be taken care of...We hadn't been able to get in touch with "Dumbo" to inform him of the agenda for the night. He was on the road to Clarksville, from his home in Chattanooga, so Rob met up with him downtown across the street from the old theater.

After a handshake and a bear hug that stopped traffic—literally, as it took place in the middle of Franklin Street on a Friday night—the two much older and wiser former co-workers told a few incredible lies and then headed off to G's for those much-anticipated flapjacks.

Jerry and I rolled into the parking lot at G's, maybe 15 minutes before "Death" and "Dumbo" stumbled into the restaurant.

G's had been the scene of what we remembered as "The Last Supper" 30 years earlier, when a guy I resembled with long and dark curly hair played the benevolent and soon-to-be betrayed central character. One hand facing up, one down. Everybody must wear shades and smoke 'em if you got 'em. A photograph in the *News Brothers* Collection captures the moment in time.

"Which saint was I?" asked Jerry, as we stepped into what we had turned into our own upper room on that night—the back room of the restaurant, reserved for all *News Brothers* gatherings—and moved toward our table.

I didn't tell my buddy the saint he most resembled now is Nick. Of course, these days, I'm also more burned-out relic than blurry-eyed miracle worker. No water into wine tonight, I thought to myself. Just water and coffee, please.

With flapjacks, butter, maple syrup and a side of sausage.

"Da Mayor," known to non-New Brothers as Rich Liebe—the dethroned ruler of Hopkinsville, Kentucky, a private eye, Harley rider, serial car buyer and raconteur by trade now—leaped from his chair and embraced us both. He didn't know Jerry, but he knew he was "Chuckles."

"God bless the *News Brothers* extra good, wherever they are," said "Da Mayor." Jerry and I looked at each other, because we knew where we were. But we let "Da Mayor" slide a bit on that one in hopes he'd foot the night's bill.

"Chuckles…Where's your silly yellow hat?" asked "Da Mayor," who sat down and began ordering up food as if he was at an all-you-can-eat Chinese buffet rather than a flapjacks joint. Two omelets, one western and one cheese, a large stack, French toast, short-stack of chocolate chip flapjacks, biscuits and gravy, potatoes, chocolate milk, sausage and bacon and coffee. Oh, and Miss, could I have some water?

"I'm trying to cut back," "Da Mayor" said, with a laugh. Then his eyes lit up. A familiar face had just entered the room.

Scott "Badger" Shelton, carrying the oxygen tank that only on this day he had gotten as a tool to keep breathing in his valiant fight with the damned cancer, walked toward our table.

"I used to be Badger *News Brother*," Scott said, with a big smile. "How do you like my new mask?" Although not comfortable with the spiders of oxygen tubes taking the life-air to his nose, the feistiest of all *News Brothers* had no complaints about his predicament.

He was playing the cards life had dealt to him. "Badger" joked about it, of course. After all, he is, even in this mortal struggle, a *News Brother*. And *News Brothers* never back down. They laugh and spit in the eye of adversity and even the darkest and meanest of foes.

In planning our annual reunion, Rob and I wanted to make sure it was convenient for Scott to participate in the camaraderie. After all, in the *News Brothers* fraternity, it's all for one, and one for all.

We knew our brother, "Badger," in the fight of his life, needed the laughter as much as the oxygen to keep fighting. And we weren't going to let him down. Witnessing his courage and grace on this particular night made all of us damn proud of him....really proud to be his friend.

Scott's wife, the fiercely loyal Elise Frederick Shelton, joined us at G's. She was right there at her husband's side, to escort him and make sure he was happy with his flapjacks. In between those duties, she even had time to give an occasional hug to "Flapjacks," "Death" and "Chuckles" *News Brother.*

"Badger, I hugged your wife, but can I hug you?" I asked Scott, knowing he'd been in the hospital recently and his immunity was probably down. I knew I was healthy enough, but I wanted to make sure I didn't make him ill.

My "brother" assured me a hug was not a problem and was more than welcome. "From you? Flapjacks, I'd love a hug," Scott responded.

As I embraced him, I was careful not to squeeze hard on his brittle and lean frame. Damn. It felt so good to hug him. Our friendship has deep roots. I knew Scott even before the *News Brothers* movie days, as he was the local radio newsman and sometimes I would hang out at the station in the hopes someone would let me have the microphone and allow me to play Beatles music. And occasionally that happened.

While I was replaying "Badger" memories in my mind, Rob walked through the door of G's with Ricky G. "Dumbo" Moore—who had missed all previous reunions, but remembered on this occasion to wear his shades and even the hat he wore in the movie. Rob greeted Elise and "Badger," while I hugged Ricky, who I hired on my sports staff more than 30 years before and who I hadn't seen in 27 years. Looked leaner, at least by comparison, than he did in the 1980s. Remember that's "leaner" .... Not "lean."

With Rob and Ricky's arrival at G's, it was time to kick off the evening of fun...So, with "Flapjacks" ceremoniously soaking his flapjacks with syrup, the telling of three decades of lies and stories—some exaggerated—commenced and continued for more than two hours..

The News Brothers talk about the old days while having coffee at the Scott Shelton residence in Clarksville.

Jim "Flash" Lindgren autographs a *News Brothers* T-shirt for his old pal, Scott "Badger" Shelton.

The News Brothers recreate their infamous Abbey Road photograph at their 11-11-11 reunion. From left are Tim Ghianni, Scott Shelton, Rob Dollar and Jerry Manley.

The News Brothers mind their own business while visiting The Roxy in downtown Clarksville, Tennessee, during their 11-11-11 reunion. From left are David Ross, Jim Lindgren, Rob Dollar, Jerry Manley, Tim Ghianni and Rick Moore.

David "Teach" Ross, wearing his St. Louis Cardinals baseball cap, the newest *News Brother*, but among the most devoted, sat between Scott and "Da Mayor."

Denny Adkins, who played "The Big Guy" in the "Flapjacks" movie, and "Little Joe" Kraeske, who only recently won rave reviews for portraying George W. Bush in a 2010 *News Brothers* video, chowed down on their flapjacks at the far end of the long table. Unable to separate the true stories from the lies, they laughed anytime anyone said anything and kept uneasily looking for the door. Denny looked like he was trying to undress the waitress with his eyes. But knowing it was another lost cause, he never made his move. She popped her bubble gum and easily outclassed him, anyway. I think Denny left a single dollar bill on the table when he left the restaurant. It was either a big tip for him, or maybe it had his phone number on it.

Arriving late from Indianapolis, and completing the group for the 11-11-11 gathering, were Jim "Flash" Lindgren and his young newspaperman son John "Flash Jr." Lindgren. The elder "Flash," in a tribute to the late Harold Lynch, wore a trench coat and black cowboy hat to the reunion. He laughingly told us he brought his boy along so "Flash Jr." could meet some "real newspapermen." During our walk down Memory Lane, the waitress danced and hopped around—while laughter mixed with melancholy—as plates of flapjacks, sausage, eggs, biscuits and gravy and omelets kept arriving at the table.

Not all the food was going to be eaten by "Da Mayor," either. Just a good portion of it.

I enjoyed a short stack of buttermilk flapjacks and two sausage patties and remembered the nights Rob and I, sometimes with Jerry, sometimes with Skipper, ended up here at this same restaurant, eating the same menu items.

"We gonna recreate 'The Last Supper shot'?" "Dumbo" asked, during a break in the lying and story-telling.

We are, just by being here, I thought to myself.

Just how many more times will we see each other?

I mean, I know I'll see these guys, but will they all ever be together in this room again? We all have our separate lives, and none of us are spring chickens anymore…Time waits for no man, you know.

Putting those thoughts away, at least for the night, it was time to leave G's.

"Da Mayor," a damn nice guy, picked up the checks for the Sheltons' meals. Mine and Rob's, too.

"God bless you extra good," he told "Badger," before jumping into his Mustang and heading home to Hopkinsville, maybe to work on his next cheating spouse case or to make a late-night stop at Dairy Queen for an ice cream cone.

The flapjacks had hit the spot for everyone, and afterward, the rest of us went over to Scott's house, where his wife, Elise, had coffee ready for the *News Brothers* entourage. It was now time for the *News Brothers* to tell some more lies and warm a brother's heart. Scott settled into his couch and allowed his old friends to entertain him and enjoy his company.

And that's what we did…. At one point, I pointed out a picture on the wall of Scott's dad, Bill Shelton, a local insurance salesman who had been among my closest "advisers." Scott looked a lot like his late dad, which made me smile.

Bill Shelton had been one of the Clarksvillians who would routinely drop by *The Leaf-Chronicle* office to let me know things we might want to write about in the newspaper. He also used to ride me for smoking, something I finally gave up years ago. "The cigarettes always win," he told me, long before I finally accepted his sound advice.

To further describe any more of our private time at the Shelton residence would never do it justice, simply because it was a house filled with love and emotion. And plenty of laughter.

Yes, I said, Rob and I are writing a book. You are all in it. They seemingly didn't believe it, but I hope they buy copies.

After an hour or so, it was time to leave Scott's house—we could see he was getting tired, but still so proud to be among us. As I climbed up his stairs from the "Man Cave," I told him I loved him. He laughed and pointed to a stack of oxygen tanks in a nearby hallway. The biggest one Elise would hook him up to in a few minutes when he got in bed.

When Rob hugged "Badger," he asked if there was anything we could do to help out. "Just send me your prayers," Scott said.

"You've got them," Rob responded.

As we went out the front door, Scott waved goodbye and said, "I wish I could go with you guys."

But the look in his eyes showed it was not possible. Next time, "Badger." Next time.

For the rest of us, the night of 11-11-11 ended at 11:11 p.m. in downtown Clarksville with a farewell salute beneath the marquee of The Roxy. It was the same marquee that 29 years earlier had neon-flashed that the amazing tale of *The News Brothers* was playing inside the stately theater. "Laugh for a good cause," the marquee proclaimed in large red letters.

They did…And, we did.

We almost missed our "11-11-11-11-11" moment because of a pair of drunken British soldiers. The strange encounter could only happen to *The News Brothers*. The two soldiers were stumbling from bar to tattoo parlor and then down the middle of the street, while cursing and hollering at no one in particular. Approaching us, one of them bellowed, "This is how we curtsy." He then demonstrated, on unsteady legs, and then ran across the street.

"I'll beat you back to the barracks," he yelled to his mate. What I had just seen reminded me of all the nights I'd had to edit or even write about dead soldiers who had fallen victim to drunken driving out on Fort Campbell Boulevard. Some things never change.

Still laughing about the "curtsy," and trying our best to imitate it, we wandered aimlessly back to the hotel where Rob and the Lindgrens were spending the night. We tried to talk about our lives now, but really, what we all wanted to share was the camaraderie of our lives then—three decades ago when we were the "Kings of the World."

When the time came for the traveling *News Brothers* to leave and the sleepers to go to their rooms (including "Dumbo," who was booked at another hotel near Interstate 24), there were more hugs and laughs.

"Don't eat the paper, Dumbo," Rob told Ricky, with a big grin. "Dumbo" is the only original *News Brother* to still be employed, full-time, by a daily newspaper.

"It was great to see yous" flew around outside the hotel. And then we were gone.

As we rolled out of town, Jerry and I passed *The Leaf-Chronicle* on Commerce Street. We noticed a sign on the front door, advertising office space for rent on the first floor of the beautiful red brick building.

"Maybe we ought to rent it and put out a real newspaper in this town again," I quipped. "They might even give two former employees, now out-of-work newspapermen, a pretty good deal."

"Naah," answered "Chuckles," with a chuckle. "Be too hard to commute."

Further on down the road, we found ourselves within a couple blocks of Scott's house. We wondered how he was doing with his oxygen.

"I don't know how many more times I can do this," I told Jerry. "Maybe this is it."

"I'm just glad we got to see Scott," said Jerry, as he turned up the heat in the cab of his truck and pushed a CD into the changer.

Springsteen's "Glory Days" blasted from the stereo as we rolled into the night, taking extra care not to run over dogs or deer.

The next morning I heard from Rob. He asked me if I'd seen The Lone Ranger lately.

"Nope," I answered. "But let's ride off into the sunset, kemosabe...Maybe, if we're lucky, we'll get a look at Badger's silver bullet."

After a courageous battle, Scott Shelton died of cancer on Monday, Jan. 23, 2012. Five days later, *The News Brothers* were honorary pallbearers at a memorial service for their beloved brother. In this photograph, from left, are Rob Dollar, David Ross, Denny Adkins, Frank White, Rich Liebe, and Tim Ghianni

Chapter 29

THE DEARLY DEPARTED

Sad as it is, for all practical purposes, *The News Brothers* aren't roaming and reporting for their suppers, anymore. It's really a damn shame, especially for the people still around who enjoy reading a good newspaper.

What follows is the official-as-it-gets "30s"—or professional obituaries—for a bunch of damn nice guys and a lovable monkey who tried their best to make a difference in a world definitely gone crazy:

Tim "Flapjacks" Ghianni has been called by some "the last newspaperman."

Of course, that's not completely true. There remain people working at newspapers. But when he walked out the door of *The Tennessean* in August of 2007, American journalism lost a treasure. At least that's the opinion of some people. Others, no doubt, remarked "good riddance" to a guy who would neither bend down nor back down.

Unlike every other journalist he could see on his lonely, armed-guard escorted exit from *The Tennessean*—actually the guards were kind and also pissed that he was leaving, partly because he took the time to actually get to know their names—all he ever wanted to be was a newspaperman, a journalist. A teller of the truth and of tales that touched the heart.

He thought himself a leader, and backed it up by ladling his loyalty on the folks who worked hard for him, rather than squandering that loyalty on the people who employed him. His attitude was that if his staff worked hard for him, then that work would make the newspaper look good, as well. But the staff, the working folks, always came first.

It was his undoing.

When Ghianni exited *The Tennessean* building—a modern urban ulcer made of glass and covered in Styrofoam or some other foul, yet soft, compound—he was putting a very quiet "30" on a career he loved.

It began, not on Sept. 12, 1974—when he first showed up for work at 200 Commerce St. in Clarksville, Tennessee, the lovely old brick building that housed *The Leaf-Chronicle*—but really when he was just a child.

The seed to a life in newspapers actually was planted by Ghianni's mother, the late Dorothy "Dot" Ghianni, who went to work in the newsrooms of Chicago back during the days of World War II.

His father, Em Ghianni, a member of "The Greatest Generation," had enlisted in the Big War as a Marine, but was forced into the U.S. Army because of color-blindness. Em Ghianni was in the Rainbow Division, but plans to have him land in Normandy were short-circuited by the opportunity to attend Officer Candidate School. It led to him becoming a first lieutenant, with a tour of duty in the Pacific during the final days of World War II and the first few years of the Occupation of Japan.

All beside the point, of course…But, Ghianni's mother had been among the women who entered the workforce because the men were at war. And her love of the newspapering way of life— she began as a cops reporter, covering the cruelty and gore on Chicago's historically rugged South Side—was instilled in her second son.

As previously mentioned in this book, the day Ghianni showed up for his *Leaf-Chronicle* interview—a week before his official first day's work—he sat in the lobby with James "Fly" Williams, a playground basketball legend. Fly was beginning his new career that day—he'd just signed a multimillion-dollar contract with the

Spirits of St. Louis. Fly's career crashed and burned, not long after it started.

Ghianni, on the other hand, was in it for the long haul, beginning with his $125 per week salary and working a variety of jobs at *The Leaf-Chronicle*, including prep writer, prep editor, sports editor, assistant city editor, special projects editor and, for many years, associate editor.

His time at *The Leaf-Chronicle* is well-documented in this book.

He was the last *News Brother* at *The Leaf-Chronicle* when he departed on a cold, rainy, late night/early morning in February of 1988.

The next night Ghianni began his job at the *Nashville Banner*, where they created a position for him—night city editor—so they could bring him on board as a full-time employee.

It should be noted his final years at *The Leaf-Chronicle* were not a wasted effort. Even though he had "lost" his friend for life, this book's co-author, as his running buddy in news adventures, and his other *News Brothers* also had departed, Ghianni continued to do what he believed in.

Still chasing his dream, he took pride in *The Leaf-Chronicle*, working usually seven nights a week to make sure the best possible newspaper was delivered to the people of the town that he had adopted and that had adopted him.

Even after the rest of *The News Brothers* left town, Ghianni continued to wear his sunglasses and yellow fedora to work and on weekends wear his Deerfield High School, Class of 1969 letter jacket, with Hawaiian shirts and red canvas Converse All-Stars sneakers.

He also began a curious habit of keeping dead roses in vases on his desk, a trait that followed him until his last night in a newsroom.

The half-decade spent after his brothers left was not without its successes. Ghianni and the newspaper won many first-place awards for journalism excellence and he twice received the state's top award for investigative or feature journalism, The Malcolm Law Award, while in Clarksville.

In his final years at *The Leaf-Chronicle*, he had only occasional contact with his comrade in adventure and journalism, Rob Dollar. Probably the most contact they had came when the hurricane hit Houston and "Flap," ever the compassionate man, called his friend and advised him to "get your ass out of there."

Ghianni, at all the newspapers where he worked, wrote an award-winning column, which was his passion. He also did his very best to help teach the younger reporters about handling the big story on deadline.

To this day, Ghianni prides himself on his ability to write a world-class lead for a story.

The biggest story he was involved with in the post-*News Brothers* era came in December 1985, when a plane-load of Fort Campbell soldiers returning from a year of peacekeeping duty in the Sinai, crashed in Gander, Newfoundland. Two-hundred and forty-eight soldiers died in the tragedy.

His boss at the time, Dee Bryant, editor of *The Leaf-Chronicle*, called him as soon as she learned about it. She primarily worked days to tend to business and corporate politics and lunch, and Ghianni handled the night shift when the paper was live.

He had probably been asleep two hours when Bryant called to report the early, unconfirmed rumors of the crash.

"Oh, shit," was his measured response, as he leaped from bed, fired up a smoke, stepped into the shower and got ready for what turned into almost a 24-hour shift covering the tragedy of all tragedies for the area communities. Yes, the shower extinguished the smoke.

Ghianni was editor and traffic cop, working with Bryant to make sure all angles of this major story were covered, and then he went out to the first memorial service that night to do a bit of writing himself.

Ever good with catchy phrasing, when Bryant asked for a "tag" to tie all of the stories together, Ghianni came up with the phrase "Fallen Eagles," which was co-opted by some of the television networks covering the tragedy.

Late in his Clarksville years, Ghianni reconnected with Jerry "Chuckles" Manley, who came to Ghianni's house every Sunday night, after his own shift was done down at *The Tennessean*, and the two old *News Brothers* would salute the dawn together.

One day, out of the blue, Ghianni got called by John Seigenthaler, the esteemed former aide to Bobby Kennedy who was chairman and editor of *The Tennessean* in Nashville. Seigenthaler wanted to see Ghianni the next morning.

A four-hour interview followed in which Seigenthaler hired Ghianni to be a night city editor as soon as that position was available in six weeks. He was able to keep his Chronicle job in the meantime and when he reported on an off-day for training at *The Tennessean*, he was told by Seigenthaler's thumbs-less managing editor that "John's crazy as shit ... there's no job here for you."

It was about six months later that Ghianni got the same job at the *Banner*.

It didn't take long for Ghianni to establish himself there, moving from night city editor to state editor, where he was in charge of news outside Metro and all government coverage, including the legislature, the governor and the Washington, D.C. delegation from Tennessee.

Ghianni was responsible for the coverage of the first Bill Clinton presidential election, after the *Banner* became the first newspaper in the country to endorse "The Man from Hope." He still carries his Secret Service security clearance card, along with IDs from all of the papers where he worked.

While at the *Banner*, he prided himself on running a staff that he thought was the best in the business, from folks adept at quirky murder stories with bizarre twists—like the murderous and obese twins who burned up their victims to a killer who with precision skinned his prey—to the reporters who handled the headline-grabbing antics of the legislature and Congress. The state desk routinely dominated the newspaper, thanks to Ghianni and his assistant, Andy Telli. Yeah, some folks may have called them "garlic-eaters," but Ghianni and Telli, the *Banner* Mafia, knew how to sniff out the big stories and handle the news.

It would be difficult for Ghianni to choose his favorite *Banner* stories, as he was the editor in charge of coverage of the 101st Airborne (Air Assault) deployment and mission in Somalia and in the Bush Sr. Gulf War. He dispatched one of his reporters, Charlie Appleton, to file dispatches from Somalia. Ghianni couldn't go himself, because of his duties, but he was happy Charlie got to go on the great adventure.

Because of his contacts at Fort Campbell, hard-won during his tenure in Clarksville, the *Banner* was the first daily newspaper (other than perhaps his pal Dollar's *New Era*) to report the full deployment of the Screaming Eagles to Bush Sr.'s Gulf War.

Ghianni also made sure every Scud attack "on *Banner* time" was properly documented during Bush Sr.'s war. "Nothing makes you happier than hearing a Scud land on *Banner* time," he joked with his boss, managing editor Tony Kessler, as they mapped out story placement and Scud locator maps.

Ghianni's famous 5 a.m. "strategy sessions"—at which he and deputy editor Mike McGehee, a genuinely good guy and versatile, ethical journalist (not surprisingly, he got shafted eventually himself), huddled over cigarettes outside the *Banner*'s entrance on Broadway—became more than the day's first smoke breaks. Often Kessler would come out to join in, though he despised smoking. If Eddie Jones – the seasoned editor who had become Ghianni's mentor and close friend -- was around, he'd almost always join in the outdoors plotting of that day's newspaper.

Ghianni's sense of humanity was never questioned, as for example, when one of his reporters covered the suicide of a Tennessee secretary of state who had been caught up in the political scandal du jour for state government. That news story was filled with passion and sadness and tawdry details. But Ghianni, who knew the dead official, then went to the fallen politician's hometown to talk with his friends and family, people who loved him despite his scandalous and tarnished end.

Because of his reputation of being a fair journalist, these people took Ghianni into their confidence and the day ended with him putting a convenience store-bought flower on the grave of the dead official. Then he drove back to the newspaper to write about the tragedy of loss deeply felt in the much-loved man's hometown.

Perhaps the most fun story he was involved in at the *Banner* occurred the night he took his night cops reporter Jose Lambiet— now a high-flying celebrity columnist in South Florida—to a farewell dinner at Lorenzo's a since-deceased mom-and-pop Italian restaurant owned by a retired wrestler who was a friend of Ghianni's godfather, Uncle Al Conte.

Anyway, the cops reporter was leaving because he had been drafted ... into the Belgian Army ... and had to go home to serve. Ghianni lost staffers to better jobs or to the company ax in the past. Heck, as well-chronicled in this book, his sidekick Rob Dollar lost his job because he "wanted" to become police chief. Still, losing a prize reporter and pal because he was drafted by Baudoin, King of the Belgians, and his brother Prince Albert II aka "Prince Albert in a can" was, to say the least, unprecedented.

Ghianni and the drafted Belgian Lambiet grabbed the portable police scanner and went to dinner, figuring they'd come back and finish things up in a couple of hours.

About 9 p.m., as the two were wrapping up their wine-soaked Chicken Parmesan dinner and preparing to head back to the office, the portable scanner began to chirp with news of a truckload of cattle that had overturned on I-440, near downtown Nashville.

"We're calling the rodeo out here to help," said one of the officers on the scanner.

A perfect story. Seems that a traveling rodeo was in town to perform at Municipal Auditorium.

The cowboys had been enlisted to go out to the closed interstate to help rescue the score or more of beef cattle that were on the loose in the heart of the city.

It was a perfect story for Lambiet—a fine police reporter with a curiosity and energy that reminded Ghianni somewhat of his pal, Rob Dollar (who was the best cops reporter he's ever known) — to go out on before his military service.

The two men rolled out to the highway and were allowed through the police blockade and witnessed a troupe of lasso-waving men in Stetsons and chaps riding their gallant steeds at full gallop up and down I-440 and the median to capture the beef cattle.

It was no Chico The Monkey story, but it too had a sad ending, as the captured cattle were bound for slaughter and dining room tables near you. And it sure made a great lead story for the next day's *Banner*.

Ghianni's habit of being called into the office to visit the publisher—something that happened with increasing frequency during his final years in Clarksville, so much so that Luther Thigpen eventually bought him a chair (just joking)—continued at the *Banner*. The publisher there frequently "hosted" Ghianni, especially if a senator or a legislator or a governor called to complain about the less-than-flattering coverage in the newspaper.

Those visits eventually led to Ghianni being shifted from state editor to features editor, but he retained his spot as the No. 2 man—behind the managing editor—in the newsroom when the paper was live.

During his years as a journalist, Ghianni's favorite politician was not Clinton nor Al Gore—although he befriended Gore's mom and pop and they held him in high regard—but Tennessee Gov. Ned McWherter.

Why? It was because when McWherter was angry with him, he didn't call the publisher and cause him to be hauled in and sworn at by an overweight, sweaty businessman. When the governor was mad, he'd just call Ghianni at home and tell him about it. Very colorfully.

As for Al Gore, well Ghianni knew and liked him fine. But he'll gladly tell you the story of the day he went into a meeting with the visiting senator, senior political writer J. Patrick Willard, the publisher and Editor Eddie Jones.

Sipping his coffee from a white Styrofoam cup—"nothing tastes as good as good old newspaper coffee," said the future Mr. Global Warming.

Since there was a deadline, Ghianni and his reporter left the meeting to go begin hammering out a story on what brought the future presidential candidate to 1100 Broadway that day.

Gore couldn't help but show his true colors. After he said his goodbyes to the publisher, Al—a former newsman of muted acclaim at *The Tennessean*— tossed out his Styrofoam cup and ambled over to Ghianni's desk and began dictating a lead.

Tim listened and then said: "No wonder you couldn't make it in this business, you worthless son of a bitch. You can't write."

Al laughed and went on to try to change the world and lose the presidency in Florida years later.

Ghianni's personality and honesty, and a hint of that big smile, even got him into the home of Pauline and Sen. Albert Gore Sr.— the future vice president's folks—on the day Clinton announced Little Al as his running mate.

Ghianni called the Gore home in Carthage, Tennessee, to ask if the proud mom would mind talking. She said she didn't know if she had time, but to come over if he wanted to.... An hour later he stood at her door. And four hours after that he left both the senior Gores laughing and offering their friendship. Course they did ask him to vote for their son "and that guy from Arkansas."

Even though their son was a former *Tennessean* staffer, it was a *Banner* writer who first got to interview the Gores about the soon-to-be-nominated offspring.

At the *Banner*, Ghianni continued the prize-winning column writing and even won one more Malcolm Law Award.

His favorite award ever was the Jerry Thompson Humanitarian Journalist Award, presented by the Conference of Christians and Jews. Thompson, a great and gritty *Tennessean* journalist who was dying of cancer, left his bed to be there to hand the award to Ghianni, the first non-*Tennessean* staffer to win the honor. It was Jerry's last time to present the award in person, but he said he had to do it for Ghianni, whose acceptance speech is the stuff of legend and said to be available on bootleg tapes.

He also earned the staff-voted Fred Russell Award at the *Banner*. Russell was one of the great sports writers of all time—considered right up there with Red Smith, Jim Murray and Grantland Rice—and the award named for Russell was to go to the editor or staffer who did the most to provide leadership and instill loyalty in the staff and for the newspaper.

Nashville Banner great Fred Russell (left) congratulates Tim Ghianni after Ghianni won the newspaper's first Fred Russell Award for journalistic excellence, newsroom leadership and dedication to his craft. Ghianni was the only one to ever receive the staff-voted award. After Ghianni won by a landslide the first year, the award was retired permanently.

After Ghianni was awarded the first Russell honor, the "annual" honor was canceled, apparently as the powers-that-be didn't like the prospect of annually allowing the staff to celebrate the eccentric and ethical journalist.

It should be noted that Mr. Russell—as Ghianni always called him— had been on a first-name basis with Babe Ruth, Jack Dempsey, Lou Gehrig, Joe DiMaggio, Jackie Robinson, Vince Lombardi, John Madden, Rocky Marciano, Wilma Rudolph, Mickey Mantle, Willie Mays, Johnny Unitas and Ben Hogan.

A great fan of and mentor for Ghianni and his writing, Mr. Russell told the younger man on more than one occasion that "the best thing the *Banner* ever did is hire you."

Ghianni carried Mr. Russell's "office"—autographs and great news clippings—out to his car on the day the older gentleman tried to quietly leave the profession. They went down an elevator, away from the newsroom, and to the parking lot. And they hugged. When Mr. Russell died, his family noted there was a picture of Ghianni's daughter, Emily, and his dog, Buddy, on the great journalist's refrigerator.

The *Banner* folded in February 1998, but Ghianni's column for the year before was judged the best in the nation by a major association of editors.

The folding of the paper that he loved left Ghianni with only one choice for continuing his career as a journalist.

He didn't want to move from Nashville because his elderly parents lived there and his mother was gradually dying from a vicious, suffocating ailment. (It should be noted here that she and Ghianni's father, along with a number of important Nashville businessmen, attended the *News Brothers* world premiere party in Clarksville in November 1982.)

Primarily, though, Ghianni didn't want to move because he and his wife, Suzanne (an accomplished journalist, with stops in Paragould, Ark., and Clarksville, Sweetwater and Murfreesboro, Tennessee), were in the middle of their second adoption of an orphan from Romania, and the home study and the paperwork all had been completed. And, for the adoption to continue, he had to have an uninterrupted stream of income and benefits.

Here is a photo of the entire newsroom staff of *The Nashville Banner* at the time the Nashville afternoon newspaper closed its doors in February 1998.

The normally shirt-and-tie *Nashville Banner* crew dressed in casual clothing — for moving out and crying — on the last day of publication on Feb. 20, 1998. Tim Ghianni (second from right) led the last daily news budget meeting plotting the lineup of stories. That last issue included coverage of the paper's death as well that of Tim's friend Grandpa Jones. From left are legendary journalist Bob Battle, handling business news (ties apparently were "casual wear" for Bob); Dan Coleman, editorial page editor; Ghianni, who questions his comrades about the day's offerings; photo editor Donn Jones; and Andy Telli, representing the news desk. Longtime news editor Tony Kessler, who generally headed these meetings, apparently was making copies of his resume.

GRANDPA JONES

Grandpa Jones's Feb. 19, 1998, death usually would have been the next day's lead story. But not when the next day was Feb. 20, 1998, when the *Banner's* death dominated the paper and Louis Marshall Jones' death was secondary.
In Ghianni's last long interview with Grandpa, the Grand Ole Opry legend talked not about banjos and "Hee Haw," but about Henry David Thoreau.

The Tennessean offered him a job on the night copy desk, and he took it, figuring he could move up.

Within a year he did move up to entertainment editor, and was in charge of entertainment features and breaking news in Music City USA.

A tough task, but Ghianni brought flair to it and along the way earned respect from a top-flight staff.

He also earned the friendship of Kris Kristofferson and Chet Atkins, not to mention the respect of Nashville music legends like Eddy Arnold, Willie Nelson, Tom T. Hall, George Jones, Bobby Bare, Vince Gill, Garth Brooks and Waylon Jennings.

It should be noted that after Atkins died, his widow brought to Ghianni the nameplate Chet had personally carved for his own desk.

"Chet loved you and would have wanted you to have this," or words to that effect, she wrote.

Ghianni also stood in for his reporter, Jay Orr, now a well-known executive at the Country Music Hall of Fame and Museum, when George Jones drove his Lexus off a bridge near his home near Franklin, Tennessee.

The fear was that Jones—who had fallen off the wagon and driven off the bridge in relatively consecutive fashion—would die. Orr "couldn't be reached," because he was enjoying his son's birthday.

So Ghianni went on in to the newspaper and covered the breaking news story. He pulled it off because he could call his old friends Porter Wagoner and Little Jimmy Dickens and others who were backstage at the Grand Ole Opry on the night of the crash.

"Thanks for caring about us old-timers," said Wagoner. "We sure hope old George is OK."

Jones, perhaps the greatest pure singer in country music history, not only survived, he invited Ghianni out to his house and says he still owes his friend the writer a steak dinner.

Ghianni's most-emotional days at the morning newspaper involved the declining health and the death of John R. Cash.

Kris Kristofferson and Tim Ghianni stand in front of the spot where Nashville's infamous Tally-Ho Tavern once had a thriving business, serving the rich and the struggling poor. Ghianni, as a writer for *The Tennessean*, wrote a great feature story that took the famous singer/songwriter for a trip down Memory Lane.

Kris Kristofferson visits with Tim Ghianni at the Country Music Hall of Fame in Nashville, Tennessee, in early August of 2007. The two silver-tongued (and silver-haired) devils have mellowed well with age, now sharing passions for music, family and peace.

Ghianni knew Cash some and had even been to his house, given a private and laugh-filled tour by the lady of the manor, June Carter Cash.

In Cash's declining years, "The Man in Black" didn't give many interviews, out of pride more than anything. He was ailing more than he cared the public to know. He did agree, however, to Ghianni's request for an interview "as soon as I get back from the coast" where Cash was recording his despairing and uplifting American Recordings.

Cash never made it to the coast. He soon went into the hospital and died.

Ghianni, with his senior music writer and friend Peter Cooper, covered the funeral, as they had with Cash's wife, June Carter Cash, three months earlier. Ghianni still occasionally visits the graves and keeps in touch with John Carter Cash, the son of John and June.

But then, at *The Tennessean*, came the shadows that seemed to follow Ghianni throughout his career, in the way of bosses who failed to understand the reason he stood up for his staff, wouldn't subject them to petty lies and tasks, tried to deflect the corporate lunacy. He allowed them—particularly his top-notch country music team of Cooper and gossip columnist/great reporter Brad Schmitt—to curse and laugh as long as their product was good and honorable.

Of course, he cursed and laughed—and even sang—with them, his easygoing demeanor helping the paper score scoop after scoop. But he wouldn't allow the bosses to stab those men in the backs or penalize them if, while doing their jobs, they happened to offend someone or step on toes, inside and outside the building.

Management was angry that not only he, but his staff, particularly Cooper, were spending too much time writing about guys like Cash, Arnold, Nelson, Tom Petty, Bob Dylan, Bruce Springsteen, The Rolling Stones, Duane Eddy, Rosanne Cash, The Beatles, Loretta Lynn, Dolly Parton, Carl Smith, Shel Silverstein, Waylon Jennings, Tom T. Hall, Elvis and Kristofferson—folks who appealed to the wrong target demographic—and not enough time and space on guys like Shaggy.

You remember Shaggy, don't you?

In fact, when Ghianni interviewed Eddy Arnold—the last interview the man, who had become a friend, ever did, sort of an "exit interview" for the country legend—Ghianni was told by his bosses he should have run it as "a brief.... No one cares."

Similarly, Ghianni's friendship with Scotty Moore, who invented rock 'n' roll guitar when he and Elvis and Bill Black recorded at Sun Studio in Memphis, was seen more as a liability than a plus. Sure, he got an interview that Moore still considers the best he's ever given, but management couldn't see the worth in devoting space to an "old guitar player."

Despite the fact his stories were not considered "worthy" by some, the artists enjoyed the interviews and the end result. Chuck Leavell, the bandleader and keyboardist for The Rolling Stones enjoyed the encounter with Ghianni enough to ask him to come backstage when the great rock band hit Nashville. Cooper and Schmitt had treated their boss to the almost-front-row ticket, and he asked them to join him with Leavell and other members of the entourage.

After about six years as entertainment editor, Ghianni was told he was "too old" and "a maverick, and Gannett doesn't need mavericks who don't think like everyone else."

With that explanation, he was moved to the job of senior entertainment writer. It was at that spot that he participated in coverage of the deaths of Waylon and Cash, whose worth in selling newspapers was finally recognized by the front office when they died.

Deaths of good people are never happy occurrences, and it's necessary to cover those stories with appropriate respect. For Ghianni, the best thing about the coverage was the fact he could call on people he liked, from legendary and affable Ramblin' Jack Elliott to Earl Scruggs, for comment. Scruggs' wife, Louise, who liked Ghianni, spent most of the day trying to track down the illusive Bob Dylan for comment about Cash's death. "If anybody can get that guy to talk to you, Tim, it's me," said Louise, who was a wonderful woman and good friend.

When the economy began to falter, Ghianni then was shifted to fill a space on the general features staff as senior features writer.

He again continued to stir things up. He had developed a friendship with the Rev. Will Campbell, a great theologian, writer and civil rights activist. The reverend would call Ghianni to talk about Waylon and Willie and the boys. But when Ghianni informed his bosses he wanted to do a story about Will, who had presided over Waylon's lonesome funeral and who had just written a book, he was almost spit on. "Everybody who cares about Will Campbell already knows about him," he was told. To which he responded: "What do you know about the good reverend?" and was greeted by an anemic shrug.

Kristofferson, who had been somewhat reclusive, and his wife, Lisa, became acquainted with Ghianni through an interview on the phone. After reading the story, the Kristoffersons contacted the writer, expressing their delight at the way it turned out. They said they'd like to meet Ghianni when they came to Nashville the next time.

That time came after Kris came to town to serve as eulogist at the Cash funeral that turned more into a celebration of a great and influential life.

Ghianni suggested that he and Kristofferson take a Sunday stroll down the lonesome city sidewalks of Music Row, which the songwriter hadn't visited by daylight in 30 years. Kris not only agreed, he brought along his son, Johnny Cash Kristofferson, who recorded the stroll for a high school project.

Because of Cash's recent death, the songsmith was in a reflective mood, remembering things he hadn't thought about in years. Again, when the story of the daylong ramble was written, Ghianni had a hard time getting it in the paper. "Who cares about Kris Kristofferson?" he was told more than asked.

Ghianni's *News Brothers* pal Jerry Manley gladly took the story and used it, probably against company wishes, to fill up a local and neighborhoods section, which "Chuckles" edited. Finally one of the big bosses read the story and said to Ghianni: "You've obviously known this guy for a long time to get him to open up to you." Ghianni replied it really was just the beginning of a friendship, that they hadn't been pals for a long time... that people just liked talking to Ghianni as much as he liked talking to them.

For a short time at *The Tennessean*, Ghianni had written a weekly column about the people of Nashville and it had gained some popularity. It was slice of life, like the prize-winning and nationally honored columns he did in Clarksville and for the *Banner*.

Without explanation, the column was suspended. A few weeks later, he was told that it would be revived if he agreed to write about the paper's target demographic (i.e., younger, upscale white people) instead of the mostly black, mostly lower-middle-class that had been his focus.

Instead of writing about mostly white suburban businessmen—as he was instructed—and putting his column slug on it, he refused, telling bosses he'd spent too many years building that column's reputation to taint it for commerce and corporate politics. His column was dead and his newspaper days on life-support.

Among his life's most-treasured honors was being named in an obituary among the survivors of one of his column topics, a kind and generous man named George Gordon. Yes, like many Ghianni topics, George was black; but Ghianni's point was that we are all the same, sharing the same hopes dreams, fears and ambitions. Apparently it was that kind of attitude that made Ghianni expendable.

Early in the winter of 2007, Ghianni was moved from features to night cops. The worst thing about the job transfer was that it took him away from his family: Emily and Joe, his two adopted kids from Romania, and his wife, Suzanne. But the economy was faltering and he knew layoffs or buyouts would be in the offing.

So, he made the most of it, enjoying the cop coverage—after all, that always had been a *News Brothers* specialty—right up until the day he got his buyout in August. Not too many reporters in their mid-50s are riding with undercover, weapons-packing vice cops or dealing, first-hand, with the carnage left by serial killers.

He was pushed harder toward the door by the task of listening to the scanner during rush hour and posting every traffic wreck or calamity online immediately ... so those who looked at their Internet before leaving work would know to avoid the congestion. Imagine some poor schmuck looking at his watch and saying: "Gotta go home, now, boss. But first let me check the newspaper's Web site to see if there are wrecks on I-40...."

Ghianni wasn't allowing anyone to push him out quite yet. "Pay me to stay or pay me to go," was his motto. He made a game of the wreck reports, not just tracking the traffic flow, but making sure to remind people in the building that there were snarls on various highways. He took his duty as wreck documenter seriously, of course. No monkey business allowed.... Or so he claims. When he left, the newspaper stopped doing those detailed reports on traffic jams. "It must have been my irreplaceable prose," he says, with a smile that would make some folks shudder.

His boss in those last months? Night City Editor Jerry Dale Manley. Yep, perhaps as punishment, poor old "Chuckles" was assigned the task of managing a stubborn and ethical old journalist. The two old brothers even did their best to put a dash of Chico The Monkey-style flavor into the late-news reports. Appropriate phrasing from the "Dirty Harry" movies and "NYPD Blue" and even "Flapjacks: The Motion Picture" appeared in some well-written and edited police stories.

But then came the call from the front office and Ghianni got the directive to pack up his stuff, including a massive stuffed dog covered with press passes and laminates from a career spent in high and low places. Just before leaving, he taped the last dead rose of his illustrious career to the desk he was vacating.

Now, a civilized discussion could take place on the reason Ghianni and a bunch of other veterans were "shown the door"— albeit with a little cash. But look at your local newspaper and you can tell it wasn't just in Nashville.

Since severing his ties with *The Tennessean*, Ghianni has become a successful, full-time freelance writer, with a heavy focus on the people, places and things of Nashville, as well as a part-time news writing educator at local universities. He's also been employed as a wire service correspondent for Reuters.

Tim Ghianni was known as "Flapjacks" to one and all.

"All I ever wanted to do was work in newspapers," the veteran journalist said, in describing his life's ambition. "Even now."

His main hobby, other than writing, is letting his hair—almost always on the shaggy, aggravate-the-bosses side—grow to decidedly anti-Korporate length.

The News Brothers have reunited as friends but also to tell their story and to document what happened to newspapers in the last four decades or so.

It should be noted that Ghianni ended his tenure at *The Leaf-Chronicle* by following an old Tony Durr tradition. On Christmases, at least the two Durr worked in Clarksville, or other holidays, he would call *The News Brothers* into his office for a Styrofoam cup filled with brandy.

It was a gesture of camaraderie, an act of special friendship, a subtle violation of sanitized newsroom policy.

The night Ghianni left *The Leaf-Chronicle*, he let the newsroom empty out, then he turned out the lights and went out to his car, where he poured himself a cup of brandy and said goodbye to Clarksville, to Tony Durr, to "Skipper," to a tumultuous era.

In the summer of 2007, after leaving *The Tennessean*, he sat in a different car, in a different parking lot, and stared up at a newspaper building that he knew would be the last one he'd ever occupy.

Ghianni no longer drinks, but on that night, he reached into the glove box and pulled out a small bottle of brandy. He looked into the Nashville night and took a long, slow pull. And he said goodbye to newspapers.

Rob Dollar and Tim Ghianni get into the act while visiting the Nashville Pickers antique store in the summer of 2011. Ghianni, now a freelance writer in Nashville, spotlighted the store and the picking business in a story for a weekly publication.

Rob "Death" Dollar left the profession of journalism on July 31, 2003, following a 24-year career as an award-winning staff writer and senior editor with six newspapers in three states.

At the time of his resignation, Dollar was working for his hometown daily newspaper, the *Kentucky New Era*, in Hopkinsville, Kentucky, where, he, over the years, held the jobs of staff writer/reporter, copy editor, copy desk chief, associate editor, managing editor and interim editor.

"I'm not leaving newspapers," Dollar said, in explaining his decision. "The sad truth is newspapers have left me."

The late David Riley, then the editor of the *Kentucky New Era*, said Dollar would be sorely missed by his colleagues at the newspaper, who came to know and respect him for his reputation as a tireless newsman always looking for the story behind the story.

"Whether he was phoning in stories to us from the Kuwaiti desert or from a courtroom in downtown Cadiz, Rob always had one group uppermost in his mind, and that was our readers," Riley said. "And, he always did (his job) with professionalism, creativity and compassion."

David Wilkison, Kentucky bureau chief for *The Associated Press* in 2003, lauded Dollar's work over the years.

"I'm sorry to hear about Rob's departure. He's been nothing but an asset to The AP during his tenure at the paper, helping provide AP–member newspapers and radio and TV stations and their readers and listeners across the state—and even the nation—news from the region," Wilkison said. "The AP counts on editors like Rob Dollar and their valuable contributions, and we'll miss him."

In his final job with the *Kentucky New Era*, that of managing editor, Dollar was responsible for planning and coordinating coverage of news events in the community and surrounding area. He also supervised the newspaper's reporting staff, edited stories, directed special projects and was a member of the newspaper's Editorial Board.

For two years, Dollar wrote "Stop the Press," a popular Friday column that appeared on the newspaper's editorial page. The Kentucky Press Association, in 2003, judged the column the best of all medium-sized newspapers in the commonwealth, presenting Dollar with a first-place award. Between 1983 and 2003, Dollar received more than 12 KPA awards for news writing, feature writing, and investigative reporting.

Hopkinsville-Christian County Historian William T. Turner said Dollar had a knack for keeping one eye on local events and the other eye on world events.

"Throughout the 20 years of my association with Rob Dollar, I've always found him to be professionally correct and very knowledgeable of the importance of the cavalcade of local events," Turner said.

The local historian said Dollar's leadership role in creating the 2002 "Hoptown Connection" and the 2003 "Great Storytellers"—*Kentucky New Era* special sections that earned record sales—was a decisive factor in spotlighting the importance of local history to area readers.

During his years at the *Kentucky New Era*, Dollar reported on many stories at the local level that made their way into the state, national and international spotlights.

He covered the Gander air tragedy that killed 248 soldiers from Fort Campbell in December 1985 and President Ronald Reagan's subsequent visit to the Army post to console grieving family members.

In June 1988, Dollar was the lead reporter in a series of stories about a major train derailment in Crofton that resulted in the release of a toxic plume that forced the evacuation of thousands in western Kentucky. Two years later, Dollar reported on the arrest and federal drug trial and conviction in Paducah of former Christian County Sheriff Bill Dillard, who was Kentucky's first elected black sheriff.

During his career as a reporter and editor, Dollar interviewed such national and international figures as Bob Hope, Oprah Winfrey, Peter Fonda, Hank Williams Jr., Melvin Belli, Army Gen. William C. Westmoreland, Vice President Al Gore and former

British Prime Minister Sir Harold Wilson. An interview he conducted with Hollywood actress Ashley Judd—done in the summer of 1986, weeks after her high school graduation—is mentioned in at least two books as being her first given to a journalist.

Dollar also was among the first civilian reporters to get an interview with then-Army Lt. Col. Richard A. Cody after his return from the Persian Gulf and Desert Storm in April 1991. As an AH–64 Apache attack helicopter pilot, Cody, at the time a battalion commander at Fort Campbell, and fellow aviators fired the first shots of the Gulf War earlier that year. Cody, who played basketball for Bobby Knight at West Point, eventually became a four-star general and later served as the Army's Vice Chief of Staff at The Pentagon during America's wars in Iraq and Afghanistan.

On two occasions as a senior editor, Dollar traveled to war zones—Kosovo, in August 2001 and Kuwait, only miles from its border with Iraq, in March 2003—to report on the missions of Fort Campbell soldiers. When Operation Iraqi Freedom was launched, Dollar was an embedded reporter with one of Fort Campbell's aviation brigades. Camp Thunder, where Dollar and the division's helicopter assets were based, was the target of the war's first missile attack by Saddam Hussein. There were no casualties.

In addition, Dollar was among only a few journalists ever invited to visit the secret compound of the 160th Special Operations Aviation Regiment (Airborne) and fly with "Night Stalker" helicopter pilots during a training demonstration.

For his work covering Fort Campbell soldiers, Dollar was made an honorary member of the 101st Airborne Division (Air Assault).

After about 10 years as a reporter, Dollar became part of the *New Era's* copy desk in the spring of 1993 and two years later was promoted to copy desk chief and associate editor.

From March 1999 through June 1999, Dollar served as the interim editor of the *Kentucky New Era*.

He briefly left the newspaper in July 1999 to work as a copy editor at *The Fayetteville Observer* in Fayetteville, N.C., returning to

Hopkinsville the following spring to become the *New Era*'s managing editor.

An honor graduate of Fort Campbell High School, Dollar attended and graduated from Hopkinsville Community College and Eastern Kentucky University in Richmond, Kentucky. He earned bachelor's degrees in both journalism and police science.

At EKU, he worked on the student newspaper, *The Eastern Progress*, for two years, serving as editor when he was a senior. Upon graduation, with honors, he received a citation for Significant Contributions to Collegiate Journalism.

Dollar joined the *Kentucky New Era* as a staff writer in December 1983 after working as a reporter for two small newspapers in Kentucky—the *Cynthiana Democrat*, a weekly, and *The Morehead News*, a bi-weekly—and a Tennessee daily, *The Leaf-Chronicle* in Clarksville, Tennessee.

At *The Leaf-Chronicle* for two years (1981-1983), Dollar was the police and courts reporter and a co-founder of *The News Brothers*.

For nearly three years in the early 1990s, Dollar also was the western Kentucky correspondent for *The Tennessean* newspaper in Nashville, Tennessee.

Dollar was a charter member of Military Reporters & Editors (MRE), which was founded in Washington, D.C., in November 2002. He also was a member of the National Society of Newspaper Columnists.

Since leaving journalism, Dollar has worked in the public sector, serving as the chief administrative aide to the Mayor of Hopkinsville and later as a Kentucky Partnership Specialist for the U.S. Department of Commerce/Bureau of the Census.

A resident of Hopkinsville, Dollar hopes to continue working in government until his retirement.

Scott "Badger" Shelton, who left radio news as a profession as a young man, enjoyed filling in at his WJZM alma mater in his later years. Of course, his biggest joy was his family, and if that meant dressing up as a tie-wearing elf at Christmas, he'd gladly do it. He celebrated life until his dying day.

Jerry "Chuckles" Manley worked more than 30 years in newspapers, ending his career as Night Editor of *The Tennessean* in Nashville, Tennessee, on June 30, 2011. He is retired and preparing to move to Lewisburg, Tennessee. "When this most honorable and decent man walked out the door at 1100 Broadway, it was a crippling blow for good and ethical journalism in Nashville and the nation as a whole," said his unbiased old friend, Tim "Flapjacks" Ghianni.

Jim "Flash" Lindgren lives in Indianapolis, Ind., with his wife, Brenda Myers, who also worked at *The Leaf-Chronicle* and a sister paper, the *Ashland City Times*. The couple has two grown children. Lindgren, after a long career as a copy editor and newsroom manager, is now the editor for Strategic Marketing & Research Inc. He also is a journalism instructor at Butler University.

Scott "Badger" Shelton worked as a broadcast journalist for more than a decade at three different radio stations, including WJZM in Clarksville, Tennessee. He also was a newspaper correspondent for *The Tennessean* in Nashville, Tennessee. For 12 years, Shelton served in the Clarksville Mayor's Office as the public affairs director for the City of Clarksville. After a courageous battle with cancer, he died on Jan. 23, 2012, at the age of 57. At the time of his death, Shelton was working as the communications coordinator for Cumberland Electric Membership Corp. (CEMC). He is survived by his wife, Elise Frederick Shelton, a former reporter for *The Leaf-Chronicle*, and two grown sons, Adam and Will.

David "Teach" Ross lives in Dover, Tennessee, where he teaches school at Stewart County High School. A one-time mayor of Dover and radio station owner, Ross worked for several newspapers during his journalism career, including *The Leaf-Chronicle*. He also worked in radio and television news.

John "Street" Staed lives in Anderson, S.C., with his family. Staed's journalism career included stops at newspapers in Tennessee, Alabama and South Carolina. The former managing editor of the *Anderson (S.C.) Independent Mail*, Staed now works part-time for the newspaper as a writer and is in school to become a respiratory therapist.

Madison Street United Methodist Church in Clarksville, Tennessee, was packed full for a memorial service that celebrated the life of Scott Shelton. The service was held on Saturday, Jan. 28, 2012.

Family members put together a poster board of photographs that illustrated Scott Shelton's wonderful life of nearly 58 years.

Billy "StrawBilly" Fields, after jobs at *The Leaf-Chronicle* and in public relations, found his niche in government. He is now a top aide to Nashville Mayor Karl Dean. Some political observers expect Fields to become mayor himself one day.

Harold "The Stranger" Lynch, a veteran newsman who covered the government beat for *The Leaf-Chronicle* during most of the 1980s, died of cancer on July 24, 1990, at the age of 43. During his newspaper career, he also had worked for the *Nashville Banner*.

Thomas Anthony "Tony" Durr, former editor of *The Leaf-Chronicle*, from March 1981 to July 1982, died on Sept. 24, 1991, in Alaska, of an apparent heart attack and perhaps despair. An empty bottle of prescription medicine—for his migraines, which caused him to miss almost as much work as did playing golf during his days in Clarksville—and a phone, off the hook, were found at his side when First Responders tried in vain to resuscitate him. He was 44 and serving in the Coast Guard Reserve.

Okey Lanahan "Skipper" Stepp, died on Dec. 2, 1992, at a nursing home in the Clarksville, Tennessee, area. He was 81. His remains were donated to Vanderbilt University Medical Center for research.

Frank Wm. "Wuhm" White lives in Clarksville, Tennessee, where he owns MediaWorks, a graphic design-based printing company. He left *The Leaf-Chronicle* in April 1984. A 23-year veteran of the military, his post *L-C* career has seen him edit religious publications in Nashville and save Kuwait from Saddam Hussein during Desert Storm (Bush Sr.'s Gulf War).

Ricky G. "Dumbo" Moore remains on life-support, still clinging to his job as the News Editor for a major Tennessee daily newspaper. He and his family reside in Chattanooga, where he works for the *Chattanooga Times Free Press*.

Chico The Monkey was found dead on Nov. 26, 1982, in the woods along Rossview Road, outside of Clarksville, Tennessee. At the time of his death, he was 17 months old. His killer was never found, and he remains dead.

Tim "Flapjacks" Ghianni gets ready to ride off on a goodwill mission at the first Leslie W. Watson Memorial Toy Run in Clarksville, Tennessee, in September 1982.

An Afterword from Tim Ghianni

The News Brothers love movies, and we made an awful lot of folks laugh—while raising money for charity—at the screening of our own epic film, "Flapjacks: The Motion Picture" back in November 1982.

A lot of the spirit and even the flavor of some of our favorite movies and television shows made it into our first, and only, motion picture, which essentially is a "buddy film."

And, as we show from our own story, not all buddy films have happy endings. Remember "Easy Rider"? The Peter Fonda-Dennis Hopper counter-culture classic helped define the lives—through its truth and wisdom—of many young men coming of age in this country in the late 1960s and early 1970s. Rob and I are not exceptions....

There's even a brief nod to that 1969 film in our movie, with me riding a big, ol' Harley in a crowd of more than 100 motorcyclists in what really was, in true *News Brothers* spirit, a Christmas Toy Run for underprivileged kids in Clarksville. I covered the Toy Run for *The Leaf-Chronicle* after pretty much giving the organizers the idea for the event. That's another story, another book down the road, perhaps.

But we thought I ought to at least ride in the Toy Run. "Born To Be Wild," which became a biker anthem thanks to "Easy Rider," plays over that scene in the "Flapjacks" movie. Steppenwolf leader John Kay, the writer and singer of that song, has become a friend of mine in recent years, symbolizing the kind of karma that has both plagued and pleased *The News Brothers*.

Anyway, not long before we started this book, Rob and I, always looking for kicks, started reenacting our favorite scene from "Easy Rider," with me taking on the lines of "Billy The Kid" (Dennis Hopper) and Rob doing his best George Hanson (Jack Nicholson). The reenactment ended up in one of our video projects promoting *The News Brothers*.

Sometimes, we fiddled slightly with the great Dennis Hopper, Peter Fonda and Terry Southern script. Other times, we were straightforward with our lines, because of the truths.

The conversation from the scene goes like this:

Rob: You know, this used to be a helluva good country. I can't understand what's gone wrong with it.

Tim: Man, everybody got chicken, that's what happened. Hey, we can't even get into like, a second-rate hotel, I mean, a second-rate motel, you dig? They think we're gonna cut their throat or somethin'. They're scared, man.

Rob: They're not scared of you. They're scared of what you represent to 'em.

Tim: Hey, man. All we represent to them, man, is somebody who needs a haircut.

Rob: Oh, no. What you represent to them is freedom.

Tim: What the hell is wrong with freedom? That's what it's all about.

Rob: Oh, yeah, that's right. That's what it's all about, all right. But talkin' about it and bein' it, that's two different things. I mean, it's real hard to be free when you are bought and sold in the marketplace. Of course, don't ever tell anybody that they're not free, 'cause then they're gonna get real busy killin' and maimin' to prove to you that they are. Oh, yeah, they're gonna talk to you, and talk to you, and talk to you about individual freedom. But they see a free individual, it's gonna scare 'em.

Tim: Well, it don't make 'em runnin' scared.

Rob: No, it makes 'em dangerous

Like some sort of two-man troupe of guerrilla theater, we've done that little scene perhaps a dozen times, outside the newspaper in Clarksville, in downtown Nashville honky-tonks, in parks, at festivals, even out front at Nashville International Airport, as the red caps watched in wonderment..

To us, it's become sort of a mantra, because freedom of the press, freedom of expression, freedom from corporate structure are important to us.

Indeed: What the hell is wrong with freedom?

Sometimes people look at us and respond with a smile of approval. Other times, people look the other way and laugh, before running off to chase their next dollar.

Maybe our unhappy ending—we fought the good fight to keep newspapers relevant, but lost the battle to the bean-counters, both in the movie and in real life—is at least an honorable wrap-up for what happened to us in the newspaper business.

The ending could have been much worse, especially if you recall another 1969 buddy flick, "Butch Cassidy and The Sundance Kid."

The Bolivian Army has Butch and The Kid pinned down in a house, and they decide to take their best shot at getting out alive.

"For a moment there I thought we were in trouble," quips Butch, while the two best friends go to their deaths, as volleys of gunfire—not raindrops—keep falling on their heads.

I guess, when you really think about it, everything ends badly, or else it wouldn't end...

-30-

Acknowledgments

This book, a love letter to their vanishing profession by two newspapermen, details their long, strange trip, punctuated by deadlines, headlines, triumph and tragedy.

Although it is the tale of two men's journeys, we weren't alone. Good newspapering requires teamwork and we want to thank those who joined us during various stages of our careers spent pursuing good journalism. Other gallant comrades we thank by bringing them back to life, if only briefly, on these pages.

We especially want to praise our wonderful families, our biggest supporters and cheerleaders. If not for their understanding and sacrifices, we could never have given up the chunks of our lives it took for us to excel as fair and ethical reporters, editors, columnists and newsroom leaders.

We also want to thank the newspapers that employed us over the course of four decades. The authors met and much of this story takes place during time spent at *The Leaf-Chronicle* in Clarksville, Tennessee. But there were other newspaper stops and lessons learned: *The Eastern Progress, Cynthiana Democrat, The Morehead News, Kentucky New Era, The Fayetteville Observer, Nashville Banner* and *The Tennessean*. If not for our associations with these fine publications, we would never have become who we are in this life.

We also want to thank the families of Kathy Jane Nishiyama and Rodney Wayne Long, not only for their grace and courage during the times of nightmarish tragedy detailed in this book but for their enduring support, friendship and humanity.

Finally, we want to single out Mary Catharine Nelson of Published by Westview for her enormous contributions in making this book possible. We will be forever grateful for her encouragement, suggestions, improvements and, most of all, for believing in us and our story.

REFERENCES

"Butch and Sundance" ending scene, Page 377, from the 1969 motion picture "Butch Cassidy and the Sundance Kid" screenplay written by William Goldman.

Chico The Monkey, Page 159-160, Excerpts from a front-page (A1) story written by Rob Dollar and published in *The Leaf-Chronicle* newspaper in Clarksville, Tennessee, on Sunday, August 15, 1982, "Deputies Go Bananas: 'Monkey At Large!'"

"Easy Rider" scene, Page 376, from the 1969 motion picture "Easy Rider" screenplay written by Dennis Hopper, Peter Fonda and Terry Southern.

"The End," Page 325, paraphrase of that classic song by The Beatles, from their 1969 album, "Abbey Road." The Beatles also are thanked for their inspiration.

"I-Feel-Like-I'm-Fixin'-To-Die Rag" and **"The Fish Cheer,"** Pages 102, 107, 108, Country Joe and The Fish. From the album "I-Feel-Like-I'm-Fixin'-To-Die." Chapter 9 title **"C'mon all you big strong men"** is from the album's title song.

"I May Smoke Too Much," Page 48, Line from singer-songwriter Kris Kristofferson's song by that title. From the album "Spooky Lady's Sideshow."

"It's A Wonderful Life," Page 168 & 176. The uplifting mood of Frank Capra's classic 1946 movie starring Jimmy Stewart and Donna Reed inspired *The News Brothers* during their Christmas episodes and life in general.

"Just Like Tom Thumb's Blues," Page 9, Line from classic Bob Dylan song by that title. From the album "Highway 61 Revisited."

"The Last Time," Page 327, lines from song of that title by The Rolling Stones, written by Keith Richards and Mick Jagger, from the album "Out of Our Heads."

The Lone Ranger Creed, Page 163, Written by Fran Striker; The Lone Ranger trademarks, characters and likenesses owned by Classic Media Inc.

Photographs throughout this book are from the personal collections of the two authors, Tim Ghianni and Rob Dollar. Some of the photographs were taken by Rob Dollar and many others were taken at various times over the past 30 years by friends and colleagues of the authors. Permission to use certain photographs was given by the Tennessee Department of Correction, Austin Peay State University and the families of Kathy Jane Nishiyama and Rodney Wayne Long. The package of photos on page 357, showing Ghianni with his friend, Kris Kristofferson, were taken by Johnny Cash Kristofferson (top photo) and by veteran photo journalist John Partipilo (his photo also used on the cover).

Rob Dollar Professional Biography, Page 366-369, Excerpts from a Page A8 story written by Rob Dollar and published in the *Kentucky New Era* newspaper in Hopkinsville, Kentucky, on Thursday, July 10, 2003, "Dollar to leave newspaper post."

"This is the End," Page 303, title of Chapter 26, from the song "The End," by The Doors from their self-titled 1967 album, "The Doors."

"To Beat The Devil," Page 37, Verse from singer-songwriter-actor Kris Kristofferson's song by that title. From the album titled "Kristofferson" and/or "Me and Bobby McGee."

The World According To Tim "Flapjacks" Ghianni, Chapter 25, Pages 261-301, includes columns and other writings that appeared elsewhere and are reproduced here with permission and proper credit. "Calling Card" columns from *The Leaf-Chronicle* in Clarksville, Tennessee: Savior of the Cosmos, 262-265, Feb. 12, 1982; Rodney's Funeral, Pages 265-267, March 5, 1982; Peace for Kathy, Pages 267-269, March 10, 1982; Me and Skipper, Pages 270-272, July 4, 1982; Skipper's Birthday, Pages 273-274, Oct. 27, 1982; Party at The Roxy, Pages 275-277, Nov. 14, 1982; The death of Chico, Pages 277-279, Dec. 10, 1982; The Lone Ranger, Pages 279-281, Jan. 16, 1983; Fighting the law, Pages 281-283, Feb. 4, 1983; Two senseless deaths, Pages 283-286, Feb. 13, 1983; Bowling for charity, Pages 286-288, Feb. 23, 1983; and City Hall shark, Pages 288-290, March 11, 1983. *Nashville Banner* opinion page: Fond farewell to the old cowboy, Pages 290-293, July 30, 1990. *Nashville Banner* "Real Life" columns: Toasting Tony Durr, Pages 293-294, Oct. 3, 1991; Saluting Skipper's voyages, Pages 295-296, Dec. 17, 1992. Tim Ghianni's "They Call Me Flapjacks" blog posts: The workingman's journalist, Pages 297-299, April 7, 2009; 'Maverick' Battle had a soul, Pages 299-301, Jan. 23, 2010.

CPSIA information can be obtained at www.ICGtesting.com
Printed in the USA
BVOW082236080412

287184BV00002BA/1/P